How to Enter and Win Clay and Glass Crafts Contests

How to Enter and Win Clay and Glass Crafts Contests /

By
ALAN GADNEY, *Alan*

Managing Editor
CAROLYN PORTER

Facts On File Publications
New York, N.Y.

How to Enter and Win
Clay and Glass Crafts Contests

© Alan Gadney 1983

Published by Facts On File, Inc. 460 Park Avenue South, New York, N.Y.
10016

In cooperation with Festival Publications

Library of Congress Cataloging in Publication Data

Gadney, Alan.
   How to enter and win clay & glass crafts
contests.

   Includes indexes.
   1. Pottery craft—Competitions.   2. Glass
craft—Competitions.   3. Pottery craft—
Scholarships, fellowships, etc.   4. Glass
craft—Scholarships, fellowships, etc.
I. Title.   II. Title: Clay and glass crafts
contests.
TT920.G3   738'.079   81-19561
ISBN 0-87196-661-1   AACR2
ISBN 0-87196-662-X (pbk.)

Printed in the United States of America

9 8 7 6 5 4 3 2 1

Computer Programming and Typesetting by Datagraphics Inc.

TO MARY M. GADNEY
whose confidence, love, and hard work
helped to make this series possible.
Thanks Mom.

EDITORIAL STAFF

Managing Editor: Dennis J. Isemonger

Senior Editors: Linda Huggins
Leigh Ducasse
Deborah Elder

Contributing Editors: Chris Moose
Alice Ober

CONTENTS

ALPHABETICAL EVENT/SPONSOR/ AWARD INDEX

SUBJECT/CATEGORY INDEX

INTRODUCTION

WELCOME . . . to How to Enter and Win CLAY & GLASS CRAFTS CONTESTS, an all new, completely up-to-date sourcebook for the contest competitor and grant seeker in the clay and glass crafts fields (ceramics, china, earthenware, enameling, glassblowing, mosaic, plastic, porcelain, pottery, raku, sculpture, stained & leaded glass, and stoneware) . . . one of an ongoing series of contest-grant books covering crafts and other related arts fields.

Each book in the series focuses in detail on an individual art or medium (Clay & Glass Crafts, Fabric & Fiber Crafts, Jewelry & Metal Crafts, Wood & Leather Crafts, Fine Arts & Sculpture, Design & Commercial Art, Color Photography, Black & White Photography, Film, Video-Audio-TV/Radio Broadcasting, Fiction Writing, Nonfiction Writing & Journalism, and so on).

And each book in the series lists complete entrance information for anyone wanting to:

- Enter their work in national and international contests, festivals, competitions, salons, shows, exhibitions, markets, tradefairs, and other award events and sales outlets.

- Apply for grants, loans, scholarships, fellowships, residencies, apprenticeships, internships, training and benefit programs, and free aids and services.

The books also have: ALPHABETICAL INDEXES listing each event, sponsor, and award by its various names. SUBJECT/CATEGORY INDEXES to the entrants' specific areas of interest. Extensive CROSS-REFERENCES and DEFINITIONS throughout. And introductory HELPFUL HINTS on how to analyze and enter the events, and possibly come up a winner!

HOW THE BOOKS BEGAN

This series of contest-grant guides actually began several years ago with the first release print of *West Texas* (a one-hour featurette I made while completing my graduate work at the USC Cinema Department). One week after our first showing, I sent our premiere print off to the first film festival, and the contest entry process started to grow from there . . . with one major problem, however: The festival contact information was almost impossible to find.

After extensive research, all I could come up with were names and addresses (and an occasional brief blurb) of intriguingly titled film events in far-off places, but with no hard facts as to their entry requirements, eligibility restrictions, awards, deadlines, fees, statistics, judging procedures, etc. That sort of vital information was practically nonexistent, unless you took the time and postage to write away to every contest you discovered an address for . . . which I did.

Through several years of continuous address researching, blindly writing off for contest entry information and periodically submitting the film, *West Texas* won 48 international film awards, and a large file of information had been collected on about 180 international festivals—quite a few of which were not even open to *West Texas* for a variety of reasons (wrong gauge, length, category, the event turned out not to be a film festival, etc.).

The need was evident for an accurate, up-to-date, and detailed entry information source to the world's Contests, Festivals and Grants . . . Thus evolved the two editions of my previous book (GADNEY'S GUIDE TO INTERNATIONAL CONTESTS, FESTIVALS & GRANTS). Their first-of-a-kind success ultimately lead to this all new series of contest-grant guides.

ABOUT THE CLAY & GLASS CRAFTS BOOK

This book (devoted solely to the field of CLAY & GLASS CRAFTS) is a single-source reference guide, providing you with vital entry information and statistics about a contest/grant before you even have to send away for the entry forms and shipping regulations (which you must always eventually do, as most require their own entry forms, and some have rather intricate shipping and customs requirements).

The 371 separate events listed in this volume were compiled through 3 years of active research on my earlier book, an additional year of research on this book, and thousands of questionnaires sent to worldwide crafts events (many requiring repeated mailings to obtain complete and up-to-date entry information). During this process, we have totally updated, revised, and expanded the scope of the original listings, added new competitions, and deleted a few which were too restricted or no longer in existence. (Other crafts events have been included in three companion volumes covering Fabric & Fiber Crafts, Jewelry & Metal Crafts, and Wood, Leather & Folk Crafts contests and grants.)

The individual events have been further grouped into 40 special-interest sub-categories (an increase in the number of subject categories over the earlier book, particularly in the areas of scholarships, fellowships, and grants). These sub-categories are further divided and cross-referenced in the SUBJECT/CATEGORY INDEX at the back of the book.

We have included two general types of events:

- Those AWARD EVENTS and SALES OUTLETS to which entrants may submit their works in order to receive SOMETHING OF VALUE in return, such as contests, festivals, competitions, salons, shows, exhibitions, markets, tradefairs, and various other award and sales programs primarily for new and unknown works.

- And BENEFIT PROGRAMS to which individuals or organizations may apply for some type of AID or SERVICE, such as grants, money and equipment loans, scholarships, fellowships, residencies, apprenticeships, internships, training programs, workshops, and so on.

Due to page length restrictions we have usually omitted those events that (1) are restricted to members of a specific organization (unless you can join that organization upon entering the contest), or limited to residents of a small city or geographical area (usually of less than state size), or (2) are not open to general entry but whose participants are nominated or invited by the sponsors or national selecting organizations. Seminars, conferences, schools, service programs, and the like, have only been listed if they are free, have free benefits attached, or encompass a contest, festival, grant, scholarship, fellowship, residency, etc.

We have listed as much detailed information about each separate event as possible (that is, as much as could be culled from the materials provided us by the event—usually including current addresses, dates, deadlines, complete entry requirements, eligibility and fee information, awards available, judging aspects, catch clauses, purpose, theme, sponsors, average statistics, where held, and various historical aspects). All information was transcribed from the questionnaires and entry materials provided us and edited to fit the format of the book. (See HOW TO USE THE BOOK for description of format.)

The information listed is the most current we could obtain, and will normally be revised and updated every two or three years in this continuing reference series.

We have also included older events when there was no direct confirmation that the events had gone out of existence. Many events come and go in an on-again, off-again manner, depending on their finances, administration changes, and other factors . . . again, good reason to ALWAYS WRITE TO AN EVENT BEFORE ENTERING YOUR WORK. Most events require entry forms, which they provide. Many have special shipping regulations. And, as we have condensed and edited their rules and regulations, it is best to write for the complete versions (especially important in interpreting the meanings of occasional tricky "catch clauses" about the use and ownership of winning entries). Also remember to send along a self-addressed, stamped return envelope (SASE), particularly to smaller events operating on tight postage budgets.

It would be almost impossible to give an exact figure for the total amount of money offered through this book. Some events give cash, others give equipment (of varying value depending on how badly you need the equipment or how much you can sell it for), and others give trophies, cups, plaques, medals, certificates, etc. (all of great value to the winner, but of little real monetary worth). Grant sources, on the other hand, may offer millions of dollars in direct financial aid. Probably the safest thing to say about the total amount of money offered through this book is that it is well into the millions.

HOW TO USE THIS BOOK

In the TABLE OF CONTENTS you will find that this volume has been divided into a series of "special-interest" SUBCATEGORIES. Each contains all those events whose primary emphasis is within that particular subcategory. The listing is usually alphabetical—first those in the United States, followed by other countries in alphabetical order.

At the start of each subcategory is an italicized INTRODUCTORY SECTION giving (1) specific contents of that subcategory, (2) definitions, and (3) "also see" CROSS-REFERENCES to similar events in other subcategories in the book.

To find additional events accepting entries in your specific interest area (but which may be listed in other subcategories because their primary emphasis is stronger in those areas), use the SUBJECT/CATEGORY INDEX at the back of the book. This lists subjects of special interest by an identifying code number for each event. The code number is located in the box above each event.

To find a specific event, sponsor, or award by name, use the ALPHABETICAL EVENT/SPONSOR/AWARD INDEX at the back of the book (again listing entries by identifying code number). In this index, sponsors and events are usually listed by full names, abbreviations, and unique titles.

EACH EVENT consists of (1) a current address and telephone number; (2) entry month; (3) introductory paragraph, including entry restrictions, month/season held, date of establishment, former names, purpose, theme, motto, sponsors, average statistics, historical information, facilities and other aspects; (4) technical entry regulations and categories; (5) eligibility requirements; (6) awards; (7) judging aspects and catch clauses; (8) sales terms; (9) entry fees; (10) deadlines. All have a similar format designed for easy use, with the five most important aspects of each event noted in bold type:

1. Identifying Code Number (in box)
2. Name of event
3. Month of entry
4. Entrant restrictions
5. Type of event and subject-category

With these five main points in mind, a potential entrant can quickly skim through a series of events to find those of particular interest.

HOW TO ANALYZE AN EVENT

We have usually provided enough information about each event to help you in making various determinations before you send away for entry forms, shipping regulations, and additional instructions. These are some of the points you should consider in your analysis.

• **When is the event held?** The month/season held is listed in the first sentence.

• **When is the entry deadline?** Months of entry are designated by bold type immediately following the address and in the DEADLINES section at the end of each event listing, and are usually well in advance of the month held. However, as deadlines do vary, the event should always be contacted about the specific entry date for the year you are applying.

• **Do I qualify?** Entrant restrictions are listed in bold type in the first sentence, and may be further clarified in the ELIGIBILITY section.

• **Does my work qualify?** The type of event and specific subject categories are listed in bold type at the beginning of the second and subsequent paragraphs. Various technical entry requirements follow each.

• **How much does it cost?** Costs and hidden costs are found in the ENTRY FEE section. The reason most events charge entry fees is usually to pay for the awards, operating costs, judges, and attendance of well-known persons. Contests and festivals can be extremely expensive to operate, and the size and scope of the event usually dictates the fee structure. Amateur competitions can range from no entry fees to very nominal ones, while the fees for more professional contests are considerably higher.

• **What are the prizes?** Found in the AWARDS section are prizes varying from trophies, cups, plaques, and medallions (of personal value), to cash, trips, equipment, and services (of a more material value—meaning you may be able to resell them at a later date if you already have better equipment, cannot take the trip, or do not want the services). Exhibition, distribution, broadcast, sale, and publication may also be offered, but should always be analyzed in terms of their financial and legal implications (what you get for what you have to give in return, and how valuable your entry may become in the future).

- **What are the catch clauses?** A few events have tricky qualifying clauses, condensed in the JUDGING section. These may involve claims to use and ownership (sometimes of all entries, and on an extensive basis), or responsibility in the event of loss, damage, nonreturn, etc.

Occasionally the actual entry forms and regulations may be rather vague as to whether the sponsors just keep a copy of your winning entry or whether they receive full ownership of the work (and for what use). Possibly, in these instances, you should write to the sponsors for further clarification.

- **How is my work judged?** The number of judges, judging procedures, and criteria are listed in the JUDGING section. It is important to understand that during preliminary judging (sometimes performed by the event's staff and aides), many entries may be immediately disqualified because of failure to adhere to the various contest regulations, or eliminated because of technical flaws or oversights (good reason always to send away for, and to read carefully, the latest rules). This is especially true of large contests that thousands enter. Sponsors have to narrow the competition as rapidly and efficiently as possible, and the first to go are the rule breakers and sloppy entries.

A program of the event or listing of past winners may give you an overall feel for the event (if it is conservative or liberal, oriented in certain directions, etc.). There is the possibility of talking to past entrants and winners in order to get an idea of specific likes and dislikes of the event and its judges. Or if you know who the judges will be, you may be able to make an educated guess as to what they will choose. However, I have found that it is almost impossible to predict how judges will act on anything other than the widest of generalities. Judges change from year to year, the philosophy of the event may alter, and single-judge contests put you at the mercy of that particular year's judge. So, you can never really outguess the judges.

- **How old is the event?** Usually included in the first sentence is the founding date, the inference being that the older the event, the more stable and reputable it is.

- **How large is the event?** Average attendance, distribution, and sales figures can often be found in the first paragraph, indicating the potential promotional and sales values of participating in the event.

- **What is the duration of an event, and how long will it tie up my entry materials?** The number of days the event is usually held is found in the first paragraph; the entry and return-of-material dates are in the DEADLINES section.

- **What is the competition?** Average statistics on number of entries, entrants, countries competing, acceptances into final competition, and winners can be found in the first paragraph, giving some idea of possible competition in future events.

- **How legitimate is the event?** This can be determined to some extent by the names of familiar sponsors, cosponsors, financial supporters, and those organizations that officially recognize the event—again, all found in the opening paragraph, and giving some idea of reputability. Also important may be the purpose, theme, and motto.

These are just a few of the aspects to examine before writing away for further information, entry forms, the most current regulations . . . and before sending away your work.

YEARLY PLANNING GUIDE

This book can also serve as a planning guide for your contest entries throughout the year. By using the SUBJECT/CATEGORY INDEX, you can get an overall picture of the various world events accepting entries in your areas of interest. We would then suggest setting up a calendar, listing those events you wish to enter by (1) the date you should write away for entry forms and current rules (several months before the actual entry month), (2) the entry dates, and (3) the dates the event is held, which will give you some indication of when the sponsor will be announcing the winners and returning your materials.

HELPFUL HINTS ON HOW TO WIN

Here are a few recommendations to enhance your chances of winning:

• ANALYZE THE STATISTICS—Look at the average statistics (found in the first paragraph of an event listing) to determine the size of your competition. Remember, you should always calculate the number of awards/honors given against the number of entrants, and not just analyze on total entrants alone. Larger events with a greater number of entrants and more awards may in reality have a higher winner-ratio than smaller events with only one award. You may also stand a better chance of winning in newer events which have not yet built up their patronage.

• ANALYZE THE TYPE OF EVENT—Based on past winner/award listings, is the event consistently conservative or liberal in its selections (or does it change moods from one year to the next)? If a contest says it leans toward contemporary or experimental works, you should take this into account before entering. You may also wish to try and analyze how the judges will vote, again based on past records and who the current judges are. (See HOW TO ANALYZE AN EVENT for additional information.)

• PATRONIZE THE SPECIALIZED EVENTS—If you have a specialized entry, while it will normally qualify for more generalized contests, you might begin by concentrating on those events which have a special interest in, or specific subject categories for your particular entry. Because of their highly specialized nature, these contests may get fewer entries, and if your work fits their interests, you should stand a better chance of winning. You might also consider patronizing those events that have changing annual themes by designing your entry to fit that particular year's needs.

• FOLLOW THE RULES—The contest rules (obtained directly from the event) should be studied carefully, first to find hidden clauses, and second to ensure you will not be inadvertently excluded because you entered the wrong category, sent an incorrect entry fee or no return postage, entered with improper technical aspects, or not enough supplementary information, etc. So read the rules and follow them, and fill out the entry forms completely. Rule breakers usually are disqualified, sometimes even before the preliminary judging. Then, to further cut down the number of competitors, most judges go strictly by the regulations, automatically discarding those entries that in any way deviate from the rules.

• KEEP IT CLEAN—Keep it technically perfect. Again, judges will usually reject sloppy entries (sometimes these don't even reach the judges, but are weeded out by the contest staff). So send only clean entries in good condition. No scratched, smudged, chipped, or broken works (and no poor-quality entry slides). All of these reflect badly on your entry's artistic content. And if the sponsors tell you they want an entry mounted, cased, or framed, you had better follow their instructions. Also, it is best to send a duplicate rather than your original work or entry slides (unless they request the original, in which case you should study their rules carefully to see if you will ever get your original back).

• SEND IT AHEAD OF TIME—Send your materials well in advance of the entry deadlines. Last-minute entries may get abbreviated handling by judges who have already looked over the earlier entries and have made up their minds. They may not get listed in the contest programs, which have already gone to the printers—and if they are shown, they may be scheduled during the least desirable exhibition times. And of course, *late* entries are usually sent back unopened.

• SEND PUBLICITY AND INFORMATION MATERIALS—Send supporting materials unless positively prohibited. (Definitely send them when they are requested.) Every little bit helps: biographical, technical, and project background information; publicity and press materials; still photos, production philosophy, synopsis, translation, transcription (and advertising materials if appropriate). The judges may occasionally use some of these in making their final decisions, and the events may use the publicity in their programs, flyers, and press rooms. Remember to send along any special technical instructions or return shipping requests you feel are needed.

• USE PROPER SHIPPING—First a word about the U.S. and international mail systems (as opposed to international Air Freight; some foreign contests even prohibit the use of air freight, as the entries may become held up in customs). Provided your entries are properly packaged, sealed, marked, stamped, and insured, and have correctly filled-out customs stickers (information about all of this is available through the U.S. Post Office), they should be able to travel almost anywhere in the world with relative safety. (This is based on personal experience. *West Texas* was mailed to a large number of film festivals all over the world, and I never lost a print or received one back damaged in transit.)

Remember always to ship by air to overseas competitions (as boat mail may take as long as three months from the U.S. to Australia, for example). On domestic U.S. shipments, you can mail at various rates lower than First Class, if you take into account the time for possible delays. (Again, contact the post office for information about mailing costs and times.)

Of course, if you have a heavy international shipment (A large sculpture for example), you may be over the postal weight limitations, and have to ship by Air Freight. In this case, it may be best to contact a customs house broker/international freight forwarder about services and charges.

Short overseas messages will travel very rapidly by international telegram. And always remember to enclose sufficient return postage and a correctly sized self-addressed stamped return envelope (SASE) when requested. Finally, if your entry arrives with "Postage Due," it could be a negative factor in the contest staff preselection process.

A WORD ABOUT GRANTS

It would take an entire volume to discuss all the "ins" and "outs" of grant solicitation. However, we can touch on a few of the more important aspects.

• FIND OUT AS MUCH AS POSSIBLE about a potential grant source before investing the time in sending a proposal. Write to the granting organization for more information—and once you have this information, analyze it and focus your energies on the most likely prospects.

• WRITE AN INQUIRY LETTER—a brief letter of introduction, to see if they are interested in your project. Include a short description of the project and its unique aspects, background information about yourself and your sponsoring organization, the proposal budget, and ask them if they would be interested in further information. Keep your introductory letter brief, to the point, well written, easy to understand, and not exaggerated. If the foundation is interested, it will request what it needs, which may run anywhere from an expanded summary to a full-scale proposal and budget.

• GET AN ORGANIZATION TO SPONSOR YOU—Many foundations restrict their granting to only nonprofit, tax-exempt organizations, institutions, etc. However, this does not necessarily prohibit you from securing a grant from them. Simply get a nonprofit organization to sponsor you and your project, and have the organization apply for the grant in their name. Many organizations offer grant solicitations as one of their services, and this can have benefits for the sponsoring organizations: You give them credit and publicity through your finished project. They have a track-record as a successful fund raiser, which may help them in obtaining future grants. And they can even be paid through your budget for handling certain administrative and bookkeeping duties.

• GET SOME NAMES ON YOUR SIDE—well-known persons in the roles of advisors, technical consultants, etc. can help greatly toward building an impressive project package.

• TRY SPECIAL INTEREST GROUPS—If you have designed a project involving a special interest (Folk Crafts, for example), rather than only approaching sources that grant your medium (Crafts), you might consider going to those grant sources that fund the special interest instead (i.e., Folk and Traditional Arts Grants). Or you may find similar money sources through special-interest organizations, associations, institutions, and businesses. The public library is a good place to start your search.

• BUILD A TRACK RECORD—A series of smaller grants, scholarships, fellowships from local or regional sources can be extremely impressive on your presentation resume when you approach the larger granting organizations. And of course, prizes and honors awarded to you and your work will help to build you as a winning grant recipient with a previous track record. Remember that many times several grants can be awarded to the same project simultaneously. So apply to as many sources (those for which you qualify) as possible, and then keep on applying.

WHY ENTER CONTESTS

Finally, a word about the positive benefits of entering your work in contests, festivals, and competitions.

To start with, it is an extremely good way to test (and prove) the artistic and commercial value of your work before professional judges, critics, and the public. There is also the challenge of the competition—the excitement and glamour of knowing that your work is being seen in contests, festivals, salons, exhibitions, and publications around the world. Your entry competes with those of your peers —and if it reaches the finals and wins, there is the great personal satisfaction and certification of acceptance.

If you do win, you can win substantial cash prizes, trips, art items, equipment, services, exhibition, distribution, broadcast, publication, sales, trophies, and other awards. There can be useful free publicity for both you and your work, through (1) press information and literature released by the event, (2) the writings and reviews of others about your work, and (3) your own promotional materials designed around your winnings.

All of this can bring valuable international exposure through the print and broadcast media, and the resulting recognition and prestige can certainly help to sell both your award-winning work and yourself as an award-winning craftsperson.

The end benefits can be sales, valuable contacts, jobs, contracts, increased fees, and the financing of other projects.

How does this translate into real terms . . . The 48 international film awards won by *West Texas* resulted directly in: (1) a large number of valuable art objects, trophies, and awards; (2) enough cash winnings to cover all the film festival entry fees, shipping, promotion, and other costs; (3) an enormous amount of free personal publicity; (4) the eventual sale and distribution of the film; (5) the writing and directing of a subsequent feature-length theatrical, *Moonchild;* (6) several paid speaking engagements; (7) a TV script assignment; (8) a stint as a film magazine contributing editor; and (9) eventually to writing this series of books on contests and grants . . . So, the entering of contests and the winning of awards in many ways can be quite profitable.

A FEW CLOSING THOUGHTS — While I have found the vast majority of events to be highly reputable and continually striving to improve their quality, there are still a few bad exceptions (lost entries, withheld awards, judging problems, etc.).

However, the interesting thing is that just as numbers and types of events change from year to year, so do most of these questionable conditions. Just when you hear someone complain about an unfair judging process, the next year the judges change, and that same person may come out a winner. Or the rules and administration change, and what was once a suspect practice disappears.

With this in mind, there has been no attempt on our part to editorialize about the occasional bad occurrences we hear of. This is strictly a reference guide (not a critical work). We list all those events which qualify, from the largest to the smallest, the oldest to the youngest, the well-known and the not so well-known. And we have tried to print enough information about each event to give you a firm basis upon which to decide whether or not to write for further information. (See HOW TO ANALYZE AN EVENT.)

It should also be stated that we do not endorse (or accept any responsibility for the conduct of) the events listed in this book.

Finally, no book of this type can ever be all-inclusive. That would be virtually impossible. Each year hundreds of new events start up, old ones lapse or go out of business, only to be replaced by similar events in a new form. As I have mentioned, there is constant growth and progression based on general changes in the art and media fields. However, considering the many individual events we have listed, each as thoroughly as possible within the edited format, and each updated and verified to the best of our knowledge based on entry materials and questionnaires provided us, we feel that we have brought you quite a comprehensive reference guide.

A special thank you to the American Library Association (the Reference and Adult Services Division, Reference Committee) for awarding the previous contest book an "OUTSTANDING REFERENCE SOURCE OF THE YEAR" ... and to the many readers and reviewers of that book for their favorable response. These honors have been extremely gratifying.

And an additional thanks and grateful appreciation to the many events, sponsors, contributors, and correspondents who have so graciously provided us with the information included in this directory.

As a final reminder, please remember that to ensure you have the latest information, complete regulations, and proper entry forms, ALWAYS WRITE TO AN EVENT BEFORE ENTERING YOUR WORK

And please advise us of any new Contests and Grants you may know of, so that we may include them in our future editions.

Alan Gadney
Festival Publications
P.O. Box 10180
Glendale, California 91209 U.S.A.

CLAY &
GLASS CRAFTS

ADVISORY ASSISTANCE

Assistance to craftspersons through counseling and planning services, administrative aid, problem solving, crafts activities and programs, conferences, workshops, libraries, legal and legislative information, grant writing, funding sources, sales and commission opportunities, promotion and publicity outlets. Includes LEGAL SERVICES, AFRO-AMERICAN, NATIVE AMERICAN, CALIFORNIA, MARYLAND, NORTH CAROLINA, BRITAIN. (Also see APPRENTICESHIPS, GRANTS, RESIDENCE GRANTS, SCHOLARSHIPS, WORKSHOPS.)

1

California Confederation of the Arts Advisory Assistance
6253 Hollywood Blvd., Suite 222
Los Angeles, California 90028 U.S.A.
Tel: (213) 469-5873

Entry dates continuous

National; **entry open to U.S.;** continuous; established 1975. Purpose: to represent and facilitate efforts of California's vital arts community to shape cultural life of the state. Have mailing lists. Also sponsor annual Arts Day Rally, annual Congress of the Arts, seminars, workshops, related programs.

CRAFTS ADVISORY ASSISTANCE: Information. Activities, funding sources, programs, legislation, regulations affecting the arts on a national, state, and local basis are available to members through bimonthly newsletter and special bulletins. Also have fine and commercial arts, photography, music, performing and visual arts information.

ENTRY FEE: Membership ranges from $5-$1500 according to individual or organizational status.

DEADLINES: Continuous.

2

Center for Arts Information Advisory Assistance
Ellen Thurston, Director
625 Broadway
New York, New York 10012 U.S.A.
Tel: (212) 677-7548

Entry dates continuous

National; **entry open to U.S.;** continuous. Purpose: to serve as information clearinghouse for and about the arts in New York State and the nation. Sponsored by Center for Arts Information. Supported by New York State Council on the Arts, NEA, Rockefeller Brother's Fund, J. M. Kaplan Fund, corporations, individuals. Publish directories, management aids. Have library facilities.

CRAFTS ADVISORY ASSISTANCE: **All Media, Information, Problem Solving.** Assistance to craftspersons, administrators by acting as source of information on funding, administration, programming, workshops, conferences, arts services through its own counseling service, library and by way of referral to appropriate sources. Services available to all branches of the arts. Also have special film-video services.

DEADLINES: Continuous.

3

Maryland Arts Council Resource Center Advisory Assistance
Cindy Kelly, Program Director
15 West Mulberry Street
Baltimore, Maryland 21201 U.S.A.
Tel: (301) 685-6740
Entry dates continuous

State; **entry open to Maryland;** continuous; established 1979. Purpose: to assist Maryland artists in obtaining information, exposure, sales and commission opportunities. Sponsored and supported by Maryland Arts Council. Average 800 registered artists. Held at Resource Center located in Maryland Arts Council offices in Baltimore. Have slide registry, resource file, library, published directory. Also sponsor travelling exhibitions.

CRAFTS ADVISORY ASSISTANCE: **Information, Exposure.** Slide Registry containing 5-10 slides of work, current resume, other supporting material per Maryland craftsperson; Resource File containing information on public and private exhibition and commission opportunities are both updated annually, and made available to registered artists, other interested individuals, groups, organizations. Also have fine and commercial art, photography sections.

DEADLINES: Registration continuous. Materials submitted within 60 days of notification of acceptance.

4

North Carolina Cultural Arts Coalition Advisory Assistance
Patricia S. Funderburk, Executive Director
407 North Person Street
P. O. Box 1310
Raleigh, North Carolina 27602
U.S.A. Tel: (919) 733-6893
Entry dates continuous

State; **entry open to North Carolina;** continuous; established 1977. Purpose: to encourage, enhance understanding of the arts throughout North Carolina. Supported by Ford Foundation, NEA, North Carolina Arts Council. Have artist referral service, job listings, arts programs. Publish *Emergence* (quarterly). Also sponsor exhibits, art and film festivals.

CRAFTS ADVISORY ASSISTANCE: **Afro-American Cultural Heritage.** Technical (including grant writing, program, development, public relations) and promotional (portfolios, brochures) assistance, help in securing scholarships, to individual members and organizations.

ENTRY FEE: Annual membership: $25 (individuals), $50 (organizations).

DEADLINES: Continuous.

5

U.S. Department of the Interior Indian Arts & Crafts Board Advisory Assistance
General Manager
Washington, DC 20240 U.S.A.
Entry dates continuous

National; **entry open to individuals, organizations who are, or are supported by, Native American groups;** continuous; established 1935. Purpose: to encourage, promote the development of native American arts and crafts. Also have employment assistance; arts and crafts promotions, demonstrations; publications, audiovisual material.

CRAFTS ADVISORY ASSISTANCE: Native American Crafts. Assistance including use of property, facilities, equipment; Advisory Services (locating sources of materials, funds; aid in planning, developing workshops, institutions), counseling; investigations of complaints. Submit project description, evidence of interest in, and expected participation of native Americans in project, budget proposal. No requests for grants, loans, other financial assistance. Competition includes fine arts.

ELIGIBILITY: Open to native American, Indian, Eskimo, Aleut individuals, organizations; state and local governments, nonprofit organizations supported by native American groups.

JUDGING: Based on relevance to agency objectives; extent to which native Americans benefit by project, have influence in project's decision making; artistic, professional quality; project feasibility.

ENTRY FEE: None.

DEADLINES: Continuous.

6

Volunteer Lawyers for the Arts Advisory Assistance
Barbara Seick Taylor, Administrator
1560 Broadway, Suite 711
New York, New York 10036 U.S.A.
Tel: (212) 575-1150

Entry dates continuous

National; **entry open to financially eligible U.S. individuals, organizations;** continuous; established 1969. Purpose: to provide free legal services to craftspersons, crafts associations unable to afford private counsel. Sponsored by Volunteer Lawyers for the Arts (nonprofit). Supported by NEA, State Councils, corporations, law firms, individuals. Publish *Art and the Law* (quarterly). Advisory assistance available in 39 regions. Also sponsor lectures, seminars, workshops, neighborhood clinics, conferences, intern programs.

CRAFTS ADVISORY ASSISTANCE: Legal Services and Information. Consultation referral (including contacts, copyright, taxes, incorporation tax exemption, labor relations, insurance, loft problems, immigration, small claims court advice, general corporate) provided for craftspersons in matters directly relating to crafts practice. Competition includes music, writing, dance, film, theater.

ELIGIBILITY: Open to financially eligible U.S. candidates determined on basis of individual's income, organization's operating budget.

ENTRY FEE: None. Referral fee: $15 individual, $25 organization, $50 nonprofit organization.

DEADLINES: Continuous.

7

British American Arts Association (U.K.) Ltd. (BAAA) Advisory Assistance
Jennifer Williams, Director
49 Wellington Street
London WC2E 7BN, ENGLAND
Tel: (01) 379-7755

Entry dates continuous

International; **entry open to Brit-**

ain, U.S.; continuous; established 1979. BAAA founded in Washington, D.C. by grant from Rockefeller Foundation. Purpose: to strengthen links and increase opportunities in all aspects of arts in Britain and U.S. Sponsored by BAAA. Supported by Rockefeller Foundation, British Council, U.S. Embassy, industry. Also sponsor fellowships, lectures, conferences, services in all areas of the arts.

CRAFTS ADVISORY ASSISTANCE: **Consultation, Counseling, Planning.** Assistance to craftspersons, administrators, associations, in organizing, financing, coordinating transatlantic projects (using its experience, knowledge of arts administration and policy) private and state funded, in both countries; matches organizers with sponsors for exhibitions, competitions.

DEADLINES: Continuous.

APPRENTICESHIPS, ASSISTANTSHIPS, INTERNSHIPS

Apprenticeships, Assistantships, Internships, Residencies, Work-Study Programs, primarily for ON-THE-JOB STUDY and TRAINING. Includes CERAMICS, GLASS, PORCELAIN, SCULPTURE. (Also see RESIDENCE GRANTS, SCHOLARSHIPS, FELLOWSHIPS.)

8

Arrowmont School of Arts and Crafts Spring and Summer Assistantships
Sandra J. Blain, Director
P. O. Box 567

Gatlinburg, Tennessee 37738 U.S.A.
Tel: (615) 436-5860

Entry January, March

International; entry open to all; annual in March-April and June-August; established 1945. Purpose: to allow artists to study, exchange ideas, perfect skills. Sponsored by and held at Arrowmont School of Arts and Crafts, located adjacent to Great Smoky Mountains National Park outside Gatlinburg for 2-5 weeks. Supported by Pi Beta Phi Fraternity, Tennessee Arts Commission, private and corporate donations. Recognized by University of Tennessee-Knoxville. Average 125 entrants (all sections). Have equipped studios, book-supply store, visiting crafts lecturers, permanent collection.

CRAFTS RESIDENCE ASSISTANTSHIPS: **Workshop Sessions** (including clay, enamel, stained glass). 10-15 spring, 12 summer tuition grants plus room and board to craftspersons with 4 years completed coursework or equivalent in experience for 2 weeks in spring (1 week class, 1 week work for school), 5 weeks in summer (3 weeks class, 2 weeks work for school). Graduate-undergraduate credit available through University of Tennessee-Knoxville. Assistants do work assignments related to general functions of school. Submit 10-20 slides of recent work, 3 references. Competition includes arts, photography, other crafts.

JUDGING: By director and program coordinator. Based on application form, references, slide portfolio.

ENTRY FEE: $10.

DEADLINES: Application, January (Spring), March (Summer). Acceptance, February, April. Assistantships, March-April, June-August.

9

Johnson Atelier Sculpture Apprenticeship Program Tuition Scholarships

Johnson Atelier Technical Institute of Sculpture
Brooke Barrie, Academic Director
743 Alexander Road
Princeton, New Jersey 08540 U.S.A.
Tel: (609) 452-2661

Entry dates continuous

International; **entry open to students;** continuous throughout year; established 1974. Institute founded by and named after J. Seward Johnson, Jr. to foster traditional sculpture casting technology; expanded to become one of most sophisticated art foundries in world. Purpose: to restore link, interplay between sculptor and founder. Sponsored and supported by J. Seward Johnson, Jr. Recognized by New Jersey State Department of Education, Veterans Administration. Average 50 2-year apprenticeships. Have advanced equipment and technology for ceramic shell and bound sand metal casting.

SCULPTURE APPRENTICE-SHIPS: Technical Training. $4800 grants available to student-apprentices for tuition costs. Require personal interview. Submit resume, slide portfolio of work. Categories: Mold Making, Waxworking, Resins, Ceramic Shell, Foundry, Sand, Metal Chasing, Structures, and Modeling-Enlarging.

ELIGIBILITY: Open to advanced students preferably with BA, BFA, MFA in sculpture and interest in casting sculpture technology.

DEADLINES: Application, continuous.

10

Moravian Pottery and Tile Works Summer Apprenticeship

Mandy Sallada
Swamp Road
Doylestown, Pennsylvania 18901
U.S.A. Tel: (215) 345-6722

Entry April

International; entry open to all; annual in June-August; established 1975. Purpose: to provide persons pursuing careers in ceramics opportunity to participate in unique production situation. Sponsored and supported by Bucks County Department of Parks and Recreation. Held at Moravian Pottery and Tile Works in Doylestown for 9 weeks.

CERAMIC APPRENTICESHIP: Summer Workshop. 5 9-week apprenticeships (including 24 hours per week supervised production at hourly wage; use of materials and facilities for own work; instruction, critiques, supervision, field trips) to ceramic apprentices. Submit 10 slides of work, biography, statement of intent for entry review. Require entrants use studio independently working within capacities of local red clay, tile orientation; provide own accommodation.

JUDGING: Based on previous experience, direction of personal work, commitment to 3 days labor following production schedule.

DEADLINES: Application, April. Notification, May. Event, June-August.

11

Peters Valley Craftsmen Internship Program

Sherrie Posternack, Director
Star Route
Layton, New Jersey 07851 U.S.A.
Tel: (201) 948-5200

Entry dates continous

International; **entry open to age 18 and over;** continuous; established 1970. Purpose: to serve as alternative or supplemental program to traditional education. Held at Peters Valley, a crafts-producing community. Sponsored by Peters Valley Craftsmen. Supported by NEA, New Jersey State Council on the Arts, Dodge Foundation. Have workshops, living accommodation, studios, kitchen facilities, sales, auctions, demonstrations, performances. Also sponsor summer studio assistantships, resident program.

CRAFTS INTERNSHIPS: Studio Work in Ceramics, Glass, Sculpture. 10-13-week internships to qualified individuals for opportunity to learn through observation and participation with resident teachers. College credit may be arranged. Submit resume, slides of work, recommendation letters, letters of intent. Competition includes photography, art, other crafts.

ENTRY FEE: $15 for annual membership.

DEADLINES: Continuous.

12

Truro Center for the Arts at Castle Hill Work-Study Program
Joyce Johnson, Director
Box 756, Castle Road
Truro, Massachusetts 02666 U.S.A.
Tel: (617) 349-3714

Entry June

International; entry open to all; annual in Summer; established 1972. Purpose: to assist financially restricted artists in augmenting their experience, exposure. Sponsored by Truro Center for the Arts. Recognized by Massachusetts Council on the Arts and Hu-

manities. Average 10 entrants (all sections). Held in Truro for 10 weeks. Have studios, workshops, weekly concerts and lectures, films, classes, visiting artists.

CERAMICS   WORK-STUDY PROGRAM: Summer Workshops in Handbuilding, Wheel, Porcelain, Stained Glass, Glaze. 10 tuition waivers to students age 14 and over for 10 weeks of art instruction in exchange for minimum 5 weeks of work at specific jobs in Center. Room and board not furnished. College credit may be arranged. Submit resume. Competition includes photography, visual arts, writing, other crafts.

JUDGING: By director.

ENTRY FEE: $10.

DEADLINES: Application, June. Study program, Summer.

CERAMICS

Ceramics usually defined as the art and technology of making clay objects by heat-treatment (fire hardening). Includes VESSEL FORM. (Also see CLAY, POTTERY.)

13

Beloit and Vicinity Exhibition
Wright Art Center
Marylou S. Williams, Director
Beloit College
Beloit, Wisconsin 53511 U.S.A.
Tel: (608) 365-3391

Entry January

Regional; **entry open to Wisconsin and neighboring states;** annual in March-April; established 1967. Purpose: to provide exposure to regional artists, encourage purchase of their work. Sponsored by Art League of Beloit, Wright Art Center of Beloit College. Average statistics (all sections): 200 entries, 6 awards, 900 attendance. Held at Beloit College for 3 weeks. Also sponsor workshops, lectures, classes, exhibitions.

CERAMICS CONTEST: All Types, original, 8 feet maximum any dimension, suitably presented for display; limit 1 per entrant (all sections). Completed in previous 2 years. Require hand-delivery. Submit slides for entry review. No work done under supervision, previously exhibited in Beloit vicinity. Competition includes photography, visual arts, fiber.

AWARDS: $2000 in Cash Awards. Beloit College Purchase Award.

JUDGING: Entry review by jury. Awards judging by 1 juror. Sponsor insures during exhibition. Not responsible for loss or damage.

SALES TERMS: Sales optional. 25% commission charge.

ENTRY FEE: $8.

DEADLINES: Entry, January. Judging, February. Event, March-April.

14

Broward Art Guild (BAG) Tri-County Watercolor and Ceramics Competition
Kirk Dressler, Executive Director
3450 North Andrews Avenue
Fort Lauderdale, Florida 33309
U.S.A. Tel: (305) 564-0121

Entry February

Regional; **entry open to Broward, Dade, and Palm Beach counties in Florida;** annual in March. Sponsored and supported by BAG (founded 1952). Held at BAG Gallery in Fort Lauderdale for 2 weeks. Publish *BAG*

Newsletter, Florida State Arts Monthly Gazette. Also sponsor All Broward Exhibition, London Workshop (7-day study tour), Abstract Show, poetry readings, other cultural events.

CERAMICS CONTEST: All Types, original; limit 3 per entrant. Require hand-delivery. May be executed by 2 artists if done from start to finish by both. No work from kits, patterns, molds, copies from another's photograph; done under supervision. Also have watercolor section.

AWARDS: $150 First, $75 Second, $25 Third Prizes. Honorable Mention Ribbon.

JUDGING: By 1 ceramicist.

SALES TERMS: Sales optional. 20% commission charge.

ENTRY FEE: $15.

DEADLINES: Entry, February. Acceptance, event, March.

15

East Central Indiana Ceramic Art Show
Sharon L. Williams, President
R. R. #2, Box 80
Warren, Indiana 46792 U.S.A.
Tel: (219) 375-2515

Entry September

International; entry open to all; annual in September; established 1956. Sponsored by East Central Ceramic Art Association. Held in Grant County 4H Fairgrounds in Marion, Indiana for 3 days. Have studio, teachers and hobbyist booths available.

CERAMICS CONTEST: All Forms, ready for display; limit 2 per category. Require hand-delivery. No props, lampshades, potted plants, felt on base. Divisions: Professional, Hobbyist, Pre-School, High School, Senior Citizens, Handicapped. Categories: Wheel; Hand-Formed; Incising; Sgraffito and Carving; Glaze Combination; Applied Decoration; Flowers; Jewelry (porcelain, ceramic, glass); Glass; Porcelain (glazed, stain, china paint); Underglaze; Stain (figurines, steins, plaques, luster and metallics, miscellaneous); Lace Draping (porcelain, stain); Creative Arrangement; China Painting; Clay Lifting; Luster and Metallics, Fired; Decoupage; Air Brush (underglaze, stain); Majolica; Freehand Brush Decoration, Mold Piece; Greenware Alterations; Stoneware; Textured Glazes; Stain-Glaze Combinations; Dolls (porcelain, ceramic); Holiday; Decals; Glaze; Special Effects (including sand painting); Boo Boos.

AWARDS: Not specified.

JUDGING: By 3 judges. Each category judged independently.

ENTRY FEE: 50¢ per work. $1.50 per set of 3 or more works.

DEADLINES: Entry, event, September.

16

Michigan Potters' Association (MPA) Ceramics Exhibition

Shirley White-Black, Vice-President
1233 Bending Road
Ann Arbor, Michigan 48103 U.S.A.
Tel: (313) 662-2287

Entry January

State; **entry open to Michigan residents age 18 and over;** annual in March-April; established 1978. Purpose: to showcase good ceramic work for benefit of artists; acquaint public with clay art. Sponsored by MPA (founded 1961). Supported by Michigan Foundation for the Arts, Michigan Council for the Arts, Detroit Artist Market. Average statistics: 225 en-

---

tries, 91 entrants, 7 awards, $4000 total sales. Held in Detroit, Michigan for 4 weeks. Also sponsor workshops, lectures. Second contact: Detroit Artist Market, 1452 Randolph Street, Detroit, Michigan 48226; tel: (313) 962-0337.

CERAMICS CONTEST: All Forms (special biennial theme even years), handcrafted, assembled, easily movable, ready for display; limit 3 per entrant. No supervised work.

AWARDS: $1200 in Cash Prizes.

JUDGING: By 1 nationally known potter-judge. Based on singular quality, sensitive use of skills, quality of enjoyment, spirit, theme. Sponsor insures during exhibition only; may photograph work for publicity.

SALES TERMS: Sales optional. 25% commission charge (under $100), 30% (over $100).

ENTRY FEE: $18.

DEADLINES: Entry, January. Judging, event, March-April.

17

Middletown Fine Arts Center American Art Exhibition

Edith Kohler, President
130 North Verity Parkway
Middletown, Ohio 45042 U.S.A.
Tel: (513) 424-2416

Entry August

National; **entry open to U.S.;** annual in September-October; established 1975. Formerly called MIDDLETOWN AREA ART SHOW, became national 1981. Purpose: to provide artistic outlet for visual artists, bring quality art exhibit to Middletown area. Sponsored by and held at Middletown Fine Arts Center for 4 weeks. Average statistics (all sections): 300 entries, 200 entrants, 1500 attendance, $200 sales per entrant. Also sponsor Mario Cooper Watercolor Workshop (October).

CERAMICS CONTEST: All Types, maximum 60x72 inches, 100lbs., wall decorations ready for hanging. Submit 35mm mounted slides for entry review. Competition includes visual arts, photography, fabric arts, metalwork.

AWARDS: $1000 to best of show (includes all sections). $100 to best ceramics.

JUDGING: Entry review by 5-member committee. Awards judging by 2 art professionals. Sponsor may photograph entries for publicity. Not responsible for loss or damage.

SALES TERMS: Sales encouraged. 33-1/3% commission charge.

ENTRY FEE: $7 per work plus return postage.

DEADLINES: Entry August. Judging, event, September-October.

18

New Orleans Triennial Competition
New Orleans Museum of Art
William A. Fagaly, Curator
P. O. Box 19123
New Orleans, Louisiana 70179
U.S.A. Tel: (504) 488-2631

Entry Spring

Regional; **entry open to Southeastern U.S.;** triennial in Spring; established 1887. Formerly called ARTIST BIENNIAL to 1980. Purpose: to give Southeastern U.S. artists opportunity for review and exposure. Sponsored by New Orleans Museum of Art, Art Association of New Orleans. Average statistics (all sections): 3700 entries, 1300 entrants. Held at New Orleans Museum of Art for 6 weeks.

CERAMICS CONTEST: All Types, original, any dimensions; limit 3 per entrant. Submit 1 (2D), 3 (3D) 35mm slides for entry review. Require paper documentation, typewritten proposals, and-or 8x10-inch monochrome photographs for conceptual works. Competition includes film, video, photography, fabrics, visual arts.

ELIGIBILITY: Open to residents of Kentucky, Tennessee, West Virginia, North Carolina, South Carolina, Georgia, Alabama, Mississippi, Arkansas, Louisiana, Texas.

AWARDS: Purchase Awards. 1-person exhibition at museum.

JUDGING: By nationally prominent authority in contemporary art. Entries insured during exhibition. Not responsible for in-transit loss or damage.

ENTRY FEE: None. No sales commission charge.

DEADLINES: Entry, event, Spring.

19

Vessels Aesthetic National Exhibition
Taft College
Jack Mettier, Exhibition Director
29 Emmons Park Drive
Taft, California 93268 U.S.A.
Tel: (805) 765-4086

Entry dates vary

National; **entry open to U.S. residents;** periodic; established 1981. Purpose: to recognize and show aesthetic versatility of clay in vessel form. Sponsored by Taft College, Downey Museum of Art. Supported by Taft College community services, industry. Average statistics: 1000 entries, 400 entrants, 75 finalists. Held at Taft College Art Gallery, and Downey Museum of Art, for 3 weeks each.

CERAMICS CONTEST: Vessel Form, Functional, Nonfunctional, original, 6 feet maximum any dimension, portable by 2 people; unlimited entry. Mixed media only where clay is dominant media. Submit 3 35mm slides (including 1 full and one detailed view) for entry review. No glass mounts, work done under supervision, fragile entries.

AWARDS: $1500 in Merit Awards. Purchase Prizes.

JUDGING: By 3 professional clay artists. Based on craftsmanship, aesthetic concept, technical execution. Sponsor may photograph entries for catalog, educational, publicity purposes; insures during exhibition.

SALES TERMS: 30% commission charge.

ENTRY FEE: $5 per work (set counts as 1).

DEADLINES: Periodic.

20

Faenza International Competition of Artistic Ceramics
Marabini Edmondo, Secretary
Municipal Palace
Place del Popolo, 31
48018 Faenza, ITALY Tel: 0546 28664

Entry April

International; entry open to all; annual in July-October; established 1930. Purpose: to encourage the pursuit of new creations of inventiveness, practical utility, and suitable techniques. Sponsored by City of Faenza. Average statistics: 3000 entries, 400 entrants, 35 countries, 20 awards. Held in Faenza for 11 weeks. Tickets: 500 L. Second contact: Bassi Piera, Palazzo Mazzolani, Corso Mazzini 93, 48018 Faenza, Italy.

CERAMICS CONTEST: All Types, any technique; limit 5 per entrant. Submit artist curriculum, photograph or slide of each work, technical description of works. No non-fired decoration; previously displayed entries.

AWARDS: 1,500,000 L Faenza Prize to best of show. 7 500,000 L Purchase Prizes (with prior authorization of the artist). President of the Republic, Regione Emilia-Romagna, Ministries' and Associations' Gold Medals.

JUDGING: By 5 art, ceramic and cultural experts. Sponsor owns winning entries for permanent display; retains photographs and curricula. Not responsible for loss or damage.

SALES TERMS: Sales optional (works for sale to be priced). 10% commission charge.

ENTRY FEE: None. Entrants pay return postage.

DEADLINES: Entry, April. Event, July-October.

21

Monte Carlo International Grand Prix of Contemporary Art
Monaco National Museum
Annette Bordeau, Secretary General
17 Avenue Princesse Grace
Monte Carlo
MONACO PRINCIPALITY Tel: (93) 30-91-26

Entry January

International; entry open to all; annual in Winter; established 1967. Purpose: to discover, encourage, make known work with potential. Sponsored and supported by Monaco National Museum. Average statistics (all sections): 4000 entries, 50 countries, 300 finalists. Held at Congress Centre Auditorium of Monte Carlo for several weeks. Also sponsor social, educational, artistic, scientific events year-round. Second contact: Dr. Helene Day, Consul of Monaco in New England, 251 Payson Road, Belmont, Massachusetts 02178; tel: (617) 489-1240.

CERAMICS CONTEST: All Trends, Techniques. Submit maximum 6 slides for entry review. Competition includes painting, drawing, prints, sculpture.

AWARDS: (Includes all sections): 10,000 F Grand Prix De S.A.S. Le Prince Rainier 111 Medal, Diploma. 3 5000 F, 1 2000 F Diplomas. 5000 F Prix de la Ville Monaco Diploma to work with subject of Principality of Monaco or Mediterranean landscape. 5000 F Diplomas to sculpture, figurative work. Prix d'Art Sacre Diploma, Medal to sacred art. 2 Diplomas and volumes of Art Awards. Honorable Mentions.

JUDGING: Entry review by selection committee. Awards judging by jury. Not responsible for loss or damage.

ENTRY FEE: 100 F per work. No sales commission charge.

DEADLINES: Entry, January. Judging, event, late Winter.

CERAMICS, GLASS

Ceramics and Glass, including CHINA, CLAY, POTTERY, MOSAIC, and BLOWN, CAST, STAINED GLASS. See CERAMICS for definition of Ceramics. (Also see other CERAMICS, GLASS CATEGORIES.)

22

Central Pennsylvania Festival of the Arts Juried Craft Exhibition
Lurene Frantz, Managing Director
Box 1023
State College, Pennsylvania 16801
U.S.A. Tel: (814) 237-3682

Entry March

International; entry open to all; annual in July-September; established 1966. Purpose: to encourage craftspersons; to enable craftspersons to present their work to the public. Average statistics: 260 entrants, 100 accepted entries. Sponsored by and held at Central Pennsylvania State University in State College for 3 months. Have banner, fiddle, poetry competitions. Also sponsor sidewalk sale, photography exhibition.

CERAMICS CONTEST: All Types, 9x5 feet maximum; limit 2 per entrant (set counts as 1). Submit 35mm slides (1 for 2D, 4 for 3D) for entry review. Competition includes other crafts.

GLASS CONTEST: All types. Requirements, restrictions same as for Ceramics.

AWARDS: $2000 in Prizes. Purchase Prize (includes all sections).

JUDGING: Entry review and awards judging by 1 crafts professional. Sponsor may photograph entries; insures work while at University.

SALES TERMS: 10% commission charge.

ENTRY FEE: $5 plus $15 refundable exhibition fee. Entrants pays return postage.

DEADLINES: Entry, March. Materials, June. Event, July-September.

23

Cooperstown Art Association Art Exhibition
Olga Welsh, Director
28 Pioneer Street
Cooperstown, New York 13326
U.S.A. Tel: (607) 547-9777

Entry June

National; **entry open to U.S.;** annual in July–August; established 1928. Purpose: to foster interest in fine and applied arts. Sponsored by and held at Cooperstown Art Association Galleries in Cooperstown for 1 month. Average statistics (all sections): 500 entries, 200 finalists, 5000 attendance, $10,000 total sales. Tickets: 50¢ (children under 12 free). Also sponsor educational art classes, weekly demonstrations. Second contact: 22 Main Street, Cooperstown, New York 13326.

CERAMICS CONTEST: All Types, original, freestanding objects maximum 48 inches greatest lateral dimension, 200lbs.; hanging objects maximum 60 inches horizontal dimension, 40lbs., ready for hanging; limit 1 per entrant. Recently produced. Competition includes fine arts, other crafts.

GLASS CONTEST: All Types. Requirements, restrictions same as for Ceramics.

AWARDS: $7350 in Awards (includes all sections).

JUDGING: Entry review and awards judging by 1 art professional. Sponsor may photograph work for publicity. Not responsible for loss or damage.

SALES TERMS: Sales optional. 20% commission charge.

ENTRY FEE: $10.

DEADLINES: Entry, June. Judging, event, July–August.

24

Grand Prairie Festival of Arts
Grand Prairie Arts Council
Mrs. Neil Maynard, President
P. O. Box 65
Stuttgart, Arkansas 72160 U.S.A.
Tel: (501) 673-7278

Entry September

International; entry open to all; annual in September; established 1957. Purpose: to encourage cultural development in Grand Prairie area. Theme: Yesterday, Today and Tomorrow. Sponsored and supported by Grand Prairie Art Council. Held at Grand Prairie War Memorial in Stuttgart for 3 days. Have talent demonstrations, entertainment, clothesline show. Also sponsor one-man show, special exhibits, Madelene Jones Oliver Memorial Scholarship.

CERAMICS-CLAY CONTEST: All Forms (including china), original, maximum 4 feet any dimension; unlimited entry. Produced in previous 2 years (adult), 1 year (youth). Divisions: Adult, Youth (Grand Prairie students only). Competition includes all crafts. Also have photography, art sections.

STAINED GLASS CONTEST: All Forms. Requirements, restrictions same as for Ceramics.

AWARDS: *Adult* (includes all crafts): $50 Best of Show. $50 Best of Grand Prairie Creative Crafts. *Youth:* Gift Certificates, Ribbons.

JUDGING: By 1 juror and popular vote. Sponsor may photograph entries for catalog, publicity. Not responsible for loss or damage.

SALES TERMS: 10% commission charge.

ENTRY FEE: $1 per work. Youth free for maximum 2 entries.

DEADLINES: Entry, event, September.

25

Hartland Art Show
Hartland Art Council
Sandy Scherba
P. O. Box 126
Hartland, Michigan 48029 U.S.A.

Entry June

State; **entry open to Michigan;** annual in June; established 1967. Purpose: to provide Michigan artists with opportunity to display, be recognized for and sell their work. Sponsored by Hartland Art Council. Supported by Hartland Foundation. Average statistics (all sections): 700 entries, 360 entrants, 175 finalists, 20 awards, 2000 attendance. Held at Hartland Art School for 1 week.

CERAMICS CONTEST: All Types, original; unlimited entry. Competition includes photography, fine arts, textiles, jewelry, other crafts.

GLASS CONTEST: All Types. Requirements, restrictions same as for Ceramics.

AWARDS: *Includes all sections:* $2000 in Purchase and Cash Awards. Excellence Awards. Winning entries displayed in private gallery (September-October).

JUDGING: By 2 art professors or museum curators. Sponsor may display award-winning entries in private gallery. Sponsor reserves right to refuse any entry.

ENTRY FEE: $8 per work. No commission charge.

DEADLINES: Entry, awards, June.

26

Marin County Fair Fine Craft Competition
Yolanda F. Sullivan, Manager
Marin Center Fairgrounds
San Rafael, California 94903 U.S.A.
Tel: (415) 499-6400

Entry May

Regional; **entry open to Northern California;** annual in July; established 1945. Sponsored by Marin County Fair and Expositions. Average statistics (all sections): 350 entries, 13 awards. Held at San Rafael. Have entertainment; photography, film, music, arts contest.

CERAMICS CONTEST: All Types (including mosaic, mixed media), original, able to be handled without mechanical assistance, ready for hanging if appropriate; freestanding items to be provided with a rectangular wood stand (with plexiglass cube cover if fragile); limit 2 per section. Require hand-delivery. No commercial kits. Also have textile, jewelry, metal, woodwork sections.

GLASS CONTEST: All Types (including hand-blown, molded, stained glass), original. Requirements, restrictions same as for Ceramics.

AWARDS: $400 and Ribbon to best of show (includes all sections). $125 and Ribbon each to ceramics, glass. $60 and Merit Ribbon to ceramics, glass. Honorable Mention Ribbons.

JUDGING: Entry review and awards judging by 3 craftspersons. Not responsible for loss or damage.

SALES TERMS: Sales optional. 20% commission charge.

ENTRY FEE: $3 per work.

DEADLINES: Entry, May. Judging, June. Event, July.

27

Richmond Art Center Designer-Craftsmen Annual Exhibition
Clayton Pinkerton, Curator
Civic Center Plaza
25th and Barret
Richmond, California 94804 U.S.A.
Tel: (415) 231-2163

Entry September

State; **entry open to California;** annual in October-November; established 1962. Purpose: to present rich and varied arts to San Francisco Bay Area public. Sponsored and held at Richmond Art Center for 1 month. Average statistics: 300 entries, 200 entrants, 10 awards, 1500 attendance. Also sponsor Annual Spring Exhibition.

CERAMICS CONTEST: All Types, original, handcrafted, portable by 1 person or divided into manageable sections, set counts as 1 entry; limit 3 per entrant (all sections). Completed in previous 2 years. Require hand-delivery. No work produced under supervision; excessively fragile entries. Competition includes glass, textiles, metal, jewelry, wood.

GLASS CONTEST: All Types. Requirements, restrictions same as for Ceramics.

AWARDS: $1000 in Cash Awards (includes all sections).

JUDGING: Entry review and awards judging by 3 judges. Sponsor may photograph entries for publicity, catalog, records; insures work during exhibition. Not responsible for loss or damage.

SALES TERMS: 25% commission charge.

ENTRY FEE: $5 per work.

DEADLINES: Entry, September. Acceptance, October. Event, October-November.

28

Santa Clara County Fair Art Exhibit
William R. Smethers,
Secretary-Manager
344 Tully Road
San Jose, California 95111 U.S.A.
Tel: (408) 295-3050

Entry July

Regional; **entry open to Santa Clara County;** annual in August. Held at Statehouse Art Building for 11 days.

CERAMICS CONTEST: All Types (including pottery), original. Require hand-delivery. Also have arts, photography, other crafts.

GLASS CONTEST: All Types (including blown, cast). Requirements, restrictions same as for Ceramics.

AWARDS: *Includes both sections:* $100 First, $50 Second Prize; Third, Fourth, Fifth Place Ribbons. $25 and Bronze Medal Special Award (includes other craft media, arts, photography).

JUDGING: By 3 jurors. Sponsor may withhold awards. Not responsible for loss or damage.

ENTRY FEE: $3 (up to 3 works). $3 per additional 3 works.

DEADLINES: Entry, July. Event, August.

29
Square Fair Arts and Crafts Gallery Contest
Garnett Branch of American
Association of University Women
(AAUW)
Cheri Kent, Chair
403 West 6th
Garnett, Kansas 66032 U.S.A.
Tel: (913) 448-6891

Entry April

International; entry open to all; annual in May; established 1972. Sponsored by Garnett Branch of AAUW, Garnett Area Chamber of Commerce. Average 120 entrants (all sections). Held in Courthouse Square for 1 day as part of Arts and Crafts Fair. Second contact: Garnett Area Chamber of Commerce, 322 South Oak, Garnett, Kansas 66032.

CERAMICS-POTTERY CONTEST: **All Forms,** handcrafted; limit 1 per contest entrant, 2 per fair exhibitor. Entrants set up own work display. No commercial work. Competition for some awards includes visual arts, other crafts.

GLASS CONTEST: **All Forms.** Requirements, restrictions same as for Ceramics.

AWARDS: $50 Best of Show Award to fair exhibitors only. $25 First, $15 Second, $10 Third Place Award to people's choice winners (includes all sections). $25 First, $15 Second, $10 Third Place Award to each media category.

JUDGING: By 1 professional and by public vote.

ENTRY FEE: Contest entrant: $3. Fair exhibitor: First entry free, second $2 (plus $12 for 8x4-foot exhibition space). No sales commission charge.

DEADLINES: Entry, April. Event, May.

30
Vahki Juried Arts and Crafts Competition
City of Mesa Cultural Activities
Department
Gerry Hulcher, Superintendent
155 North Center Street
P. O. Box 1466
Mesa, Arizona 85201 U.S.A.
Tel: (602) 834-2198

Entry May

State; **entry open to Arizona;** annual in June; established 1979. Named after Vahki phase of Hohokum people (300 B.C. to 100 A.D.), period noted for introduction of new cultural traits into Gila River Basin. Purpose: to provide Arizona artists opportunity to exhibit, sell work. Sponsored and supported by City of Mesa Cultural Activities Department, and held in their Gallery for 3 weeks. Have workshops, lectures, panel discussions.

CERAMICS CONTEST: **All Types,** original, 3D fully assembled, 2D framed, ready for hanging if appropriate; limit 4 per entrant (set counts as 1). Completed in previous 2 years. Submit slides for entry review. No entries previously exhibited in any Arizona juried show. Competition includes visual arts, photography, other crafts.

GLASS CONTEST: **All Types.** Requirements, restrictions same as for Ceramics.

AWARDS: $500 in Cash Awards (all sections).

JUDGING: By 3 professionals. Not responsible for loss or damage.

SALES TERMS: Sales optional. 15% commission charge.

ENTRY FEE: $5 per work.

DEADLINES: Entry, judging, May. Event, June.

CERAMICS, GLASS, SCULPTURE

Ceramics, Glass, Sculpture, including CLAY, POTTERY, and BLOWN, CAST, STAINED GLASS. See CERAMICS for definition of Ceramics. (Also see other CERAMICS, GLASS, SCULPTURE CATEGORIES.)

31

Beverly Art Center Art Fair and Festival
Beverly Art Center and Vanderpoel Art Association
Pat McGrail, Manager
2153 West 111th Street
Chicago, Illinois 60643 U.S.A.
Tel: (312) 445-3838

Entry April

International; entry open to all; annual in June; established 1975. Purpose: to bring art to people and people to art. Sponsored and supported by Beverly Art Center and Vanderpoel Art Association. Average 130 entries (all sections). Held at Beverly Art Center in Chicago for 2 days. Have 2-story gallery, 460-seat theater, classrooms, workshops. Also sponsor drama, film, literature, music contests.

CERAMICS CONTEST: All Types, original; unlimited entry (all sections). Submit 5 35mm slides (4 full view, 1 detail) for entry review. No copies, kits, commercial molds, manufactured products. Competition in-

cludes photography, visual arts, fiber, jewelry, metalsmithing.

GLASS CONTEST: All Types. Requirements, restrictions same as for Ceramics.

SCULPTURE CONTEST: All Types. Requirements, restrictions same as for Ceramics.

AWARDS: *Includes all sections:* $400 to best of show. 8 $200 Excellence Awards.

JUDGING: Entry review by 5 art professionals. Awards judging by 3 judges. Sponsor may withhold awards. Not responsible for loss or damage.

ENTRY FEE: $7.50 jury fee plus $15 (refundable). Entrants pay return postage. No sales commission charge.

DEADLINES: Entry, April. Acceptance, May. Judging, event, June.

32

Gateway to the Delta Invitational Arts Competition
Yazoo County Chamber of Commerce
P. O. Box 172
Yazoo City, Mississippi 39191 U.S.A.

Entry September

Regional; **entry open to Mississippi, Alabama, Arkansas, Louisiana, Tennessee Craftsmen's Guild members;** annual in October; established 1972. Sponsored by Yazoo County Chamber of Commerce. Have arts-crafts fair and sale, tours, music.

CERAMICS-SCULPTURE CONTEST: All Types, original; limit 3 per entrant (all sections). Produced in previous 3 years. Entrants provide and attend sales displays. Submit 3 35mm slides (or studio photographs) for entry review. No kits, commercial molds, patterns. Competition includes wood, metal, arts, photography, other crafts.

GLASS CONTEST: All Types. Requirements, restrictions same as for Ceramics-Sculpture. Competition includes fiber, embellished fabrics, leather, jewelry, arts, photography.

AWARDS: $150 First, $75 Second, $25 Third Prizes each to ceramics and sculpture (includes wood, metal), glass (includes fiber, embellished fabric, leather, jewelry,). *All sections:* $200 Best in Show. Purchase Awards, Honorable Mentions.

JUDGING: Entry review by committee. Awards judging by 1 judge.

ENTRY FEE: $23 for 12x12-foot booth space.

DEADLINES: Entry, September. Event, October.

33

North Dakota Art Exhibition
Minot Art Gallery
Shelly Ellstrom, Director
P. O. Box 325
North Dakota State Fairgrounds
Minot, North Dakota 58701 U.S.A.
Tel: (701) 838-4445

Entry February

National; **entry open to U.S.;** annual in March; established 1970. Purpose: to provide opportunity for children and adults to participate in visual arts. Sponsored by Minot Art Gallery and Association. Supported by North Dakota Council of the Arts and Humanities, NEA. Held at Minot Art Gallery for 3 weeks. Also sponsor annual outdoor Art Fair, regular exhibitions.

CERAMICS CONTEST: All Types, maximum 6 feet, 100lbs.; limit 2 per entrant. No plaster, excessively

fragile works. Competition includes arts, photography, other crafts.

GLASS CONTEST: All Types. Requirements, restrictions same as for Ceramics.

SCULPTURE CONTEST: All Types. No plaster. Other requirements, restrictions same as for Ceramics.

AWARDS: $1000 in Cash, Purchase Awards.

JUDGING: By craft professional. Sponsor may photograph entries for publicity; insures accepted works. Not responsible for loss or damage.

SALES TERMS: Sales optional. No commission charge.

ENTRY FEE: $6.

DEADLINES: Entry, February. Event, March.

34

Rochester-Finger Lakes Crafts Exhibition
Memorial Art Gallery
University of Rochester
490 University Avenue
Rochester, New York 14607 U.S.A.
Tel: (716) 275-4755

Entry April

State; **entry open to New York residents age 18 and over;** biennial in May-June (even years). Sponsored by and held at University of Rochester Memorial Art Gallery for 6 weeks.

CERAMICS CONTEST: All Types, original, 2D works framed; limit 2 per entrant (collaborated work counts as 1). Completed in previous 2 years. No excessively large works. Competition includes painting, drawing, prints, photography, film and video, other crafts.

GLASS CONTEST: All Types (including stained glass). Requirements, restrictions same as for Ceramics.

SCULPTURE CONTEST: All Media (including ceramics). Requirements, restrictions same as for Ceramics.

ELIGIBILITY: Residents, age 18 and over, of Allegany, Cayuga, Chemung, Cortland, Genesee, Livingston, Monroe, Onondaga, Ontario, Orleans, Oswego, Schuyler, Seneca, Steuben, Tioga, Tompkins, Wayne, Wyoming, and Yates Counties.

AWARDS: $3500 in Cash Prizes (includes all sections).

JUDGING: By well-known artist, director, professor. Sponsor may reject entries of excessive size, complexity, requiring special installation. Sponsor insures during exhibition only; not responsible for loss or damage in-transit.

SALES TERMS: Sales optional. 30% commission charge.

ENTRY FEE: $10.

DEADLINES: Entry, April. Event, May-June.

35

**San Jose Art League
3-Dimensional Art Regional
Exhibition**
482 South Second Street
San Jose, California 95113 U.S.A.
Tel: (408) 294-4545

Entry May

State; **entry open to California residents over age 18;** annual in May-June; established 1970. Formerly called ART REGIONAL to 1976. Purpose: to give recognition to emerging artists, craftspersons. Sponsored by San Jose Art League (nonprofit organization). Supported by Santa Clara Music and Arts Foundation, Fine Arts Commission, City of San Jose. Average statistics (all sections): 250 entries, 100 entrants. Held at San Jose Art League Galleries for 1 month. Also sponsor 2D Art Regional Exhibition, Art Festival, monthly exhibitions, lectures, demonstrations.

CERAMICS CONTEST: All Forms (including fired pottery), original, maximum 50 inches wide, 150lbs., ready for display or hanging; unlimited entry. Require hand-delivery. No supervised work, fragile entries. Competition includes glass, sculpture, metal, fiber and woodwork.

GLASS CONTEST: Blown, Cast. Requirements, restrictions same as for Ceramics.

SCULPTURE CONTEST: All Media (except plaster, other perishable material), original, maximum 50 inches wide, 150lbs.; bas relief minimum 3-inch projection, ready for display or hanging; unlimited entry. Other requirements, restrictions same as for Ceramics.

AWARDS: $1000 in Cash Awards at jurors' discretion.

JUDGING: By 2 art professionals. Based on quality. Not responsible for loss or damage.

SALES TERMS: Sales optional. 25% commission charge.

ENTRY FEE: $5 per work (set counts as 1).

DEADLINES: Entry, May. Event, May-June.

36

Tahoe Ehrman Mansion Art Show and Crafts Fair
North Tahoe Fine Arts Council
Eileen Janowitz-Ward, Coordinator
P. O. Box 249
Tahoe Vista, California 95732 U.S.A.
Tel: (916) 546-5562

Entry July

International; entry open to all; annual in August; established 1967. Purpose: to provide high quality fine arts show. Sponsored by North Tahoe Fine Arts Council, Lake Tahoe State Park Advisory Committee. Average $5000 total sales (all sections). Held at Ehrman Mansion (Sugar Pine Point State Park) for 1 week. Have reception, music. Publish *Arti-facts* (semimonthly). Also sponsor Outdoor Arts and Crafts Fair.

CERAMICS CONTEST: Free Form, Slab, Wheel-Thrown, original, framed and ready for hanging if appropriate; limit 2 per adult, 1 per child-high school. No commercial work. Divisions: Adult, Children-High School. Categories: Functional, Nonfunctional. Competition includes visual arts, photography, other crafts.

STAINED GLASS CONTEST: All Types, 48 inches wide maximum, framed, ready for hanging. Other requirements, restrictions, divisions same as for Ceramics.

POTTERY CONTEST: Free Form, Slab, Wheel-Thrown. Requirements, restrictions, divisions, categories same as for Ceramics.

SCULPTURE CONTEST: Clay, Mixed Media, maximum 3 feet, 100lbs. Other requirements, restrictions, divisions same as for Ceramics.

AWARDS: Cash Awards. First Place Awards to each division.

JUDGING: By 3 art professionals.

SALES TERMS: Sales optional. 20% commission charge.

ENTRY FEE: Adults, $6 per work. Children-high school, free.

DEADLINES: Entry, July. Judging, event, August.

CERAMICS, GLASS, SCULPTURE, ENAMEL, PLASTIC
Ceramics, Glass, Sculpture, Enamel, Plastic, including CLAY, PORCELAIN, EARTHENWARE, STONEWARE, and TABLEWARE. ENAMEL usually defined as glassy substance or glaze applied by fusion to surface of ceramics, glass, or metal. See CERAMICS for definition of Ceramics. (Also see other CERAMICS, GLASS, SCULPTURE, ENAMEL, and PLASTIC CATEGORIES.)

37

Arkansas Arts Center Prints, Drawings and Crafts Exhibition
Townsend Wolfe, Director
MacArthur Park
P. O. Box 2137
Little Rock, Arkansas 72203 U.S.A.

Entry April

Regional; **entry open to South-Central U.S.;** annual in May-June; established 1968. Sponsored by Arkansas Arts Center, founded in 1941 to establish and maintain growth, understanding of arts. Supported by City of Little Rock. Recognized by Arkansas State Board of Education, American Association of Museums. Held at Arkansas Arts Center in Little Rock for 4 weeks. Have book and film library, traveling seminars, concerts, workshops, visiting artists programs. Also sponsor Toys Designed by Artists Exhibition, Delta Art Exhibit; instruction, exhibitions and scholarships in photography, filmmaking, drama, dance, arts, and crafts.

CERAMICS CONTEST: All Types; limit 2 per entrant (all sections). Competition for some awards includes other fine arts, other crafts. Also have jewelry, metal, textiles, wood, photography sections.

GLASS CONTEST: All Types. Requirements same as for Ceramics.

PLASTICS CONTEST: All Types. Requirements same as for Ceramics.

MIXED MEDIA CONTEST: All Types. Requirements same as for Ceramics.

ELIGIBILITY: Open to residents of Arkansas, Louisiana, Mississippi, Missouri, Oklahoma, Tennessee, Texas.

AWARDS: 1 $200 Purchase Award to ceramics, general crafts. $2000 in additional Purchase Awards (includes all sections).

JUDGING: By a judge. Sponsor retains winning entries for permanent collection.

ENTRY FEE: $7.50 per work.

DEADLINES: Entry, April. Event, May-June.

38

Butler Institute of American Art Ohio Ceramic, Sculpture and Craft Show
Joan Chopler, Public Relations Coordinator
524 Wick Avenue

Youngstown, Ohio 44502 U.S.A.
Tel: (216) 743-1107, 743-1711
Entry December

State; **entry open to residents, former residents of Ohio;** annual in January-February; established 1947. Purpose: to provide annual representation of contemporary visual art. Sponsored and supported by Butler Institute of American Art (nonprofit organization). Average statistics (all sections): 350 entries, 110 finalists, 6 awards, 3500 attendance. Held at Butler Institute in Youngstown for 6 weeks. Have galleries, cases and stands. Also sponsor national midyear Area Artists' Annual Show.

CERAMICS CONTEST: All Types; limit 3 per entrant (pair or set counts as 1). No fragile, poorly constructed, previously sold work. Competition includes jewelry, fiber, metalwork.

GLASS CONTEST: All Types. Restrictions same as for Ceramics.

SCULPTURE CONTEST: All Types (including clay and glass). Restrictions same as for Ceramics.

ENAMEL CONTEST: All Types. Restrictions same as for Ceramics.

AWARDS: (Includes all sections): $1500 Butler Institute Purchase Prizes. Friends of American Art Purchase Prize. $100 Sidney S. Moyer Award to sculpture. $50 Youngstown Junior League Award.

JUDGING: By 1 nationally known artist, Institute staff. Sponsor may withhold awards. Not responsible for loss or damage.

SALES TERMS: Sales optional. 10% commission charge.

ENTRY FEE: $1 per work plus $3

per mailed container. Entrants pay return postage.

DEADLINES: Entry, judging, December. Event, January-February.

39

Mid-Michigan Art Exhibition
Midland Art Council of the Midland Center for the Arts
Toni Pott & Linda Wingfield, Chairs
1801 West St. Andrews Street
Midland, Michigan 48640 U.S.A.
Tel: (517) 631-3250

Entry January

State; **entry open to Michigan residents age 18 and over;** annual in January-February; established 1959. Sponsored and supported by Midland Art Council of the Midland Center for the Arts, Michigan Foundation of Arts. Average statistics (all sections): 750 entries, 300 entrants, 200 finalists, 2000 attendance. Held at Midland Center for the Arts for 1 month. Publish *Art Scape* (quarterly).

CERAMICS CONTEST: All Types, 2D work ready for hanging, large constructions assembled by artist; limit 3 per entrant (all sections). Produced in previous 2 years. Require hand-delivery. No work done under supervision. Competition includes photography, arts, other crafts.

SCULPTURE CONTEST: All Types. Requirements, restrictions same as for Ceramics.

ENAMEL CONTEST: All Types. Requirements, restrictions same as for Ceramics.

PLASTIC CONTEST: All Types. Requirements, restrictions same as for Ceramics.

AWARDS: Kathryn Rave Award (includes all crafts). *Includes all sections:* $750 First, $500 Second, $300 Third Prize. Viewers' Choice Award. Up to $400 in Honorable Mentions.

JUDGING: By 1 curator. Not responsible for loss or damage. Sponsor may withdraw entries from exhibition.

ENTRY FEE: $15. No sales commission charge.

DEADLINES: Entry, January. Event, January-February.

40

Northwest Regional Crafts Exhibition
Allied Arts of Seattle Visual Arts Committee
107 South Main Street, Suite 202
Seattle, Washington 98104 U.S.A.
Tel: (206) 624-0432

Entry May

Regional; **entry open to Pacific Northwest U.S.A.;** biennial (even years) in September-October; established 1982. Purpose: to bring recognition to quality crafts produced in Northwest. Sponsored and supported by Allied Arts of Seattle. Average statistics: 1000 entries, 500 entrants, 200 finalists, 20 awards. Held at Museum of History and Industry in Seattle for 3 weeks.

CERAMICS CONTEST: All Forms, original, 200lbs. maximum; limit 3 per entrant (all sections). Completed in previous 2 years. Submit 35mm slides for entry review (objects designed for wearing should be shown by at least 1 slide of item worn). No work produced under supervision; work requiring special installation, handling without prior consent. Competition includes all crafts.

GLASS CONTEST: All Forms. Requirements, restrictions same as for Ceramics.

ENAMEL CONTEST: All Forms. Requirements, restrictions same as for Ceramics.

PLASTICS CONTEST: All Forms. Requirements, restrictions same as for Ceramics.

AWARDS: One-Person Shows held at Contemporary Crafts in Portland, Oregon to outstanding craftspersons. Cash, Merit, and Purchase Awards.

JUDGING: By 3 crafts specialists. Sponsor insures for 80% of sales price for duration of exhibition; may photography entries for publicity, catalog, educational purposes.

SALES TERMS: Sales encouraged. 25% commission charge.

ENTRY FEE: $8 plus return postage.

DEADLINES: Entry, May. Acceptance, June. Materials, August. Exhibition, September-October.

41

Ohio Designer Craftsmen Winterfair Exhibition
JoAnn H. Stevens, Director
1981 Riverside Drive
Columbus, Ohio 43221 U.S.A.
Tel: (614) 486-7119

Entry July

National; **entry open to U.S.;** annual in December; established 1977. Purpose: to present an outstanding pre-Christmas crafts fair organized by and for craftspersons. Sponsored and supported by Ohio Designer Craftsmen Enterprises, Ohio Arts Council. Average statistics (all sections): 275 entrants (maximum), 30,000 attendance, $552,000 total sales. Held at Ohio State Fairgrounds for 4 days. Have parking facilities, retail consignment shop and wholesale marketing program, craft tour guides, comprehensive promotion campaigns, exhibition display tables (3x8 feet), chairs, electrical hookups. Tickets: $2.50. Also sponsor Cleveland Designer Craftsmen Fair, Cincinatti Crafts Fair.

CERAMICS CONTEST: All Types, original concept, design, execution; unlimited entry (2 media categories maximum per booth). Entrants provide and attend sales displays. Submit 4 slides per category for entry review; 1 entry (optional) for comprehensive exhibition. No commercial molds, manufactured artwork. Competition includes photography, fiber, metal, wood.

GLASS CONTEST: All Types. Requirements, restrictions same as for Ceramics.

SCULPTURE CONTEST: All Types. Requirements, restrictions same as for Ceramics.

ENAMEL CONTEST: All Types. Requirements, restrictions same as for Ceramics.

MIXED MEDIA CONTEST: All Types. Requirements, restrictions same as for Ceramics.

AWARDS: 7 $100 Excellence Awards. $100 Awards each to outstanding design, outstanding craftsmanship, best general booth display.

JUDGING: Entry review and awards judging by outstanding craftspersons and Fair Advisory Council. Sponsor may photograph entries for publicity, publication.

SALES TERMS: Sales compulsory. No commission charge.

ENTRY FEE: $5 screening fee. $115 for 10x10-foot booth space, $145 for end-of-aisle booth, $185 for double booth.

DEADLINES: Entry, July. Acceptance, August. Event, December.

42

San Mateo County Fair International Visual Arts Competition

San Mateo County Fair Arts Committee
Lois Kelley, Administrator
171 Flying Cloud Isle
Foster City, California 94404 U.S.A.
Tel: (415) 394-2787

Entry August

International; entry open to all; annual in September; established 1934. Sponsored by San Mateo County Fair Arts Committee. Held at County Fairgrounds in San Mateo for 19 days. Average 200,000 attendance. Also sponsor scholarship competitions to San Francisco Academy of Art College, and Instituto Allende in Guanajuato, Mexico.

CERAMICS CONTEST: All Types (including earthenware, porcelain. stoneware), size to fit through art room double doors, portable by 2 persons. Also have arts, photography, video, writing, dance, other crafts.

GLASS CONTEST: All Types. Requirements, restrictions same as for Ceramics.

SCULPTURE CONTEST: All Types (including mobiles). Requirements, restrictions same as for Ceramics.

ENAMEL CONTEST: All Types. Requirements, restrictions same as for Ceramics.

AWARDS: $100 and First Place Trophy, $50 Second, $25 Third Prize each to ceramics (including glass and enamel) and sculpture. *Includes all sections:* $100 and First Place Trophy, $50 Second, $25 Third Prize to Thoroughbred horse interpretations. $100 and First Place Trophy, $35 Merchan-dise Certificate Second, $25 Third Prize to best floral interpretations. $50, 2 Marine World Africa, U.S.A. Gold Passes, and Trophy to first place; 6 Regular Passes to second; 2 Regular Passes to third for best interpretations of Marine World Africa, U.S.A.

JUDGING: Entry review, awards judging by crafts professional. Sponsor may photograph entries for publicity. Not responsible for loss or damage.

SALES TERMS: Sales optional. 20% commission charge (tax-exempt donation).

ENTRY FEE: $6 per work (plus $3 handling charge for shipped entries).

DEADLINES: Entry, August. Notification, event, September.

43

Royal Dublin Society Crafts Competition and Exhibition

Betty Searson, Arts Administrator
Ballsbridge
Dublin 4
IRELAND Tel: 01-680645, ext. 312

Entry July

National; **entry open to Ireland;** annual in July-August; established 1925. Formerly called NATIONAL ART COMPETITION, 1925-1967. Purpose: to encourage and develop craft industry in Ireland. Sponsored by Royal Dublin Society. Supported by Commissioners of Charitable Donations and Bequests from R. R. de la Branchardiere and Queen's Institute Fund; Irish American Cultural Institute; Royal Dublin Society. Held in Ballsbridge. Also sponsor Taylor Art Competition.

CERAMICS CONTEST: All Forms (including tableware, sculpture, architecture), original, 6 feet maximum any dimension; limit 1 per category. Completed in previous 2 years in Ireland. Submit detailed description of work for entry review. No commercial kits, copies, identification marks on work. Competition includes other crafts.

GLASS CONTEST: Architectural, Decorative, Domestic, original; limit 1 per category. Other requirements, restrictions same as for Ceramics.

ENAMEL CONTEST: All Forms. Other requirements, restrictions same as for Ceramics.

AWARDS: IR£100 First, £50 Second, £25 Third Prizes to each category. *Includes all sections:* Scholarship or Development Grant to entrant with most outstanding ability. California Gold Medal to best first-prize winner. Crafts Council of Ireland Medal to any prizewinner with work of outstanding merit. Royal Dublin Society Certificates. Special Prizes to selected categories. Exhibition of works at current year's annual Horse Show and other events.

JUDGING: By 5 judges. Based on standard of design, workmanship, competence. Sponsors may reduce, withhold awards. Not responsible for loss or damage.

SALES TERMS: Sales optional. 20% commission charge.

ENTRY FEE: IR£2 per work (£1 per student) plus return postage.

DEADLINES: Entry, July. Event, July-August.

CERAMICS, GLASS, SCULPTURE, GENERAL CRAFTS, MIXED MEDIA

Ceramics, Glass, Sculpture, General Crafts, including CLAY, BLOWN GLASS, PLASTER, POTTERY, MARBLE and STONE SCULPTURE. See CERAMICS for definition of Ceramics. (Also see other CERAMICS, GLASS, SCULPTURE, GENERAL CRAFTS CATEGORIES.)

44

La Mirada Festival of Arts Competition and Exhibition
Sheila Krotinger, Publicity Director
P. O. Box 233
La Mirada, California 90637 U.S.A.
Tel: (213) 941-3066, 943-0627

Entry May

National; **entry open to U.S.;** annual in June; established 1960. Formerly called LA MIRADA FIESTA DE ARTES to 1980. Purpose: to provide opportunity for artists to compete. Sponsored by City of La Mirada. Average statistics (all sections): 1000 entries, 500 entrants, 21 awards. Held at La Mirada Civic Theatre and grounds for 10 days. Have theater, food facilities, entertainment. Tickets: $1. Also sponsor annual Artists Village.

CERAMICS CONTEST: All Types, original, 72 inches maximum any dimension, portable by 1 person (can be exceeded by special arrangement). No fragile entries. Divisions: Juried (unlimited entry), Open (limit 3 per section), Young Artists (limit 3 per entrant, all sections). Competition includes fine art, graphics, photography. Also have fine art, graphics, photography sections in Open Show.

SCULPTURE CONTEST: All Media. Requirements, restrictions same as for Ceramics.

CRAFTS CONTEST: All Media.

Requirements, restrictions same as for Ceramics.

AWARDS: *Juried Show (includes all sections):* $2000 Purchase Award. 2 $500 Jurors' Awards, 6 Honorable Mentions. *Open Show:* 2 $100 Awards. 3 Honorable Mentions. *Young Artists (includes all sections):* $100 to best of show. Seniors (14-18): $75 Award, 2 $40 Awards, 6 Honorable Mentions. Juniors (9-13): $35 Award, 2 $20 Awards, 6 Honorable Mentions. La Mirada Mall Purchase Award (includes Open and Juried Shows).

JUDGING: Entry review (Juried Show) and awards judging (Juried, Open Shows) by 3 judges from different art disciplines. Awards judging (Young Artists) by art educator. Not responsible for loss or damage.

SALES TERMS: Sales optional. 30% commission charge.

ENTRY FEE: $5 per work plus $2 handling charge for Juried, Open Shows. $1 per work plus $2 handling charge for Young Artists.

DEADLINES: Entry, May. Event, June.

45

Mid-States Craft Exhibition
Evansville Museum of Arts and Science
411 South East Riverside Drive
Evansville, Indiana 47713 U.S.A.
Tel: (812) 425-2406

Entry January

Regional; entry open to residents of Indiana or within 200-mile radius of Evansville; annual in February-March; established 1961. Purpose: to promote excellence in crafts, give craftspersons opportunity to exhibit and sell work. Sponsored and supported by Evansville Museum of Arts and Sciences. Average statistics (all sections): 325 entries, 190 entrants, 125 exhibits, 98 exhibitors, 10 awards, 10,000 attendance. Held at Evansville Museum of Arts and Sciences for 5 weeks.

CERAMICS CONTEST: All Types, original; limit 2 per entrant. Completed in previous 3 years. Request presence of award winners or representatives at awards presentation. Competition includes textiles, metalwork, miscellaneous handcrafts.

GLASS CONTEST: All Types. Requirements, restrictions same as for Ceramics.

MIXED MEDIA CONTEST: All Types. Requirements, restrictions same as for Ceramics.

AWARDS: (Includes all sections): $1000, 3 $500, $300 Museum Purchase Awards. 2 $100, $75, 2 $50 Merit awards.

JUDGING: By craft professional. Based on inventiveness, imagination, practicality as well as unusualness of pieces. Sponsor insures works at exhibition.

SALES TERMS: Sales optional. 20% commission charge.

ENTRY FEE: $5 plus return postage.

DEADLINES: Entry, January. Judging, February. Event, February-March.

46

Parents Without Partners International Adult Talent Awards Program
Jan Williams
7910 Woodmont Avenue
Bethesda, Maryland 20814 U.S.A.
Tel: (301) 654-8850

Entry December

International; **entry open to all (club membership required);** annual. Purpose: to encourage and promote cultural interest; display adult talent in the area of crafts. Sponsored and supported by Parents Without Partners (nonprofit). Held at chapter, regional, zone, international levels. Also sponsor International Youth Talent Awards Program for members' children.

CERAMICS CONTEST: Decoration of Clay, Plaster; unlimited entry at chapter level (only 1 each category can progress to further levels). Submit 3-5 photographs, project description of each work for entry review. Competition includes all crafts. Also have art, music, writing, science, photography sections.

CRAFTS CONTEST: All Forms. Requirements, restrictions same as for Ceramics.

AWARDS: First, Second, Third Place Prizes (type varies) to each category (at chapter, regional, zone levels). First through Fourth Place Certificates to each category (at international level).

JUDGING: Based on originality, quality, craftsmanship, color, function at each level.

ENTRY FEE: None.

DEADLINES: Entry, December.

47

Pletcher Village Art Festival and Competition
Amish Acres, Inc.
Richard Pletcher, President
1600 West Market Street
Nappanee, Indiana 46563 U.S.A.
Tel: (219) 773-4188

Entry April

International; entry open to all; annual in August; established 1962. Average 200 entrants (maximum all sections). Held in Amish Acres grounds in Nappanee for 4 days. Have electricity for demonstration, entertainment, security, participation events, guided tours, demonstrations, style shows. Tickets: $1.75 (children under 10 free).

CERAMICS CONTEST: All Forms (including blown glass, pottery), original; 3 per entrant (all sections). Submit 3 35mm slides, description for entry review (preference to crafts representing second half of 19th century). Entrants provide and attend sales displays; demonstrate craft skills. No agents, dealers, imports, manufactured or kit jewelry, commercial kits or molds, craft supplies. Categories: 2D, 3D. Competition includes visual arts, other crafts.

SCULPTURE CONTEST: Clay. Requirements, restrictions same as for Ceramics.

CRAFTS FAIR: All Media. Entrants provide and attend sales displays; demonstrate craft skills. Requirements, restrictions same as for Ceramics.

AWARDS: $600 Best of Show Purchase Prizes each to 2D, 3D. $100 First, $50 Second, $25 Third Prize, Honorable Mentions to ceramics, sculpture, contemporary and traditional crafts. $100 Best of the Marketplace, $50 Second, $25 Third, Honorable Mention to booth displays. $100 First, $50 Second, $25 Third Prizes each to visitor popular piece, popular booth.

JUDGING: By professionals, popular vote. Booth presentations based on costume display, total work, salesmanship signs, festival compatibility. Sponsor owns winning entries; provides security.

SALES TERMS: Sales compulsory. 10% commission charge.

ENTRY FEE: $40 for 12x15-foot booth.

DEADLINES: Entry, April. Judging, event, August.

48

South Carolina State Fair Fine Arts Juried Show
Meg McLean, Superintendent of Fine Arts
505 Winston Road
Columbia, South Carolina 29209
U.S.A. Tel: (803) 766-4698

Entry October

State; **entry open to South Carolina;** annual in October; established prior to 1957. Purpose: to exhibit fine art by professionals, amateurs, children. Sponsored by the State Fair Association. Held at the Fairgrounds Cantey Building in Columbia for 10 days. Tickets: $2.

CERAMICS CONTEST: **Hand-Built or Wheel-Thrown,** of permanent materials, 150lbs. maximum, ready for hanging (with instructions if appropriate); limit 1 per entrant (all sections). Divisions: Professional, Amateur. Also have drawing, painting, print, collage-mixed media sections.

SCULPTURE CONTEST: **All Types.** Requirements, restrictions, divisions same as for Ceramics.

CRAFTS CONTEST: **Open Media** (including glass). Requirements, restrictions, divisions same as for Ceramics. Competition includes Fiber, Jewelry.

AWARDS: $1000 State Fair Purchase Award, State Record Mint Award (all sections). 1-year subscription to *Ceramics Monthly Magazine*

(includes both divisions). *Professional:* $100 First, $50 Second, $25 Third Place Prize to each section. $350 Pioneer Purchase Award to rural life theme; Pioneer Merit Award (all sections). $50 Richtex Merit Award to ceramic sculpture. *Amateur:* $50 First, $25 Second, $10 Third Place Prize to each section. $250 Pioneer Purchase Prize to rural life theme; Pioneer Merit Award (all sections).

JUDGING: Entry review by 3 local professional artists (each section). Awards judging by 1-out-of-state judge. Sponsor may photograph winners for publicity.

ENTRY FEE: None. Entrant pays return postage. No sales commission charge.

DEADLINES: Entry, event, October.

49

Southern California Exposition Art in All Media Exhibition
Lolly Stuckenschneider, Exhibit Supervisor
Entry Office Fairgrounds
Del Mar, California 92014 U.S.A.

Entry May

State; **entry open to Southern California;** annual in June-July; established 1890. Oldest art exhibition in San Diego County. Purpose: to present finest exhibition of arts and crafts in Southern California. Sponsored and supported by Southern California Exposition. Average statistics: 2300 entries, 1400 entrants, 600 finalists, 100,000 attendance, $8000 total sales. Held during the Southern California Exposition in Del Mar for 3 weeks.

CERAMICS CONTEST: **All Types,** original, maximum 6x8 feet (wxh) 250lbs. any component; limit 3 per entrant. Produced recently, suitable for family viewing. No crafts kits, copies, work produced under supervision; unsafe or electrical entries; work requiring special hooks. Also have painting and graphics sections, other crafts.

SCULPTURE CONTEST: Ceramic, Stone, Marble, Other Media. Requirements, restrictions same as for Ceramics.

CRAFTS CONTEST: Any Media, Mixed Media. Requirements, restrictions same as for Ceramics.

ELIGIBILITY: Open to residents of San Diego, Imperial, Oregon, Riverside, Los Angeles, San Bernardino, Ventura, and Santa Barbara counties.

AWARDS: $250 each to best sculpture, best craft work in show (includes all crafts media). $100 First, $50 Second, $25 Third Prize each to sculpture, general crafts (includes all media), ceramics.

JUDGING: By 3 art professionals. Sponsor may photograph entries for catalog, publicity purposes. Not responsible for loss or damage.

SALES TERMS: Sales optional. 25% commission charge.

ENTRY FEE: $4 each work.

DEADLINES: Entry, acceptance, May. Event, June-July.

50

Union Street Gallery Annual Competition
Jill Manton, Director
1909 Union Street
San Francisco, California 94123
U.S.A. Tel: (415) 921-7160

Entry April

International; entry open to all; annual in July-August; established 1981.

Purpose: to provide opportunity for new artists to exhibit their work. Sponsored and supported by Union Street Gallery. Held in San Francisco for 2 months.

CERAMICS CONTEST: All Forms, 6 feet maximum any dimension; ready for display; limit 10 per entrant. Require hand-delivery. Request entrant attendance. Submit 10 slides for entry review. Competition includes painting, watercolor.

GLASS CONTEST: Blown Glass. Requirements, restrictions same as for Ceramics.

SCULPTURE CONTEST: All Forms. Requirements, restrictions same as for Ceramics.

MIXED MEDIA CONTEST: All Forms. Requirements, restrictions same as for Ceramics.

ELIGIBILITY: No entrants affiliated with art galleries in San Francisco.

AWARDS: $1000 in Cash Awards; 1- or 2-person show (includes all sections).

JUDGING: By 3 Gallery Board Directors.

SALES TERMS: Sales compulsory. 50% commission charge.

ENTRY FEE: $10.

DEADLINES: Entry, April. Materials, June. Judging, event, July-August.

CERAMICS, SCULPTURE

Ceramics and Sculpture, including CLAY and IN COLOR. See CERAMICS for definition of Ceramics. (Also see other CERAMICS, SCULPTURE

CATEGORIES.)

51

**Butler Institute of American Art
Area Artists Annual**
524 Wick Avenue
Youngstown, Ohio 44502 U.S.A.
Tel: (216) 743-1107

Entry October

Regional; **entry open to residents
(past and present) within 40-mile radius of Youngstown;** annual in November; established 1938. Sponsored
by and held at Butler Institute of
American Art in Youngstown for 1
month. Average statistics (all sections): 600 entries, 8 awards.

CERAMICS   CONTEST: **All
Types,** framed if appropriate; limit 2
per entrant each of 3 sections (set
counts as 1). Require hand-delivery.
Competition includes photography,
fine arts, other crafts.

SCULPTURE CONTEST: **All Me-
dia.** Requirements, restrictions same
as for Ceramics.

AWARDS: (Includes all sections):
Cash and Purchase Prizes. Youngs-
town Federation of Women's Club
Award.

JUDGING: By 1 local professional.
Sponsor may photograph entries for
publicity. Not responsible for loss or
damage.

SALES TERMS: Sales encouraged.
10% commission charge.

ENTRY FEE: $1 per work.

DEADLINES: Entry,   October.
Event, November.

52

Faber Birren Color Award Show
Stamford Art Association
39 Franklin Street
Stamford, Connecticut 06905 U.S.A.

Entry October

International; entry open to all; an-
nual in November; established 1981.
Purpose: to inspire interest in color.
Sponsored by and held at Stamford
Art Association Galleries for 23 days.
Supported by Faber Birren Endow-
ment. Have demonstrations, panel
discussions, scholarships.

CERAMICS CONTEST: **Color in
All Forms,** original, 40x72 inches
(wxh) maximum, framed, ready for
hanging; 3D 60lbs. maximum; limit 1
per entrant. Require hand-delivery.
Competition includes visual arts, photography, other crafts.

SCULPTURE CONTEST: **Color in
All Forms,** original, maximum 40x72
inches (wxh), 60lbs., ready for hanging if appropriate; limit 1 per entrant.
Other requirements same as for Ceramics.

AWARDS: $500,   Certificate,
Plaque or Medal for distinguished and
creative expression with color (includes all sections).

JUDGING: By 1 prominent gallery
curator. Sponsor insures work (maximum $1000) during exhibition. Not
responsible for loss or damage.

ENTRY FEE: $10.

DEADLINES: Entry,   October.
Event, November. Materials returned,
December.

53

Ink and Clay Exhibition
California State Polytechnic
University (Cal Poly) Art Department
Diane Divelbess, Coordinator
3801 West Temple Avenue
Pomona, California 91768 U.S.A.
Tel: (714) 598-4567

Entry October

State; **entry open to California;** annual in January; established 1972. Purpose: to provide university with exhibition of outstanding contemporary art. Sponsored by Cal Poly, Pomona Art Department, Library. Average statistics (all sections): 200 entries, 150 entrants, 7 awards, 1500 attendance. Held at University Library Gallery in Pomona for 3 weeks. Second contact: Madelyn Mellon, University Library, Cal Poly, Pomona, California 91768.

CERAMICS CONTEST: Clay (may be combined with other material), maximum 90 inches, 300lbs.; limit 2 per entrant (all sections). Entrants more than 100 miles from Cal Poly may submit slides for entry review. Competition includes ink drawings, and paintings.

SCULPTURE CONTEST: Clay. Requirements, restrictions same as for Ceramics.

AWARDS: $1500 minimum in Purchase Prizes for James Jones Collection at Cal Poly.

JUDGING: By 1 clay specialist. Not responsible for loss or damage.

SALES TERMS: Sales optional. 20% commission charge.

ENTRY FEE: $8 plus return postage.

DEADLINES: Entry, October (slides), December (works). Judging, event, January.

54

Island Arts Council Choochokam Art Exhibition
Richard Proctor, President
120 First Street
P. O. Box 1
Langley, Washington 98260 U.S.A.
Tel: (206) 321-5240

Entry June

State; **entry open to Washington;** annual in July; established 1976. Purpose: to provide community with quality exhibition, area artists with opportunity to express talents. Sponsored and supported by Island Arts Council. Average statistics (all sections): 600 entries, 300 entrants, 10 awards. Held on Widbey Island in Langley for 2-4 days. Have food, entertainment. Also sponsor Choochokam Arts and Pleasure Fair.

CERAMICS CONTEST: All Types, original, ready for hanging or display; limit 2 per entrant (all sections). Require hand-delivery. No copies, molds, kits. Competition includes visual arts, photography, textiles, jewelry.

SCULPTURE CONTEST: All Types. Requirements, restrictions same as for Ceramics.

ELIGIBILITY: Open to residents from Puget Sound area, Choochokam artists.

AWARDS: $1000 minimum in Cash Awards (includes all sections).

JUDGING: By 3 professional artists, art educators. Based on quality, content. Sponsor may photograph works for publicity, archival purposes. Not responsible for loss or damage.

SALES TERMS: Sales optional. 10% commission charge. Works sold may be replaced with reserve pieces.

ENTRY FEE: $5.

DEADLINES: Entry, June. Judging, event, July.

55

Mondak Historical and Arts Society Annual Art Show

J. K. Ralston Museum and Art Center
Anne Schneider, Director
P. O. Box 50
221 Fifth Street S.W.
Sidney, Montana 59270 U.S.A.
Tel: (406) 482-3500

Entry September

National; **entry open to U.S. artists age 14 and over;** annual in Fall; established 1975. Purpose: to give exposure, recognition to contemporary artists. Sponsored and supported by Mondak Historical and Arts Society, J. K. Ralston Museum and Art Center. Recognized by Art Museum Association. Average statistics (all sections): 44 entries, 25 entrants, 6 awards, 200 attendance. Held at Art Center for 3-4 weeks. Also sponsor Annual Quilt Show.

CERAMICS CONTEST: All Types, original, maximum 4x6x2 feet, 100lbs.; limit 3 per entrant. Completed in previous 3 years. Competition includes fabrics. Also have drawing, painting, and print sections.

SCULPTURE CONTEST: All Types. Requirements, restrictions same as for Ceramics.

AWARDS: (Includes all sections): $250 in Cash and Purchase Awards. First, Second, Third Place Prizes.

JUDGING: By 3 judges. Based on originality, design, creativity, craftsmanship. Not responsible for loss or damage.

SALES TERMS: Sales optional. 25% commission charge.

ENTRY FEE: $5 per work plus return postage.

DEADLINES: Entry, September. Event, October-November.

56

Shreveport Art Guild National Exhibition

Friends of the Meadows Museum of Art
2911 Centenary Boulevard
Shreveport, Louisiana 71104 U.S.A.

Entry September

International; entry open to all; annual in January-February; established 1924. Sponsored by Shreveport Art Guild, Friends of Meadows Museum of Art (founded 1975). Held at Meadows Museum in Shreveport for 1 month.

CERAMICS CONTEST: All Types, original, ready for hanging if appropriate; unlimited entry. Completed in previous 2 years. Submit maximum 3 35mm color slides per work for entry review. No supervised works. Competition includes textiles, visual arts.

SCULPTURE CONTEST: All Types, original; unlimited entry. Submit maximum 3 35mm color slides per work for entry review. No supervised works. Competition includes textiles, visual arts.

AWARDS: (Includes all sections): $1000 Best of Show , $500 Second Place Awards. $1000 in Merit Awards.

JUDGING: Entry review and awards judging by professional. Sponsor may photograph entries for catalog, publicity; retains slides. Not responsible for loss or damage.

SALES TERMS: 10% commission charge.

ENTRY FEE: $10 first 3 works, $1 each additional.

DEADLINES: Entry, September. Event, January-February.

CLAY

Includes CONTEMPORARY CERAMICS, POTTERY, SCULPTURE, WALL HANGINGS. (Also see CERAMICS, POTTERY.)

57

Chicago Vicinity Clay Competition
Lill Street Gallery
Kristin Poole
1021 West Lill Street
Chicago, Illinois 60614 U.S.A.
Tel: (312) 284-4414

Entry August

Regional; **entry open to 150-mile radius of Chicago;** annual in October; established 1981. Sponsored by Lill Street Gallery. Supported by Illinois Arts Council, Chicago Council of Fine Arts, Continental Bank Inc. Average 88 accepted entries. Held at Lill Street Gallery in Chicago for 1 month. Also sponsor workshops.

CLAY CONTEST: All Forms; limit 2 per entrant.

AWARDS: Purchase Prizes.

JUDGING: By 2 professional ceramicists. Sponsor may photograph entries for catalog; insures work while in gallery.

SALES TERMS: 10% commission charge.

ENTRY FEE: $5 per work.

DEADLINES: Entry, August. Acceptance, September. Event, October.

58

Clay, Fiber, Paper as Medium
Octagon Center for the Arts
Martha Benson, Director
427 Douglas
Ames, Iowa 50010 U.S.A. Tel: (515) 232-5331

Entry December

Regional; **entry open to residents age 18 and over within 500 miles of Ames, Iowa;** annual in January-February; established 1968. Formerly called CLAY AND PAPER, alternating with CLAY AND FIBER from 1974-1981. Purpose: to present viewers with impressive cross-section of work done in these areas. Sponsored by and held at Octagon Center for the Arts in Ames for 1 month. Average statistics (all sections): 150 entries, 100 entrants, 13 awards. Also sponsor Regional Scholastic Art Award Competition, workshops, classes.

CLAY CONTEST: All Forms (including pottery, sculpture), original; limit 3 per entrant (all sections). Produced solely by artist in previous 2 years. Competition for some awards includes fiber, paper.

AWARDS: $200 Best of Show (includes all sections). $100 Best in Clay. Honorable Mentions.

JUDGING: By an experienced artist-teacher. Sponsor insures during exhibition.

SALES TERMS: Sales optional. 25% commission charge.

ENTRY FEE: $15 plus return postage (except award-winning works).

DEADLINES: Entry, December. Exhibition, January-February.

59

Earthworks Clay Exhibit
South County Art Association
1319 Kingstown Road
Kingston, Rhode Island 02881 U.S.A.
Tel: (401) 783-2195

Entry April

State; **entry open to Rhode Island;** annual in May; established 1975. Purpose: to exhibit quality new ceramic works. Sponsored by South County Art Association. Recognized by Arts Rhode Island, Federal Arts Fund. Average statistics: 120 entries, 50 entrants, 4 awards. Held at Helme House in Kingston for 2 weeks.

CLAY CONTEST: All Forms (including wall hangings), original, ready for hanging if appropriate, 20lbs. maximum; limit 6 per entrant. Work need not be functional. Require hand-delivery.

AWARDS: $100 First, $75 Second, $50 Third, $25 Fourth Place Awards. Honorable Mentions.

JUDGING: By out-of-state jurors. Not responsible for loss or damage.

SALES TERMS: Sales optional 20% commission charge.

ENTRY FEE: $3 per work.

DEADLINES: Entry, April. Event, May.

60

West Michigan Juried Competition
Muskegon Museum of Art
Mary Riordan, Director
296 West Webster Avenue
Muskegon, Michigan 49440 U.S.A.
Tel: (616) 722-2600

Entry March

Regional; **entry open to West Michigan adults;** annual in March-April; established 1926. Purpose: to encourage regional artists to produce work of exhibition caliber. Sponsored by Muskegon Museum of Art (formerly Hackley Art Gallery). Average statistics (all sections): 400 entries, 125 finalists, 10 awards, 3000 attendance. Held at Muskegon Art Gallery for 5-6 weeks.

CLAY CONTEST: All Forms, original, portable by 1 person, framed, mounted, ready for hanging if appropriate, dry, assembled; limit 2 per entrant. Completed in previous 2 years. Competition includes photography, visual arts, metal, wood, fiber, paper.

AWARDS: $1000 Cash Awards (includes all sections).

JUDGING: By 1 art professional. Sponsor may photograph entries for publicity. Not responsible for loss or damage.

SALES TERMS: Sales optional. 25% commission charge.

ENTRY FEE: $5 first, $2.50 second work plus return postage.

DEADLINES: Entry, March. Event, March-April.

61

Westwood Clay National Exhibition
Downey Museum of Art
Lukman Glasgow, Director
10419 South Rives Avenue
Downey, California 90241 U.S.A.
Tel: (213) 861-0419

Entry May

National; **entry open to U.S.;** annual in July-August; established 1980. Purpose: to show versatility of clay as a medium for functional and aesthetic expression. Sponsored and supported by Westwood Ceramic Supply Company, U.S. Gypsum, Feldspar Corporation, Olympic Kilns, others. Average statistics: 1000 entries, 800 entrants, 10 awards, 1500 attendance, $1000 total sales, $150 sales per entrant.

CLAY CONTEST: Contemporary Ceramics (including pottery, sculpture), original, functional or nonfunctional, maximum 12x12 feet, portable by 2 people; unlimited entry (set counts as 1). Can be mixed media if emphasis is on clay. Submit maximum 3 35mm color slides (1 full view, 1 detail) for entry review. Require work be available for tour after exhibition. No craft series, work done under supervision.

AWARDS: Purchase and Cash Awards.

JUDGING: By 1 artist, 1 critic. Based on craftsmanship, aesthetic concept, technical execution. Sponsor may photograph entries for exhibition catalog, publicity, educational purposes.

SALES TERMS: Sales optional. 30% commission charge.

ENTRY FEE: $7 per work plus shipping and insurance.

DEADLINES: Entry, May. Entry review, June. Event, awards, judging, July-August.

CLAY, GLASS, ENAMEL

Clay, Glass, Enamel, including CERAMICS, PORCELAIN, EARTHENWARE, STONEWARE, MOSAIC, and BLOWN, ETCHED, MOLDED, and STAINED GLASS. ENAMEL usually defined as glassy substance or glaze applied by fusion to surface of ceramics, glass or metal. (Also see other CLAY, GLASS, ENAMEL CATEGORIES.)

| 62 |

California Exposition and State Fair Craft Show
Peter Scott, Chief of Exhibits
Art Department, Building 7,
Exposition Center
1600 Exposition Blvd., P. O. Box 15649
Sacramento, California 95813 U.S.A.
Tel: (916) 924-2015

Entry June

State; **entry open to California;** annual in August-September. Originally agricultural fair; now includes industry, culture, science and arts. Sponsored by California State Fair, California State General Fund. Average statistics (all sections): 2000 entries, 1200 entrants, $15,000 in awards, 755,000 attendance. Held at California State Fairgrounds in Sacramento for 18 days. Tickets: $4.

CLAY CONTEST: All Types (including ceramics, earthenware, porcelain, stoneware), a set counts as 1 entry, for dinnerware 1 place setting considered 1 entry; structurally supported for presentation; limit 2 per entrant (all sections). Also have fine arts, photography, agriculture, other crafts sections.

GLASS CONTEST: All Types (including blown, forms, stained glass), structurally supported for presentation; limit 2 per entrant (all sections).

GENERAL CRAFTS CONTEST: Miscellaneous; limit 2 per entrant (all sections). Competition includes fiber, wood.

AWARDS: $300 and State Fair Plaque First, $200 and State Fair Ribbon Second, $150 and Ribbon Third, $100 and Ribbon Fourth, $50 and Ribbon Fifth Place Awards to each section. $100 and Wine Goblet to best of show (includes fiber, metal, wood). Maximum 15 Honorable Mention Ribbons to each section.

JUDGING: Entry review and awards judging by 3 craft professionals. May withhold awards, duplicate awards in case of tie. Not responsible for loss or damage.

SALES TERMS: Sales optional. No commission charge.

ENTRY FEE: $5 per work each section. Entrant pays return postage.

DEADLINES: Entry, June. Judging, July. Event, August-September.

63

Colorado Artist-Craftsmen Annual Juried Exhibition
Cathy Cohen, President
P. O. Box 4382
Denver, Colorado 80204 U.S.A.
Tel: (303) 778-6427

Entry May

State; **entry open to Colorado;** annual in June-July. Purpose: to promote professionalism in crafts, give crafts better exposure. Sponsored by Colorado Artist-Craftsmen. Supported by Colorado Arts Centers, businesses. Recognized by Colorado Council on the Arts and Humanities. Average statistics: 600 entries, 200 entrants, 12 awards, $200 average sale. Held in different Colorado Art Centers for 1 month. Publish *Craft Range* (bimonthly). Also sponsor annual sale, forums, workshops. Second contact: Carmon Slater, 7317 South Silverhorn

Drive, Evergreen, Colorado 80439.

CLAY CONTEST: All Forms, original; limit 3 per entrant. Produced in previous 2 years. Competition includes other crafts.

GLASS CONTEST: All Forms. Requirements, restrictions same as for Clay.

ENAMEL CONTEST: All Forms. Requirements, restrictions same as for Clay.

AWARDS: (Includes all sections): Minimum $500 in Cash Awards. $200 in Material Awards. $500 in Purchase Awards.

JUDGING: By 2 out-of-state jurors. Sponsor may photograph entries for publicity; insures work during exhibition.

SALES TERMS: Sales compulsory. 30% commission charge.

ENTRY FEE: $12 plus return postage.

DEADLINES: Entry, May. Event, June-July.

64

Coos Art Museum Crafts Now Juried Exhibit of Functional Art
Maggie Karl, Director
515 Market Avenue
Coos Bay, Oregon 97420 U.S.A.
Tel: (503) 267-3901

Entry May

National; **entry open to U.S.;** annual in July; established 1974. Purpose: to help support the arts in Southwestern Oregon. Sponsored by Coos Art Museum. Recognized by Oregon Art Commission. Held at Coos Bay Art Museum for 1 month. Also sponsor Juried Photographic Exhibition; Juried Nonfunctional and

Functional Art Exhibitions, art students' and special functions exhibitions; art, crafts, dance classes, and workshops.

CLAY CONTEST: Functional, original; limit 2 per entrant. Completed in previous year. No supervised work, kits, copies, patterns. Competition includes all functional crafts.

GLASS CONTEST: Functional. Requirements, restrictions same as for Clay.

ENAMEL CONTEST: Functional. Requirements, restrictions same as for Clay.

MOSAIC CONTEST: Functional. Requirements, restrictions same as for Clay.

AWARDS: Exhibition of winners. Invitational show for 15 outstanding craftspersons (held 1-1/2 years later), possible Purchase Awards by Coos Art Museum. Honorable Mentions.

JUDGING: By 2 jurors. Based on integration of form and function, craftsmanship. Sponsor insures for 50% of sales price during exhibition. Not responsible for loss or damage.

SALES TERMS: Sales optional. 25% commission charge.

ENTRY FEE: $7.50.

DEADLINES: Entry, May. Event, July.

| 65 |

Electrum Contemporary Craft Show
Helena Arts Council
Nadine M. Shafer, Director
P. O. Box 1231
Helena, Montana 59624 U.S.A.
Tel: (406) 442-6400

Entry September

International; **entry open to U.S., Canada;** annual in October; established 1972. Purpose: to recognize man's search for beauty in the arts. Sponsored and supported by Helena Arts Council (nonprofit organization). Average statistics (all sections): 450 entries, 250 entrants, 175 finalists, 45 awards, 5000 attendance. Held at Helena Civic Center as part of 3-day art festival. Have Marketplace art gallery for display of work ($40 for 8-foot space), nonjuried show, concerts, performances, demonstrations, lectures. Also sponsor Electrum Medallion Design Competition, Electrum Juried Art Show, Electrum Juried Photography Show. Second contact: Sally Starnes, Electrum, 814 Gilbert, Helena, Montana 59601; tel: (406) 442-9666.

CLAY CONTEST: Coiled, Modeled, Slab or Wheel-Thrown, original, ready for display or hanging; limit 4 per entrant (includes all sections). Completed in previous year. No commercial molds; extremely fragile, poorly mounted or oversized work. Competition includes jewelry, leather, fiber, metal, and woodcrafts.

GLASS CONTEST: Blown, Etched, Molded or Stained. Requirements, restrictions same as for Clay.

COLLAGE ASSEMBLAGE CONTEST: Multimedia. Requirements, restrictions same as for Clay.

AWARDS: (Includes all sections): Cash Awards. Electrum Medallion and Cash Award to best of show. Electrum Honorarium.

JUDGING: By 3 jurors. Sponsor may photograph work for publicity, publication. Not responsible for loss or damage.

SALES TERMS: Sales optional. 20% commission charge (none on Marketplace sales).

ENTRY FEE: $4 per work. Sponsor pays return postage of award winners.

DEADLINES: Entry, September. Judging, event, October.

| 66 |

Greater Hazleton Creative Arts Festival

Arts Council of Greater Hazleton
Alice Luptka, President
Mezzanine, Northeastern Building
Hazleton, Pennsylvania 18201 U.S.A.
Tel: (717) 459-2975

Entry April

National; **entry open to U.S.;** annual in May; established 1966. Sponsored and supported by Arts Council of Greater Hazleton. Supported by Pennsylvania Council on the Arts. Average statistics (all sections): 14 awards, 20,000 attendance. Held at Hazleton Campus, Pennsylvania State University, for 3 days. Have nonjuried indoor Open Art Show, demonstrations, children's events, performances, workshops. Also sponsor juried Sidewalk Show.

CLAY CONTEST: All Types (including mixed media), 4x5 feet maximum, framed, ready for hanging if appropriate; limit 5 per entrant (all sections). Completed in previous 18 months. Also have visual arts, photography, fiber, metalwork, leather, wood sections.

GLASS CONTEST: All Types (including mixed media). Requirements, restrictions same as for Clay.

AWARDS: $75 First each to mixed media (includes all sections), clay, glass.

JUDGING: By 2 jurors from Philadelphia Arts College. Not responsible for loss or damage.

SALES TERMS: Sales optional. 10% commission charge.

ENTRY FEE: $3 per work.

DEADLINES: Entry, April. Judging, event, May.

| 67 |

Topeka Crafts Exhibition

Topeka Public Library
Larry D. Peters, Gallery Director
1515 West 10th Street
Topeka, Kansas 66604 U.S.A.
Tel: (913) 233-2040, ext. 27

Entry March

Regional; **entry open to residents of Kansas, metropolitan Kansas City, Saint Joseph in Missouri;** annual in April; established 1977. Purpose: to promote and support artists in the area. Sponsored by Topeka Public Library. Supported by Topeka Public Library, Friends of the Library, Kansas Craftsmen Association. Average statistics (all sections): 300 entries, 100 entrants, 58 finalists, 12 awards. Held at Topeka Public Library for 1 month. Also sponsor art shows.

CLAY CONTEST: All Types (including mixed media); limit 3 per entrant (all sections). Competition includes glass, enamel, fiber, metalwork, wood crafts.

GLASS CONTEST: All Types (including mixed media). Restrictions same as for Clay.

ENAMEL CONTEST: All Types (including mixed media). Restrictions same as for Clay.

AWARDS: Cash and Purchase Prizes. No awards under $50.

JUDGING: By 1 academic. Based on design, craftsmanship.

SALES TERMS: Sales optional. 20% commission charge.

ENTRY FEE: $10 plus return postage.

DEADLINES: Entry, March. Event, April.

68

West Michigan Seaway Festival Juried Art Show

Gilbert P. Buckley, Executive Director
470 West Western Avenue
Muskegon, Michigan 49440 U.S.A.
Tel: (616) 722-6520

Entry March

International; entry open to all; annual in July; established 1961. Purpose: to promote artists in Muskegon area. Sponsored and supported by West Michigan Seaway Festival, Inc. Average statistics (all sections): 250 entrants, 20,000 attendance, 35 works displayed (indoor show). Held at Muskegon Museum of Art for 3 weeks. Have food, concerts, contests, parade, fireworks, sports. Also sponsor Outdoor Art Fair, Village Market.

CLAY CONTEST: All Forms, original, portable by 1 person, dry and assembled; limit 2 per entrant. Completed in previous 2 years. Require hand-delivery of accepted works. Submit 1 slide per work for entry review. Competition includes painting, drawing, graphics, photography, other crafts.

GLASS CONTEST: All Forms. Requirements, restrictions same as for Clay.

AWARDS: $500 First, $300 Second, $200 Third Place Awards (includes all sections). $100 Awards to each section. $100 People's Choice Award. Cash and Purchase Awards.

JUDGING: By panel of qualified judges. Not responsible for loss or damage.

SALES TERMS: 25% commission charge.

ENTRY FEE: $5, 1 entry. $7.50, 2.

DEADLINES: Entry, acceptance, March. Event, judging, July.

CLAY, GLASS, ENAMEL, SCULPTURE, PLASTIC

Clay, Glass, Enamel, Sculpture, Plastic, including CERAMICS, STONE, and WESTERN. (Also see other CLAY, GLASS, ENAMEL, SCULPTURE, and PLASTIC CATEGORIES.)

69

Art in Arizona Show

White Mountain Fine Arts Association (WMFAA)
Pinetop, Arizona 85935 U.S.A.

Entry May

National; entry open to U.S.; annual in June; established 1973. Sponsored and supported by WMFAA. Held at Pinetop Lakes Country Club for 3 days. Have artists' and collectors' reception, awards banquet, food, shops. Also sponsor Outside Show and Sale, National Show, Cowboy Artists of America Exhibition, Guest Artists Exhibition.

CLAY CONTEST: All Forms, original; limit 5 per entrant. Submit slides of entries exceeding 75lbs. No supervised work, facsimilies, copies.

Competition includes other crafts. Also have fiber, fine arts, photography sections.

SCULPTURE CONTEST: All Media. Requirements, restrictions same as for Clay.

WESTERN WORKS CONTEST: All Media. Requirements, restrictions same as for Clay.

AWARDS: $6500 in Cash Awards and Prizes (includes all sections).

JUDGING: By 3 arts professionals. Not responsible for loss or damage.

SALES TERMS: 20% commission charge, including purchase awards.

ENTRY FEE: $3 per work, plus return postage.

DEADLINES: Entry, June (oversize, May). Judging, event, June.

OUTSIDE SHOW AND SALE: Arts and Crafts, original. 50 artists maximum. Submit photo samples. Entrants provide and attend sales displays. $100 Best of Show Award; $25 First Place Awards; Second and Third Place Ribbons. 20% sales commission charge. $20 entry fee. Deadlines: Entry, May.

| 70 |

Creative Crafts Council Biennial Exhibition
Marcia Jestaedt, Co-Chair
13300 Forest Drive
Mitchellville, Maryland 20716 U.S.A.
Tel: (301) 464-8513

Entry February

Regional; **entry open to sponsoring guild members in Washington, D.C. area;** biennial (even years) in June-July; established 1952. Sponsored by Ceramic Guild of Bethesda, Enamelists Guild, Kiln Club, Montgomery Potters, Potomac Craftsmen, Washington Guild of Goldsmiths. Average statistics: 800 entries, 230 entrants. Held in Washington, D.C., for 1 month. Also sponsor lectures. Second contact: Doramay Keasbey, 5031 Alta Vista Road, Bethesda, Maryland 20814.

CLAY CONTEST: All Forms, original; limit 4 per entrant (set counts as 1). Produced in previous 2 years. Require hand-delivery. No work previously exhibited in a juried show; work completed under supervision. Competition for some awards includes glass, plastic, enamel, fiber, paper, metal, leather, wood.

GLASS CONTEST: All Forms. Requirements, restrictions same as for Clay.

ENAMEL CONTEST: All Forms. Requirements, restrictions same as for Clay.

PLASTIC CONTEST: All Forms. Requirements, restrictions same as for Clay.

ELIGIBILITY: Entry open to craftspersons or students in Washington, D.C., Maryland, Virginia; members of sponsoring organizations.

AWARDS: Ceramics Monthly Purchase Award. First, Second, Third Prizes (includes all sections).

JUDGING: By 3 judges. Not responsible for loss or damage.

SALES TERMS: Sales optional. 25% commission charge.

ENTRY FEE: $5 per work, students $4.

DEADLINES: Entry, February. Materials, judging, March. Event, June-July.

71

Louisiana Craftsmen Exhibit
Louisiana Crafts Council
P. O. Box 44247
Baton Rouge, Louisiana 70804
U.S.A. Tel: (504) 925-3880

Entry date not specified

State; **entry open to Louisiana;** annual in April; established 1968. Purpose: to show range of Louisiana crafts. Sponsored by Louisiana Crafts Council. Supported by Louisiana Department of Culture, Recreation and Tourism. Recognized by Handweavers Guild of America. Held at J. Broussard Memorial Gallery in Old State Capitol for 3 weeks.

CLAY, GLASS, PLASTICS CONTEST: All Forms. Competition includes photography, prints, and other crafts.

AWARDS: 3 $400 Awards of Excellence (includes all sections).

JUDGING: By 1 art academic.

ENTRY FEE: Not specified.

DEADLINES: Event, April

72

Mamaroneck Artists Guild Juried Exhibition
Cynthia Doyle, Chair
150 Larchmont Avenue
New York, New York 10538 U.S.A.
Tel: (914) 834-1117, 948-8385,
961-9050

Entry dates vary

National; **entry open to U.S.;** annual in Spring; established 1953. Purpose: to show best available work covering broad spectrum of styles. Sponsored by Mamaroneck Artists Guild, Inc. Average statistics (all sections): 850 entries, 500 entrants, 220 finalists, 23 awards, 550 attendance. Held at Community Unitarian Church in White Plains, New York, for 2 weeks. Also sponsor solo shows, lectures, demonstrations.

CLAY CONTEST: All Types, original; hanging pieces 75lbs. maximum, ready for hanging; limit 2 per entrant (all sections). Produced recently. Require hand-delivery. Competition includes photography, arts, other crafts.

GLASS CONTEST: All Types, original. Other requirements, restrictions same as for Clay.

SCULPTURE CONTEST: All Types, original, freestanding work attached to base (artist supplies pedestals), hanging pieces 75lbs. maximum, ready for hanging; limit 2 per entrant (all sections). Submit 3 8x10-inch photographs of sculpture exceeding 150lbs. Other requirements same as for Clay.

PLASTIC CONTEST: All Types. Requirements, restrictions same as for Sculpture.

MIXED MEDIA CONTEST: All Types. Requirements, restrictions same as for Sculpture.

AWARDS: $1500 minimum in Cash Awards (includes all sections).

JUDGING: By 4 judges. Not responsible for loss or damage.

SALES TERMS: Sales optional. 30% commission charge.

ENTRY FEE: $12 for 1 entry, $16 for 2 entries.

DEADLINES: Entry, varies. Event, Spring.

73

Summit Art Center Juried Show
Perijane Zarembok, Chair
68 Elm Street
Summit, New Jersey 07901 U.S.A.
Tel: (201) 273-9121

Entry January

International; entry open to all; annual in January-February; established 1980. Sponsored by Summit Art Center. Average statistics (all sections): 400 entries, 125 finalists, 6 awards. Held for 1 month. Also sponsor monthly art exhibitions, classes.

CLAY CONTEST: Ceramics, Constructions; freestanding, maximum 7 feet high (including base), 12 square feet floor area, 75lbs., assembled, mounted, ready for display; wall pieces 50x70 inches maximum framed, ready for hanging; limit 1 per entrant (includes all sections). Competition includes visual arts, photography, paper and metal sculpture, jewelry, mixed media (paper or metal).

GLASS CONTEST: All Types (including stained glass). Requirements, restrictions same as for Clay.

SCULPTURE CONTEST: Clay, Glass. Requirements, restrictions same as for Clay.

MIXED MEDIA CONTEST: One-Half Clay or Glass. Requirements, restrictions same as for Clay.

AWARDS: 6 $200 Cash Prizes (includes all sections).

JUDGING: By art professionals. Sponsor insures for $500 maximum.

SALES TERMS: 30% commission charge.

ENTRY FEE: $8 plus return postage.

DEADLINES: Entry, judging, January. Event, January-February.

74

Three Rivers Arts Festival
Carnegie Institute
John Jay, Executive Director
4400 Forbes Avenue
Pittsburgh, Pennsylvania 15213
U.S.A. Tel: (412) 687-7014

Entry March

Regional; **entry open to residents age 18 and over of Pennsylvania, Ohio, West Virginia, Western New York;** annual in June; established 1960. Purpose: to offer best of visual, performing arts in parklike setting. Sponsored by Carnegie Institute. Supported by businesses, city and county government, Art Institute of Pittsburgh, Pittsburgh History and Landmarks Foundation. Recognized by NEA. Average statistics (all events, sections): 1500 entrants, 300 artist market participants, 300,000 attendance, 200 performances. Have musical, dance, theatrical performances; environmental projects; sky sculpture; food, children's activities. Held at Gateway Center in Pittsburgh, and Point State Park, for 10 days.

CLAY CONTEST: 3-Dimensional, original; limit 3 per entrant per section (maximum 2). Submit 3 35mm slides (1 of detail) per work for entry review. No commercial, molded, kit-assembled, seasonal entries. Competition includes film, video, photography, visual art, other crafts.

GLASS CONTEST: 3-Dimensional. Requirements, restrictions same as for Clay.

STONE CONTEST: 3-Dimensional. Requirements, restrictions same as for Clay.

MIXED MEDIA CONTEST: 3-Dimensional. Requirements, restrictions same as for Clay.

CRAFT FAIR: All Media. Submit 5 35mm slides of 5 representative works for entry review, publicity information; picture of display unit. Entrants provide and attend sales displays; limit 1 5-day period. No agents, dealers, commercial entries.

ELIGIBILITY: Residents age 18 and over of Pennsylvania, Ohio, West Virginia, and Western New York State (Allegany, Cattaraugus, Chautauqua, Erie, Genesee, Niagara, Orleans, and Wyoming counties).

AWARDS: Cash Awards exceeding $4000; 4 $150 Awards for fair displays of 2D and 3D works (includes all sections).

JUDGING: Entry review by art professionals. Awards judging by 1 2D, 2 3D specialists. Not responsible for loss or damage of craft fair entries; sponsor insures contest entries at sale price up to $250 during exhibit.

SALES TERMS: All work (both events) must be for sale. 25% commission charge (contest only).

ENTRY FEE: $13 jury fee (both events). $130 for 8x8-foot booth space (fair).

DEADLINES: Entry, March. Notification, April. Events, judging, June.

CRAFTS (General)

General Crafts in all media, including CERAMICS, CHINA, POTTERY, SCULPTURE. (Also see other CRAFTS CATEGORIES.)

75

Baton Rouge FestForAll Juried Show

Arts and Humanities Council of Greater Baton Rouge
Richard Sabino, Director
427 Laurel Street
Baton Rouge, Louisiana 70801
U.S.A. Tel: (504) 344-8558

Entry March

National; **entry open to U.S.;** annual in May-June, established 1981. Sponsored by Greater Baton Rouge Arts and Humanities Council, Broussard Galleries. Held in Jay R. Broussard Galleries of Old State Capitol in Baton Rouge for 3 weeks. Also sponsor FestForAll Short Story Contest, Art Festival; Goudchaux's Design Competition.

CRAFTS CONTEST: All Media, 2D matted or framed, ready for hanging; limit 3 per entrant. Submit 3 slides maximum per 3D entry. Competition includes photography, visual arts.

AWARDS: (Includes all sections): $300, $200, $100 Cash Awards. 5 Honorable Mention Ribbons.

JUDGING: By 1 art executive. Broussard Galleries retains slide entries; insures during exhibition.

SALES TERMS: Sales optional. No commission charge.

ENTRY FEE: $5.

DEADLINES: Entry, March. Judging, May. Event, May-June.

76

Felician College Art Festival
Iris G. Klein, Director
P. O. Box 546105
Surfside, Florida 33154 U.S.A.
Tel: (305) 868-6870

Entry January

International; **entry open to professionals;** annual in July; established

1972. Purpose: to raise money for Felician College. Sponsored by Felician College and Sisters of the College. Average statistics (all sections): 112 entrants, 10,000 attendance. Held in Chicago for 1 day.

CRAFTS CONTEST: All Media. Submit slides or prints for entry review. Competition includes photography, fine art.

AWARDS: $250 in Purchase Prizes.

JUDGING: Entry review by art fair director. Awards judging by panel. Not responsible for loss or damage.

ENTRY FEE: Not specified.

DEADLINES: Entry, January. Acceptance, June. Judging, event, July.

77

Lake Superior Crafts Exhibition
Duluth Art Institute
Bob Dearmond or Jennifer Link
506 West Michigan Street
Duluth, Minnesota 55802 U.S.A.
Tel: (218) 727-8013

Entry March

National; **entry open to U.S.**; biennial in June-August; established 1973. Alternates with Arrowhead Exhibition. Purpose: to offer national exposure to regional artists, show state of the crafts in upper Midwest. Sponsored by Duluth Art Institute, Tweed Museum at University of Minnesota, Duluth. Supported by Duluth Art Institute, Tweed Museum at University of Minnesota-Duluth, NEA, Arrowhead Regional Arts Council. Held at Tweed Museum for 1 month, then travels to 5 Northwest locations. Also sponsor classes, films, exhibitions, lectures, workshops, demonstrations. Second contact: Larry Gruenwald, Tweed Museum of Art, University of Minnesota-Duluth, Duluth, Minnesota 55812.

CRAFTS CONTEST: All Media; limit 2 per entrant. Recent work. Submit maximum 3 35mm color slides per work for entry review.

AWARDS: 6 $500 Cash Awards. Merit Commendations.

JUDGING: By crafts professional. Sponsor insures works at exhibition.

SALES TERMS: 25% commission charge.

ENTRY FEE: $10 plus return postage.

DEADLINES: Entry, March. Acceptance, May. Event, June-August.

78

Orange County Art Association (OCAA) All Media Juried Exhibition
Harmon Avera, Coordinator
P. O. Box 3279
Fullerton, California 92631 U.S.A.

Entry October

National; **entry open to U.S.**; annual in November-December; established 1966. Purpose: to provide juried exposure to artists in all media. Sponsored by OCAA, City of Brea. Supported by OCAA. Average statistics (all sections): 625 entries, 335 entrants. Held at Brea Civic Cultural Center Art Gallery in California for 5 weeks.

CRAFTS CONTEST: All Media, maximum 60 inches any dimension (including frame), 100lbs. (maximum 6x8 feet installation works); framed or edged, ready for hanging if appropriate; unlimited entry. Submit slides (except for hanging works), description and-or explanatory diagram of unusual media, specialized entries, installation works for entry review. No wet works. Competition includes visual arts.

AWARDS: $200 Veta Carr Memorial Award to ceramics. *Includes visual arts:* $300 Juror's Award. $200 OCAA Award. $50 Popular Choice Award.

JUDGING: By 1 nationally prominent juror. Sponsor may photograph entries for publicity; insure during exhibition only. Not responsible for loss or damage.

SALES TERMS: Sales optional. 30% commission charge.

ENTRY FEE: $10 each work plus return postage.

DEADLINES: Entry, October, Event, November-December.

79

Quinebaug Valley Council for the Arts and Humanities (QVCAH) All Arts Festival
Mark Winetrout, Executive Director
111 Main Street
Southbridge, Massachusetts 01550
U.S.A. Tel: (617) 764-3341,
764-7613

Entry April, May

International; entry open to all; annual in June; established 1978. Purpose: to encourage appreciation of and participation in arts, crafts. Sponsored by QVCAH, local businesses. Average statistics (all sections): 1000 entries, 100 entrants, 5000 attendance. Held at QVCAH Cultural Center in Southbridge, for 2 days (fair), 1 month (juried exhibit). Fair has performing arts programs, demonstrations.

CRAFTS CONTEST: All Media (including ceramics), original, 4x5 feet maximum, framed, ready for hanging if appropriate. Require hand-delivery. Also have visual arts, photography sections.

CRAFTS FAIR: All Media. Entrants provide and attend sales displays. Submit 3-10 slides or prints of work and display for entry review. No dealers. Division: Adult, Youth. Also have fine arts, photography sections.

AWARDS: Contest: $600 Cash Award. Fair: Cash, Gift Certificates to each division; Popular Vote Award (includes all sections).

JUDGING: By art professionals. Not responsible for loss or damage.

ENTRY FEE: $8 per work (exhibit); $15 Adult, $3 Youth (fair). No sales commission charge.

DEADLINES: Entry, April (fair), May (exhibit). Events, June.

80

Salon of the 50 States Prix de Paris
Ligoa Duncan
P. P. 2115 Washington Avenue E 17
Miami Beach, Florida 33139 U.S.A.
Tel: (305) 673-5012

Entry dates continuous

International; **entry open to U.S., Canada;** monthly; established 1957 in New York and Paris by Raymond Duncan. Purpose: to encourage young and old, known and unknown creative artists in all media. Sponsored by Musee des Duncan (founded 1948). Recognized by Akademia Raymond Duncan (founded 1911, in Paris). Average statistics (all sections): 15,000 entries, 300 entrants, 50 awards. Held in Paris and various U.S. cities each year. Have series of 2-week salons, artist contact service.

CRAFTS CONTEST: All Media (including pottery); limit 2-4 per entrant. Submit 35mm slides for 1 or more salons and automatic participation in Prix de Paris-Raymond Duncan Competition; biography stating source of inspiration, etc. Competition includes fine art, photography, fiber crafts.

AWARDS: Prix de Paris (an audiovisual presentation at Musee des Duncan) to all winners (monthly). Annual Diplomas.

JUDGING: By jury of artists, critics, public vote. Based on selection of wide range of styles.

SALES TERMS: 33-1/3% commission charge.

ENTRY FEE: $15 for 2 or $25 for 4 works.

DEADLINES: Entry, continuous. Notification, salons, October-September (monthly). Diplomas, June. Slides returned, September.

81

Tibbits Art and Crafts Show
Tibbits Opera Foundation and Art Council
Larry Carrico, Director
14 South Hanchett Street
Coldwater, Michigan 49036 U.S.A.
Tel: (517) 278-6029

Entry February

National; **entry open to U.S. artists age 18 and over;** annual in March; established 1975. Purpose: to provide showcase for new and established artists. Sponsored by Tibbits Opera Foundation and Arts Council. Average statistics: 200 entries, 65 entrants, 500 attendance. Held at Tibbits Theatre & Gallery in Coldwater for 1 month. Second contact: Donna Yoatsey, Gallery Chair, 125 Marshall Street, Coldwater, Michigan 49036; tel: (517) 278-6586.

CRAFTS CONTEST: All Media (including pottery, sculpture), original, matted and-or framed, ready for display; limit 3 per entrant. Produced in previous year. Competition includes visual arts, other crafts.

AWARDS: (Includes all sections): Minimum $200 in Cash Prizes. "One Man Show" to best overall.

JUDGING: By 1 academic, museum curator. Based on originality, workmanship, good design, strength of statement.

SALES TERMS: Sales optional. 15% commission charge.

ENTRY FEE: $10.

DEADLINES: Entry, February. Event, judging, March.

82

Waupaca Art and Craft Show
Waupaca Fine Arts Festival
Carolyn Gusmer, Administrative Chair
122 Shadow Lake Drive
Waupaca, Wisconsin 54981 U.S.A.
Tel: (715) 258-2685

Entry April

International; entry open to all; annual in April; established 1963. Purpose: to bring fine arts to Waupaca area, encourage local artists. Sponsored by Waupaca Fine Arts Festival. Supported by Waupaca Foundry, individuals. Average statistics (all sections): 450 entries, 160 entrants, 18 awards, 2000 attendance, $1500 total sales. Held at Waupaca Armory for 5 days. Also sponsor annual community chorus and orchestra, music, dance. Second contact: Gerald Knoepfel, Route 1, Waupaca, Wisconsin 54981.

CRAFTS CONTEST: All Media (including ceramics, china painting, sculpture), original, ready for display; unlimited entry. Completed in previous 3 years. Divisions: Professional, Nonprofessional, High School Students. Categories: 2D, 3D. Competition includes other crafts.

AWARDS: Professional: $100 First, $60 Second, $40 Third Prize. Nonprofessional: $60 First, $40 Second, $30 Third Prize. High School Students: $20 First, $10 Second, $5 Third Prize. $5 Popular Vote (includes all 3D sections). $5 Popular Vote to high school students (includes all sections).

JUDGING: By 1 crafts specialist. Sponsor insures during exhibition.

SALES TERMS: Sales optional. 15% commission charge.

ENTRY FEE: $10 Professional, $6 Nonprofessional, $3 High School Student, for any 3 works.

DEADLINES: Entry, event, April.

CRAFTS (Regional-State)

General Crafts in all media, limited to specific Region or State. Includes CALIFORNIA, COLORADO, FLORIDA, NEW MEXICO, WEST VIRGINIA, WISCONSIN, ONTARIO, and MIDWEST, NEW ENGLAND, SOUTHEAST. (Also see other CRAFTS CATEGORIES.)

83

A-B Jamboree Crafts Contest and Fair
Acton-Boxborough Community Education Program
William L. Ryan
16 Charter Road
Acton, Massachusetts 01720 U.S.A.
Tel: (617) 263-2607

Entry May, July

Regional; **entry open to New England;** annual in July-August; established 1979. Purpose: to provide quality arts and crafts show. Sponsored by Acton-Boxborough Community Education Program. Average statistics (all sections): 150 entries (contest), 85 entrants (fair), 20,000 attendance. Held at Acton-Boxborough Regional High School for 2 days. Have security. Second contact: Contest: Jeanne Rotalante, Art Director, 4 Seneca Court, Acton, Massachusetts, 01720; tel: (617) 263-4248; Fair: Peggy Stegeman, 16 Meeting House Road, Acton, Massachusetts 01720; tel: (617) 263-4038.

CRAFTS CONTEST: All Media, original, hanging works maximum 4x6 feet, freestanding works 250lbs., 8 feet (height); limit 3 per entrant. Require hand-delivery. Categories: Freestanding, Mixed Media. Competition includes visual art, photography, all crafts.

CRAFTS FAIR: All Media, original. Submit 3 35mm slides or photos for entry review. Entrants provide and attend sales displays. No kits, manufactures items. Competition includes all crafts.

AWARDS: *Contest (includes all sections):* $100 each to freestanding works, mixed media. $50 to best of show. $50 People's Choice Award. $50 Jenks Youth Award to first, $25 to second Acton-Boxborough youth under age 21. *Fair (includes all craft sections):* $100 to first, $75 to second, fee refund to third best display.

JUDGING: By 3 jurors. Contest judging based on originality, creativity. Not responsible for loss or damage.

SALES TERMS: Contest: Sales optional, 20% commission charge. Fair: Sales compulsory.

ENTRY FEE: Contest: $6 per work

($4 Seniors, Youths). Fair: $50 booth fee.

DEADLINES: Entry, May (fair), July (contest). Event, July-August.

84

Albuquerque United Artists (AUA) Craftworks Competition

Ellen Klein, Project Director
P. O. Box 1808
Albuquerque, New Mexico 87103
U.S.A. Tel: (505) 243-0531

Entry March

State; **entry open to New Mexico;** annual in April-May; established 1979. Began as Albuquerque metropolitan exhibition. Purpose: to showcase contemporary crafts by New Mexico craftspersons in an exhibition format. Sponsored by AUA, Albuquerque Designer Craftsmen. Supported by New Mexico Arts Division, NEA. Average statistics (all sections): 500 entries, 150 entrants, 2000 attendance. Held at AUA Downtown Center for the Arts for 1 month. Also sponsor exhibitions of works in all media, performances, literary events. Second contact: Karen Reck, Administrative Director, Downtown Center for the Arts, 216 Central S.W., Albuquerque, New Mexico.

CRAFTS CONTEST: All Media, sized to pass through 33x83-inch door, portable by 2 people; slides of work acceptable; limit 3 per entrant (set counts as 1). Completed in previous 2 years.

AWARDS: Cash Prizes.

JUDGING: By crafts professional. Sponsor may photograph works for publicity and documentation, insures against fire and theft during show.

SALES TERMS: Sales optional. No commission charge.

ENTRY FEE: $5.

DEADLINES: Entry, judging, March. Event, April-May.

85

Broward Art Guild (BAG) All Broward Exhibition

Kirt Dressler, Executive Director
3450 North Andrews Avenue
Fort Lauderdale, Florida 33309
U.S.A. Tel: (305) 564-0121

Entry January

Regional; **entry open to South Florida artists;** annual in February. Sponsored and supported by BAG (founded 1952). Held at BAG Gallery for 3 weeks. Have demonstrations, talks. Tickets: free. Publish *BAG Newsletter, Florida's Art News Monthly Gazette.* Also sponsor Tri-County Watercolors and Ceramics Exhibition, London Workshop (7-day study tour), Abstract Show, poetry readings, other cultural events.

CRAFTS CONTEST: All Media, original; 2D to be matted, framed, ready for hanging; limit 3 per entrant. May be executed by 2 artists if done so from start to finish. Require hand-delivery. No works from kits, patterns, molds, copied from photograph; done under supervision. Competition includes fine arts.

AWARDS: $150 to best in show. 2 $50 Merit Awards. 2 $25 Judge's Recognition Awards. $25 People's Choice Award.

JUDGING: By 1 artist. People's Choice award by popular ballot.

SALES TERMS: Sales optional. Optional 20% donation to BAG on sales.

ENTRY FEE: $15.

DEADLINES: Entry, January. Acceptance, event, February.

86

Copper Country Gallery Art Exhibit

Copper Country Community Arts Council
Madelyn Weaver
P. O. Box 236
Houghton, Michigan 49931 U.S.A.
Tel: (906) 482-2042

Entry dates not specified

Regional; **entry open to Midwest;** annual in May; established 1977. Purpose: to encourage artists in competition. Sponsored by Copper Country Community Arts Council. Supported by local merchants. Average statistics: 120 entries, 35 entrants, 7 awards. Held in Suomi College in Hancock, Michigan. Also sponsor Copper Country Summer Arts Festival, "Poor Artists" sale., Copper Country Gallery juried show. Second contact: Mary Ann Predebon, 401 Dodge Street, Houghton, Michigan 49931.

CRAFTS CONTEST: All Media, one-of-a-kind works; limit 4 per entrant. Submit slides for entry review. Competition includes visual arts.

ELIGIBILITY: Entry open to Wisconsin, Michigan, Minnesota, Ohio, Indiana, Illinois.

AWARDS: $100 Best of Show. 6 $50 Awards of Excellence. $50 Community Award. Purchase Awards.

JUDGING: By 1 museum curator.

ENTRY FEE: Not specified.

DEADLINES: Event, May.

87

Exhibition 280

Huntington Galleries
Don Silosky, Curatorial Assistant
Park Hills
Huntington, West Virginia 25701
U.S.A. Tel: (304) 529-2701

Entry January

Regional; **entry open to age 18 and over, within 280 miles of Huntington;** annual in March-April; established 1952. Works On Walls (even years) alternates with Works Off Walls (odd years). Supported by Huntington Galleries (nonprofit organization accredited by American Association of Museums), Arts and Humanities Commission of West Virginia Department of Culture and History, NEA. Average 100 entries (all sections). Have 100-seat auditorium, studio workshops, library.

CRAFTS CONTEST: All Media; limit 2 per entrant. Produced in previous 3 years. Competition includes photography, arts.

AWARDS: 3 $2000 Excellence Awards. $3000 in Purchase Awards.

JUDGING: By 3 art professionals. Based on excellence and creativity. Sponsor insures during exhibition only. Not responsible for in-transit loss or damage.

ENTRY FEE: $10 plus return postage. No sales commission charge.

DEADLINES: Entry, January. Judging, February. Awards, event, March-April.

88

Gilpin County Arts Association Annual Exhibition

Kay Russell, Secretary
Box 98
Central City, Colorado 80427 U.S.A.
Tel: (303) 582-5952

Entry April

State; **entry open to Colorado;** annual in June-September; established

1947. Purpose: to promote and show work of Colorado artists. Sponsored by Gilpin County Arts Association. Average statistics (all sections): 1000 entries, 350 entrants, 200 finalists, 30,-000 attendance, $40,000 total sales. Held at Gilpin County Arts Association Gallery in Central City for 3 months. Have bin sale. Second contact: Charlene Mantel, 4275 South Forest Court, Englewood, Colorado 80110.

CRAFTS CONTEST: All Media, maximum 5x5 inches, 300lbs.; limit 3 per entrant (10 craft items or 1 hanging craft counts as 1). Require hand-delivery. Accepted entrants may submit 15 bin works without charge. Competition includes photography, visual arts.

AWARDS: $1500 in Cash Awards. Honorable Mentions.

JUDGING: By out-of-state academic. Sponsor may reproduce entries for publicity; not responsible for loss or damage.

SALES TERMS: Sales compulsory. 35% commission charge (including bin sale).

ENTRY FEE: $6 per work.

DEADLINES: Entry, April. Event, June-September.

89

Graduate School for Community Development All Media Juried Exhibition
568 Fifth Avenue
San Diego, California 92101 U.S.A.
Tel: (714) 236-1521

Entry September

Regional; **entry open to San Diego;** annual in October; established 1977. Purpose: to promote local artists. Sponsored by Graduate School for Community Development. Average statistics: 250 entries, 3 awards, 1000 attendance, $1500 total sales. Held at Multiculture Arts Institute Gallery in San Diego for 1 month. Also sponsor Annual Festival of the Arts, Photography Juried Art Exhibition, various art shows.

CRAFTS CONTEST: All Media, maximum 6 feet any dimension, 300lbs. (larger work requires gallery approval), framed and wired for display if appropriate; limit 3 per entrant. Completed in previous year. Competition includes visual arts.

AWARDS: $200 First, $100 Second, Third Prizes and three-person show (includes all sections).

JUDGING: By 3 established local artists or art administrators. Sponsor may photography entries for publicity.

SALES TERMS: Sales optional. 25% commission charge.

ENTRY FEE: $5 per work.

DEADLINES: Entry, September. Event, October.

90

LeMoyne Southeast Crafts Competition
LeMoyne Center for the Visual Arts
Judith M. Stauffer, Artistic Director
125 North Gadsden Street
Tallahassee, Florida 32301 U.S.A.
Tel: (904) 224-2714

Entry dates not specified

Regional; **entry open to 10 states in Southeast U.S.;** annual in June; established 1979. Purpose: to promote fine craftspersons of southeastern states. Average statistics (all sections): 400 entries, 175 entrants, 75 finalists, 4 awards. Held in LeMoyne Center for the Arts for 4 weeks.

CRAFTS CONTEST: All Media.

AWARDS: $500 Best of Show, $300 First, $200 Second, $100 Third Merit Awards (includes all sections).

JUDGING: By 1 art educator.

SALES TERMS: Sales optional. 33-1/3% commission charge.

ENTRY FEE: Not specified.

DEADLINES: Event, June.

91

Mint Museum Exhibition of Piedmont Crafts
Jane Kessler, Assistant Curator
501 Hempstead Place
P. O. Box 6011
Charlotte, North Carolina 28207
U.S.A. Tel: (704) 334-9723

Entry October

Regional; **entry open to Southeast U.S. adults;** biennial in January-March; established 1963. Alternates with Biennial Exhibition of Piedmont Painting and Sculpture. Purpose: to identify the best work being produced in Southeast U.S. Sponsored by Mint Museum. Average statistics (all sections): 1000 entries, 250 entrants, 30 finalists, 10 awards. Held at Mint Museum in Charlotte for 2 months.

CRAFTS CONTEST: All Media, original; limit 4 per entrant. Executed in previous 2 years; not previously shown at Mint Museum. Submit maximum 2 35mm color slides per work for entry review.

ELIGIBILITY: Open to residents, age 18 or over, of Alabama, Florida, Georgia, Kentucky, Louisiana, Mississippi, North Carolina, South Carolina, Tennessee, Virginia, West Virginia.

AWARDS: Over $4000 in Mint Museum Purchase Awards.

JUDGING: Entry review by crafts professional. Sponsor may photograph, reproduce works for catalog, educational and publicity purposes. Not responsible for loss or damage.

SALES TERMS: Sales optional. 30% commission charge.

ENTRY FEE: $10.

DEADLINES: Entry, October. Judging, acceptance, November. Event, January-March.

92

River City Arts Festival Visual Arts Competition
Arts Assembly of Jacksonville
632 May Street
Jacksonville, Florida 32204 U.S.A.
Tel: (904) 633-3748

Entry January

Regional; **entry open to residents age 18 and over;** annual in April; established 1972. Formerly called JACKSONVILLE ARTS FESTIVAL. Purpose: to provide opportunity for artists to display, sell their work. Sponsored by Arts Assembly and City of Jacksonville, Fine Arts Council of Florida. Supported by NEA. Maximum 100 participants. Held in downtown Jacksonville for 5 days. Also sponsor concurrent film-video, poetry contests, Street Artists Market.

CRAFTS CONTEST: All Media, 100lbs. maximum; 2D framed, ready for hanging, plexiglass preferred; limit 2 per entrant. Submit maximum 5 35mm slides of work for entry review. Competition includes fine art, graphics, photography.

ELIGIBILITY: Open to residents, age 18 and over, of Florida, Georgia, North and South Carolina, Alabama, Louisiana, Mississippi.

AWARDS: $6000 total cash prizes (includes all sections).

JUDGING: Entry review and awards judging by 1 known art director-curator. Not responsible for loss or damage.

ENTRY FEE: $20 ($10 refundable if not accepted).

DEADLINES: Entry, January. Acceptance, February. Awards judging, event, April.

93
Roseville Art Center Annual Open Show
Phyllis Kozlen, Director
424 Oak Street
Roseville, California 95678 U.S.A.
Tel: (916) 783-4117

Entry March

Regional; **entry open to Sacramento and surrounding counties;** annual in April; established 1974. Purpose: to provide meaningful showcase for craftspersons. Sponsored by and held at Roseville Art Center for 3 weeks. Average statistics (all sections): 200 entries, 75 entrants, 12 awards.

CRAFTS CONTEST: All Media, original, 48x48 inches maximum, ready for hanging or presentation; limit 3 per entrant. Require hand-delivery. Competition includes visual arts, photography, all crafts.

AWARDS: $250 Best of Show Award. $50 High Merit Award. $25 Merit Award. Honorable Mentions.

JUDGING: By 1 art professional.

SALES TERMS: Sales optional. 30% commission charge.

ENTRY FEE: $4 per work.

DEADLINES: Entry, March. Event, April.

94
Wisconsin Designer Craftsmen Annual Exhibit
Barbara Pelowski, President
2742 North 95th Street
Milwaukee, Wisconsin 53222 U.S.A.
Tel: (414) 774-6861, 425-2465

Entry October

State; **entry open to Wisconsin;** annual in November-December; established 1921. Purpose: to show excellence in craftsmanship. Sponsored by Wisconsin Designer Craftsmen, various museums. Average statistics: 90 entries, 60 entrants, 5 awards. Held at different location each year for 1 month. Also sponsor Morning Glory Fair, theme exhibits, lectures, workshops, demonstrations. Second contact: Ingrid Regula, 6980 North Crestwood Drive, Milwaukee, Wisconsin 53209.

CRAFTS CONTEST: All Media, handcrafted, maximum 12 feet any dimension, ready for display; limit 2 per entrant. Require membership of Wisconsin Designer Craftsmen upon acceptance. No work produced under supervision, previously exhibited in any Wisconsin juried shows.

AWARDS: 5 $200 Prizes minimum. Milwaukee Art Commission Purchase Award.

JUDGING: By 3 jurors. Based on excellence of craftsmanship. Sponsor insures for duration of exhibition; may photograph entries for publicity. Not responsible for loss or damage.

SALES TERMS: 15% commission charge.

ENTRY FEE: $10 plus $16 membership fee (refundable).

DEADLINES: Entry, jurying, October. Event, November-December.

| 95 |

Ontario Crafts Council Provincial Exhibition
346 Dundas Street West
Toronto, Ontario M5T 1G5 CANADA

Entry dates vary

Regional; **entry open to Ontario Crafts Council members;** annual in June-December. Purpose: to exhibit the best in Ontario crafts. Sponsored and supported by Ontario Crafts Council. Publish *Craft News* (monthly). Held at various locations in Ontario for 4 weeks each. Also sponsor various grants, awards.

CRAFTS CONTEST: All Media, original, handcrafted, ready for exhibition; 35lbs. maximum; limit 3 per entrant (set counts as 1). Completed in previous 2 years. Submit entries to 6 regional competitions. No kits, unaltered patterns, excessively fragile entries. Competition includes all crafts.

AWARDS: C$3000 in Awards at Provincial Exhibition. Various Regional Prizes.

JUDGING: Not specified. Sponsor insures accepted entries; not responsible for in-transit loss or damage; may photograph entries for publicity, publication, archives.

SALES TERMS: Sales preferred. 33-1/3% commission charge.

ENTRY FEE: Varies with location. Entrant pays return postage on unaccepted entries.

DEADLINES: Entry, varies with location. Event, June-December.

CRAFTS (Specific Subject-Type)

General Crafts in all media, limited to specific Subject or Type. Includes ARCHITECTURAL EMBELLISHMENT, ART AND THE LAW, CHANGING THEMES, MOVED BY WIND, PUBLIC BUILDING WORKS, RELIGIOUS, ROSEMALING (Folk Painting). (Also see other CRAFTS CATEGORIES.)

| 96 |

Art and the Law Exhibition
West Publishing Company
50 West Kellogg Boulevard
St. Paul, Minnesota 55102 U.S.A.
Tel: (612) 228-2514

Entry May

National; **entry open to U.S. residents;** annual in September-October; established 1979. Purpose: to encourage artists to create works interpreting and illuminating the law. Average statistics: 1200 entries, 600 entrants. Sponsored by West Publishing Company (law book publisher). Held at Landmark Center in St. Paul for 1 month; then tours nation for 1 year.

CRAFTS CONTEST: Art and the Law in Any Media, 2-Dimensional, original, 72x72 inches maximum (unframed size), framed, ready for hanging if appropriate; limit 2 per entrant. Submit 1 slide per work for entry review. No multiples, sculpture. Competition includes fine arts, photography.

AWARDS: $25,000 minimum in Purchase Awards, artists' promotional travel expenses, $500, 15 complimentary reproductions of winning entry for winners'use or sale.

JUDGING: Entry   review   and

awards judging by artists, art professionals, publishers. Sponsor owns exclusive rights to winning entries; may retain entries for 1-year travel exhibit.

ENTRY FEE: None. Sales compulsory.

DEADLINES: Entry, May. Acceptance, judging, July. Event, September-October. National touring exhibition, from November for 1 year.

97

Bainbridge Arts and Crafts Annual Juried Show
P. O. Box 10161
Bainbridge Island, Washington
98110 U.S.A. Tel: (206) 842-3132
Entry September

Regional; **entry open to Alaska, Washington, Oregon residents age 18 and over;** biennial in Autumn; established 1969. Alternates with Fine Arts Juried Show. Average 120 entries. Held in Pauli Dennis Gallery for 4-6 weeks.

CRAFTS CONTEST: **Changing Theme,** original; limit 3 per entrant. No work done under supervision.

AWARDS: $150 First, $100 Second, $75 Third Prize. Bainbridge Arts and Crafts Purchase Award. $125 First, $75 Second Bainbridge Music and Arts Award to Island artists only.

JUDGING: By 3 professionals. Not responsible for loss or damage.

SALES TERMS: Sales compulsory. 40% commission charge.

ENTRY FEE: $5.

DEADLINES: Entry, September. Event, Autumn.

98

Iowa Arts Council Art in State Buildings Program
State Capitol Complex
Des Moines, Iowa 50319 U.S.A.
Tel: (515) 281-4451
Entry dates continuous

International; **entry open to age 18 and over (Iowa residents preferred);** continuous; established 1978. Established by state legislature reserving 1/2% of funds for new, substantially renewed state buildings, for purchase of artwork. Formerly called ART IN STATE ARCHITECTURE to 1981. Sponsored and supported by Iowa state funds. Average 20 assignments annually. Also sponsor artists-in-schools, expansion arts, grants-in-aid, solo artists, program touring arts team, touring exhibitions and performers.

CRAFTS CONTEST: **Works for Public Buildings,** original, high quality. Submit 5 35mm slides for continuous review, or submit separate applications. Divisions: Open Competition, Limited Competition (artists on slide registry only). Preference given to Iowa artists. Competition includes visual art, all crafts.

AWARDS: Purchase of existing work, commissioned contacts.

JUDGING: By Building Arts Selection Committee. Based on quality, media, style and nature of artwork, permanence, artist's background.

ENTRY FEE: None.

DEADLINES: Continuous.

99

Louisville Art Center Association Juried Exhibition
James S. Adams, Administrator
The Water Tower
3005 Upper River Road

Louisville, Kentucky 40207 U.S.A.
Tel: (502) 896-2146

Entry August

Regional; **entry open to residents age 18 and over living within 250-mile radius of Louisville;** annual in September-October; established 1981. Purpose: to expose work of regional artists. Sponsored by Art Center Association (founded 1909), oldest visual arts organization in Louisville. Average statistics (all sections): 100 entrants, 24 finalists. Held at Art Center Association, Old Louisville Pumping State #1 (national historic landmark) in Louisville for 1 month. Have lectures, studio tours, workshops, other exhibitions, productions, performances (10 per year). Also sponsor Annual Showcase Exhibition.

CRAFTS CONTEST: Changing Theme, All Media (including ceramics, blown glass, stained glass, sculpture), rotating theme in 4-year cycle (Water, Earth, Air, Fire), ready for exhibit, able to fit through 80x72-inch door; limit 2 per entrant. Require hand-delivery, entrants provide exhibit displays. Submit 2 slides of work (full view, detail) for entry review. Competition includes arts, other crafts.

AWARDS: Purchase and Merit Awards.

JUDGING: By nationally known professional artist. Based on technical relation to theme. Sponsor insures work at exhibition only. Not responsible for loss or damage.

SALES TERMS: Sales optional. 30% commission charge.

ENTRY FEE: $10 plus return postage.

DEADLINES: Entry, August. Judg-

ing, September. Event, September-October.

100

Religious Art and Architecture Competition
Interfaith Forum on Religion, Art and Architecture
Judith A. Miller, Administrative Assistant
1777 Church Street, N.W.
Washington, DC 20036 U.S.A.
Tel: (202) 387-8333

Entry date not specified

International; entry open to all; annual in May; established 1939. Purpose: to promote design excellence in architecture for religious use. Sponsored and supported by Interfaith Forum on Religion, Art and Architecture. Recognized by American Institute of Architects. Average statistics (all sections): 500 entries, 3 countries, 12 awards. Held at different locations each year for 3-5 days. Publish *Faith and Form, The In Between* (biannual). Also sponsor 3 conferences each year.

CRAFTS CONTEST: Religious Use. Competition includes visual arts, all crafts.

AWARDS: Design Award Certificate (includes all sections).

JUDGING: By 2-3 architects, artists, clergy each.

ENTRY FEE: None.

DEADLINES: Entry, date not specified. Event, May.

101

Vesterheim Norwegian-American Museum Rosemaling Exhibition
Marion John Nelson, Director
502 West Water Street
Decorah, Iowa 52101 U.S.A.
Tel: (319) 382-9681

Entry July

International; **entry open to U.S., Canada (5-year residents);** annual in July; established 1967. Originally painted on wood only, now expanded to include all traditional Norwegian decorative painting. Purpose: to raise standards of rosemaling in America. Sponsored and supported by Vesterheim Norwegian-American Museum. Average statistics: 180 entries, 120 entrants, 12 awards, 8000 attendance, 95 total sales. Held during Decorah Nordic Fest at the museum in Decorah for 3 days. Have program of related cultural activities, rosemaling workshops. Publish *Rosemaling Letter, Norwegian Tracks* (quarterly). Also sponsor weaving contest.

CRAFTS CONTEST: **Rosemaling** (folk painting on ceramics, porcelain, other media), original (except for base object), 8 inches minimum in 1 direction; limit 2 per entrant. Completed in previous 5 years. Artists working in contemporary style or on ceramics, porcelain may submit 1 additional entry for exhibition only.

AWARDS: $25, $15, $10 Prizes to entries deserving special recognition. Ribbons. Medals of Honor, Exhibition at Invitation Exhibit to artist having accumulated a certain number of ribbon prize points.

JUDGING: By 1 Norwegian, 1 American artist, 1 established American rosemaler. Based on technique, design. All entries viewed in their entirety.

SALES TERMS: Sales optional. 20% commission charge.

ENTRY FEE: $3 per work, plus return postage.

DEADLINES: Entry, event, July.

102

Windtoys, Weathervanes and Whirligigs National Juried Exhibition
Kentuck Association of Northport Center
Georgine Clarke, Director
P. O. Box 127
501 Main Avenue
Northport, Alabama 35476 U.S.A.
Tel: (205) 759-3202

Entry February

National; **entry open to U.S.;** annual in April-May; established 1981. Purpose: to exhibit crafts objects moved by wind. Sponsored by Kentuck Association of Northport. Average statistics (all sections): 60 entries, 30 entrants, 4 awards, $10,000 total sales. Held at Kentuck Center in Northport for 2 months. Have gallery, museum shop, studio space for resident craftspersons. Also sponsor exhibitions, educational programs.

CRAFTS CONTEST: **Moved by Wind, All Media;** limit 3 per entrant. Completed in previous 2 years. Submit maximum 2 slides for entry review.

AWARDS: Cash and Purchase Prizes (includes all sections).

JUDGING: By 1 crafts specialist. Sponsor may photograph entries for publicity, catalog, records; insures while on premises.

SALES TERMS: Sales encouraged. 30% commission charge.

ENTRY FEE: $10 plus return postage.

DEADLINES: Entry, February. Materials, March. Event, April-May.

103

Wonderworks Exhibit
Centennial Art Center
Ann Horan, Director
Metro Nashville Parks and
Recreation
Nashville, Tennessee 37201 U.S.A.
Tel: (615) 259-5538
Entry date not specified

Regional; **entry open to Southeast U.S. by invitation;** annual in October; established 1975. Purpose: to create opportunity for public to see quality work done by professional artists. Sponsored by Metropolitan Board of Parks and Recreation in Nashville. Average statistics (all sections): 70 entries, 40 entrants, $3000 total sales. Held at Centennial Art Center in Nashville for 1 month. Also sponsor monthly shows. Second contact: Paul L. Downey, Cultural Recreation, Centennial Park Office, Nashville, Tennessee 37201.

CRAFTS CONTEST: Varying Types, Media. Competition includes visual arts, all crafts.

AWARDS: Purchase Prizes.

JUDGING: By art critics, teachers.

SALES TERMS: Sales compulsory. 20% commission charge.

DEADLINES: Event, October.

104

Saltire Society Art in Architecture Awards
Ian Kinniburgh, Honorary Secretary
Saltire House
13 Atholl Crescent
Edinburgh, EH3 8HA SCOTLAND
Entry dates continuous

International; entry open to all; triennial; established 1936. Purpose: to promote Scottish culture by encouraging new endeavors in architecture, arts and crafts. Sponsored by Scottish Development and Education Departments. Supported by Scottish Arts Council. Held at Glasgow University. Have select bibliography; library; publications, recordings for sale; advisory service. Also sponsor Saltire Society and Royal Bank Scottish Literary Award, Competition for Senior School Choirs, Chambers Oral History Award, Robert Hurd Scholarship, Agnes Mure Mackenzie Award for Published Historical Research, Saltire Civil Engineering Award, Saltire Housing Award, School Study Schemes, conferences, exhibitions.

CRAFTS CONTEST: Architectural Embellishment (such as decorative glass, sculpture), works forming integral part of building project. Competition includes other crafts.

AWARDS: Saltire Art in Architecture Awards, Commendations.

JUDGING: By panel of distinguished crafts experts.

ENTRY FEE: None.

DEADLINES: Entry, continuous. Awards ceremony, February.

DESIGN
Crafts Design, including MEDALLION, STORE ITEMS, TOYS, and CERAMICS BY WOMEN.

105

Arkansas Arts Center Toys Designed by Artists Exhibition
Townsend Wolfe, Director
MacArthur Park, P.O. Box 2137
Little Rock, Arkansas 72203 U.S.A.

Entry October

National; **entry open to U.S.;** annual in December-January; established 1973. Sponsored by Arkansas Arts Center, founded 1941 to establish and maintain growth, understanding of arts. Supported by City of Little Rock. Recognized by Arkansas State Board of Education, American Association of Museums. Held at Arkansas Arts Center in Little Rock for 1 month. Have book and film library, traveling seminars, concerts, workshops, sales, visiting artists programs. Also sponsor Delta Art Exhibit; Prints, Drawings and Crafts Exhibition; instruction, exhibitions and scholarships in photography, filmmaking, drama, dance, arts, and crafts.

DESIGN CONTEST: **Toys in Ceramic, Enamel, Glass,** 2D or 3D; limit 3 per entrant (all sections). Competition includes fabric, metal, paper, wood.

AWARDS: Up to $1000 in Purchase Awards.

JUDGING: By Arkansas Arts Center jurors.

ENTRY FEE: $7.50 per work.

DEADLINES: Entry,   October. Event, December-January.

| 106 |

Electrum Medallion Design Competition
Helena Arts Council
Nadine M. Shafer, Director
P. O. Box 1231
Helena, Montana 59624 U.S.A.
Tel: (406) 442-6400

Entry May

International; **entry open to U.S., Canada;** annual in June. Purpose: to select annual official symbol of Electrum Competitions. Sponsored by Helena Arts Council (nonprofit organization). Also sponsor Electrum Juried Art Show, Electrum Juried Photography Show, Electrum Contemporary Craft Show. Second contact: Kay Lytle, 1816 Wilder, Helena, Montana 59601; tel: (406) 443-7609.

DESIGN CONTEST: **Festival Medallion in Ceramics, Glass, Plastic, etc.,** maximum 4 inches in diameter, 3oz. net weight, wearable around neck; limit 1 per entrant. Prefer design incorporating symbols depicting Electrum (e.g., 'E'), capable of being reproduced into 9 medallions. Design to include 32-inch chain, ribbon, or facsimile. Competition includes designs in all media.

AWARDS: $25 Cash Award (plus $20 each additional medallion ordered by Helena Arts Council) to winner. Winning medallion becomes official Electrum symbol for 1 year; placed in Helena Arts Council archives as part of permanent collection.

JUDGING: Not specified.

ENTRY FEE: None. Sponsor pays return postage of nonwinning entries.

DEADLINES: Entry, May. Judging, notification, June.

| 107 |

Goudchaux's Design Competition
Goudchaux's Department Store
P. O. Box 3478
1500 Main Street
Baton Rouge, Louisiana 70821
U.S.A.

Entry March

National; **entry open to U.S.;** annual in May; established 1979. Purpose: to encourage original designs marketable through retail department stores. Sponsored by Goudchaux's

Department Store. Held in conjunction with Baton Rouge FestForAll for 2 days. Average 150,000 attendance. Second contact: Arts and Humanities Council of Greater Baton Rouge, 427 Laurel Street, Baton Rouge, Louisiana 70801; tel: (504) 344-8558.

DESIGN CONTEST: Retail Department Store Items (including china, housewares, gifts), original, unpublished; unlimited entry. Submit 35mm color slides and-or diagrams, detailed drawings, 5x7-inch minimum glossy photographs of proposed design (by mail only). No kits, molds, samples, cooperative work. Also have other media design sections.

AWARDS: $600 First, $300 Second, $100 Third Prize. 5% royalty of cost on items sold above cost to originator of entries if produced and marketed by Goudchaux. Winning entries, other outstanding entries exhibited at Baton Rouge FestForAll.

JUDGING: Entry review by marketing and design specialists. Awards judging by marketing consultant. Sponsor reserves right to negotiate with artists to market entry.

ENTRY FEE: None. Entrant pays return postage.

DEADLINES: Entry, March. Event, May.

| 108 |

Women in Design International (WIDI) Competition
Connie M. Carnell, Executive Director
P. O. Box 984
Ross, California 94957 U.S.A.
Tel: (415) 457-8596

Entry April

International; **entry open to women;** annual in Fall; established 1981. Purpose: to promote visibility of outstanding women designers; compile illustrated profile of women's design accomplishments worldwide. Sponsored and supported by WIDI (founded 1977). Recognized by NEA's Design Arts Program. Average statistics: 6500 entries, 500 entrants, 16 countries. Publish *WIDI Journal* (quarterly), *Women in Design International Compendium* (annual). Have seminars, lectures, exhibits, special events, international conference. Also sponsor WIDI National Exhibition. Second contact: 530 Howard Street, Second Floor, San Francisco, California 94105; tel: (415) 285-9106.

DESIGN CONTEST: Ceramics; limit 3 categories per entrant. Submit maximum 12 professional quality 35mm slides per category in slide sleeve or box. Do not submit art works. Competition includes visual arts, fiber, textiles, jewelry, furniture, industrial products, photography, miscellaneous.

AWARDS: Certificates of Outstanding Achievement. Winners' profiles published in *Women in Design International Compendium.*

JUDGING: By international panel of prominent contributors to design world. Sponsor owns entries; may photograph entries for exhibitions, publication.

ENTRY FEE: $40 first, $20 each additional category.

DEADLINES: Entry, April. Event, Fall.

| 109 |

Ontario Crafts Council John Mather Award
Committee Chair
346 Dundas Street West
Toronto, Ontario M5T 1G5 CANADA

Entry June

Provincial; **entry open to Ontario residents (2 years);** annual in September; established 1977. Named after John Mather, founding member of Ontario Crafts Council, crafts collector. Purpose: to acknowledge service to crafts scene over extended period. Held in Toronto. Also sponsor various grants, Provincial Exhibition.

DESIGN CONTEST: Presentation Medal, Token, All Media, suitable for reproduction and presentation as a crafts medal.

AWARD: $1000 Mather Award.

ENTRY FEE: $10.

DEADLINES: Entry, June. Commission, September.

EXHIBITIONS

Juried crafts exhibitions, usually with no awards (items must be for sale). Includes CERAMICS, GLASS, and JEWELRY.

110

A Gather of Glass Exhibition
Mindscape Gallery and Studio Inc.
Deborah Farber-Isaacson, Exhibition Coordinator
1521 Sherman Avenue
Evanston, Illinois 60201 U.S.A.
Tel: (312) 864-2660

Entry June

National; **entry open to U.S.;** annual in October-November; established 1976. Named after stage in glassmaking process. Purpose: to present significant, national cross-section of glass art by second, third gen-

eration glass artists within contemporary American studio glass movement. Sponsored by and held at Mindscape Gallery and Studio Inc. for 6 weeks. Average statistics: 120 entries, 20 entrants, 5000 attendance, $30,000 in total sales, $1500 sale per entrant. Publish *Mindscape Glass* (monthly). Also sponsor glass collector's seminar-slide lecture series, workshops, conferences for artists and collectors, invitation exhibitions.

GLASS EXHIBITION: Functional, Sculptural, 6-10 per entrant. Multimedia work incorporating blown glass is acceptable. Submit slides for entry review; monochrome prints, personal-professional statement, information concerning process, for publicity and promotion.

JUDGING: By 5 professional glass-artists. All works viewed in their entirety. Based on imaginative use of media, cohesive approach to design, definition of personal statement, craftsmanship. Sponsor insures for duration of exhibition.

SALES TERMS: Sales compulsory. 45% commission charge.

ENTRY FEE: None. Entrant pays return postage.

DEADLINES: Entry, June. Event, October-November.

111

Westlake Gallery American Glass Exhibition
Cathy Westlake, Gallery Director
210 East Post Road
White Plains, New York 10601
U.S.A. Tel: (914) 682-8123

Entry February

National; **entry open to U.S.;** annual in May; established 1977. Purpose: to promote glass as collectable fine art. Sponsored by Westlake Gallery. Average statitics: 150 entrants, 50 finalists. Held at Westlake Gallery in White Plains for 4 weeks. Also sponsor Wood Exhibition, Ceramics for Collectors Exhibition, Fiber and Fabric Fantasy Exhibition.

GLASS   EXHIBITION: Blown Glass. Submit minimum 6 colored slides or photographs for entry review; biography, 2 copies of resume, business cards, technical information, 8x10-inch monochrome photographs for publicity purposes. No production work.

JUDGING: Entry review by Westlake Gallery. Based on originality, quality of craftsmanship.

SALES TERMS: Sales compulsory. Commission charges: 50% for items valued at $500 or less; 40% for items $500 or more.

ENTRY FEE: None. Sponsor pays return shipping of unsold items.

DEADLINES: Entry, judging, February. Event, May.

112

Westlake Gallery Ceramics for Collectors
Cathy Westlake, Gallery Director
210 East Post Road
White Plains, New York 10601
U.S.A. Tel: (914) 682-8123

Entry June

National; **entry open to U.S.;** annual in September-October; established 1977. Purpose: to promote ceramics as collectable fine art, show variety of contemporary works available. Sponsored by Westlake Gallery. Average statistics: 300 entries, 50 finalists. Held at Westlake Gallery in White Plains for 5 weeks. Also sponsor Wood Exhibition, Fiber and Fabric

Fantasy Exhibition, American Glass Exhibition.

CERAMICS   EXHIBITION: All Forms. Submit minimum 6 colored slides or photographs for entry review; biography, technical information, 8x10-inch monochrome photographs for publicity purposes.

JUDGING: Entry review by Westlake Gallery. Based on originality, quality of craftsmanship.

SALES TERMS: Sales compulsory. Commission charges: 50% for items valued $500 or less; 40% for items $500 or more.

ENTRY FEE: None. Sponsor pays return shipping on unsold items.

DEADLINES: Entry, judging, June. Event, September-October.

113

International Exhibition of Multi-Media, Nonprecious Jewellery
British Crafts Centre
Diana Hughes, Exhibition Director
43 Earlham Street
London WC2H 9LD
ENGLAND Tel: (01) 836-6993

Entry April

International; entry open to all; annual in October-November; established 1982. Purpose: to showcase creativity of contemporary jewelers, forced by economics to use wide range of inexpensive materials. Sponsored by and held at British Craft Centre in London for 6 weeks, and at subsequent tour venues for approximately 2 years. Have International Seminar at Opening Celebration. Also sponsor program of member exhibitions, International Exhibitions of Miniature Textiles (proposed).

JEWELRY EXHIBITION: All Media (including, ceramics, glass, plastic); limit 6 per entrant. Editions or multiples may be submitted. Produced in previous 6 months. No precious jewelry.

JUDGING: Entry review by 7 international selectors. Sponsor insures accepted work from time of acceptance.

SALES TERMS: Sales compulsory. Unspecified commission charge.

ENTRY FEE: £12.

DEADLINES: Entry, April. Event, October-November (London). Tour, 2 years.

GLASS

Includes BLOWN, ETCHED, and STAINED GLASS. (Also see other GLASS CATEGORIES.)

114

Corning Museum of Glass New Glass Review
William Warmus, Assistant Curator
Museum Way
Corning, New York 14831 U.S.A.
Tel: (607) 937-5371

Entry January

International; entry open to all; annual in January; established 1976. Purpose: to encourage communication among glassmakers, present overview of innovations in glassmaking. Sponsored and supported by Corning Museum of Glass. Average statistics: 848 entrants, 28 countries, 100 awards. Have seminar on glass.

GLASS CONTEST: All Forms; limit 3 per entrant (design series constitutes 1 work). Require slides suitable for reproduction. Submit 35mm slides for entry review. Completed in previous year.

AWARDS: Winners published in *New Glass Review.*

JUDGING: By committee of 4 (artist, museum director, curator, critic). Based on degree of innovation in function, subject, aesthetics, technique. Sponsor owns all slide entries; reserves right to photograph and sell.

ENTRY FEE: None.

DEADLINES: Entry, judging, event, January.

115

Glass Art Hawaii Juried Show
Stained Glass Association of Hawaii (SGAH)
Merrie Carol Grain
P. O. Box 22126
Honolulu, Hawaii 96822 U.S.A.
Tel: (808) 947-9555

Entry February

State; **entry open to Hawaii;** annual in May; established 1979. Purpose: to encourage finest development and greater appreciation of the art of stained glass. Sponsored by SGAH. Supported by SGAH and Pacific Guardian Life. Held at Davies Pacific Center Building in Honolulu for 2-1/2 weeks. Have professional sitters for booths. Publish *SGAH News.* Also sponsor seminars, social activities. Second contact: Robbie Byrd, Exhibit Chair; tel: (808) 638-8610.

GLASS CONTEST: Stained (including leaded flat glass, sandblasted, etched, beveled, faceted, painted, laminated, copper foil, slumped, layered, fused), original, 54x24 or 54x72 inches maximum (size may include more than one entry), framed with wood, zinc or metal and strongly constructed; ready for hanging; limit 3 per entrant. 3D works to have clearance from existing window. Require artists to attend or provide substitute or contribute to sitter fee. Submit 35mm slides (1 overall, 1 or more of detail) for outer island entrant (other than Hawaii). No supervised, collaborative work, lampshades, jewelry boxes or sculptural free-standing object; work previously exhibited in juried Hawaiian competition.

AWARDS: First, Second, Third Place Awards. Honorable Mentions.

JUDGING: Not responsible for loss or damage.

SALES TERMS: Sales compulsory (excepting one). 20% commission charge.

ENTRY FEE: $15. $15 sitter fee.

DEADLINES: Entry, February. Judging, March. Event, May.

116

Glassmasters Guild Art Glass Competition
Lili Lihn, Retail Division Manager
621 Avenue of Americas
New York, New York 10011 U.S.A.
Tel: (212) 924-2868

Entry June

National; **entry open to U.S. residents;** annual in September; established 1977. Became national 1982. Purpose: to increase public's exposure to contemporary stained glass. Sponsored and supported by Glassmasters Guild (division of Glassmasters Inc.). Average statistics: 400 entries, 150 entrants, 40 finalists, 7 awards, $7500 total sales. Held at Glassmasters Guild for 1 month. Also sponsor Street of Glass Exhibitions, lectures, permanent displays.

GLASS CONTEST: All Forms (including enameled, etched, foiled, fused, laminated, leaded, sandblasted, slumped), original; limit 3 per entrant. Submit 2 color slides (full view, detail) per work for entry review. Divisions: Amateur, Professional.

AWARDS: $500 Grand Prize to best of show. $200 First, $100 Second, $50 Third Prize to each division. Winners exhibited.

JUDGING: Entry review and awards judging by 5 businesspersons, writers, art professionals. Sponsor retains slides; insures entries while hung at gallery.

SALES TERMS: Sales optional. 25%-40% commission charge.

ENTRY FEE: $5 plus return shipping.

DEADLINES: Entry, June. Event, awards judging, September.

117

Marin Art Glass Festival
Arthur Hoffman, M.D.
30 Bayview Avenue
Mill Valley, California 94941 U.S.A.
Tel: (415) 388-6700

Entry dates vary

International; entry open to all; periodic; established 1973. Formerly called MILL VALLEY ART GLASS FESTIVAL. Purpose: to provide forum for interchange of ideas among glass artists, sales outlet. Sponsored and supported by Arthur M. Hoffman, M.D. Average statistics: 200 entries, 35 entrants, 3 countries, 400 attendance, $500 average sales per entrant. Held at Falkirk Mansion in San Raphael for 1 day. Have chamber music. Also sponsor Marin Vintage Auto Show.

GLASS   CONTEST: Blown,

Etched, Leaded. Submit 5 slides, photographs for entry review. Require entrant attendance. No trinkets.

AWARDS: $350 Best of Show. $150 Nervo Distributor's Certificate. $100 Stained Glass Shop Certificate. $100 Architect's Award. $50 Glass Depot Certificate. $50 Uroboros Glass Studio Certificate.

JUDGING: By participating artists. Architect's Award by 1 architect. Sponsor may photograph entries for publicity.

ENTRY FEE: $30.

DEADLINES: Various.

GLASS, POTTERY, SCULPTURE, ENAMEL

Glass, Pottery, Sculpture, Enamel, including CERAMICS, MOSAIC TILE, PORCELAIN, STAINED GLASS. Pottery usually defined as ceramic containers. (Also see other GLASS, POTTERY, SCULPTURE, ENAMEL CATEGORIES.)

118

All Oregon Art Exhibiticn
Oregon State Fair
Lyn and Steven Nance-Sasser, Directors
State Fairgrounds
2330 17th Street N.E.
Salem, Oregon 97310 U.S.A.
Tel: (503) 378-3247

Entry July

State; **entry open to Oregon;** annual in August-September. Sponsored and supported by Oregon State Fair (founded 1866), Oregon Arts Commission, NEA. Average statistics (all sections): 300 entries, 100 finalists, $3500 in awards, 500,000 attendance. Held at Oregon State Fairgrounds in Salem for 11 days. Tickets: $3. Have art gallery, 2 $300 honoraria for site-related projects. Also sponsor Oregon Salon of Photography, International Exhibition of Photography.

GLASS CONTEST: All Types, original, 84x108 inches maximum; limit 1 per entrant per division. Completed in previous 2 years. Submit 3 slides of work (in plastic sheet) for entry review. Require hand-delivery of accepted works. No special hanging requirements or excessive weight; no work from models or kits, supervised work. Divisions: Professional, Amateur, Student (junior-senior high school), Young Art (age 12 and under). Competition includes textiles, jewelry, photography, arts, environmental-conceptual work.

POTTERY CONTEST: All Types. Requirements, restrictions, divisions same as for Glass.

SCULPTURE CONTEST: All Types. Requirements, restrictions, divisions same as for Glass.

MIXED MEDIA CONTEST: All Types. Requirements, restrictions, divisions same as for Glass.

AWARDS: *Professional:* 5 $300, 5 $200, 5 $100 Awards. *Amateur:* 5 $100, 5 $50, 6 $25 Awards. 2 Special Projects up to $300.

JUDGING: Entry review, awards judging by 3 jurors. Not responsible for loss or damage.

ENTRY FEE: Amateur, $2.50. Students, $1. Professional, Young, free.

DEADLINES: Entry, July. Judging, August. Event, August-September.

119

Baycrafters Annual Juried Art Show
Sally Price
28795 Lake Road
Huntington Metropark
Bay Village, Ohio 44140 U.S.A.
Tel: (216) 871-6543
Entry August

Regional; **entry open to Ohio residents age 18 and over;** annual in August-September; established 1963. Sponsored and supported by Baycrafters (founded 1948). Held during Renaissance Fair at Baycrafters Gallery House in Bay Village for 2 weeks. Have shops, picture rental gallery. Also sponsor Renaissance Fair, Octoberfair, Higbee Show, Emerald Necklace Art Competition, Biennial Arts and Science Festival, Highschool Art Competition, art classes, traveling exhibitions, scholarships.

GLASS CONTEST: All Types, original; limit 6 per entrant (all crafts sections). Completed in previous 2 years. Competition includes textiles, jewelry, metalwork, fine and commercial arts, photography.

POTTERY CONTEST: All Types. Requirements, restrictions same as for Glass.

ENAMEL CONTEST: All Types. Requirements, restrictions same as for Glass.

AWARDS: (Includes all sections): $350 Best of Show, $300 First, $200 Second, $150 Third Prize. Purchase Awards.

JUDGING: Not specified. Sponsor may photograph entries for publicity. Not responsible for loss or damage.

SALES TERMS: Sales optional. 25% commission charge.

ENTRY FEE: $5.

DEADLINES: Entry, August. Event, August-September.

120

Equinox Arts Festival Juried Arts and Crafts Show
Arts Council of Snohomish County
Karen Charnell, Director
P. O. Box 5038
Everett, Washington 98206 U.S.A.
Tel: (206) 252-7469
Entry date not specified

State; **entry open to Washington residents;** annual in September; established 1981. Formerly WATERFRONT ARTS SHOW, EVERYMAN'S FAIR. Purpose: to recognize outstanding artists. Sponsored by Snohomish County Arts Council and Crafts Guild, Everett Park and Recreation Department. Sponsored by the Herald, local businesses. Average 3000 attendance. Held in Everetts Park for 2 days. Also sponsor Equinox Poster Contest, concurrent Arts and Crafts Fair.

GLASS CONTEST: 3D, original; limit 3 per entrant (all sections). Produced in previous 2 years. Competition includes textiles, jewelry, wood, and metal crafts, fine and commercial arts, photography.

POTTERY CONTEST: 3D, original, ready for hanging if appropriate. Other requirements, restrictions same as for Glass.

AWARDS: First, Second, Third Place Monetary Awards. Purchase Prizes (includes all sections).

JUDGING: By 2 professionals. Not responsible for loss or damage.

SALES TERMS: Sales compulsory. 15% commission charge on sales over $250.

ENTRY FEE: $2 per work.

DEADLINES: Entry date not specified. Event, September.

121

Fountain Festival of Arts and Crafts
Fountain Hills Chamber of Commerce
John D. Taska, Manager
P. O. Box 17598
Fountain Hills, Arizona 85268 U.S.A.
Tel: (602) 837-1654

Entry November

International; **entry open to U.S., Canada, Mexico;** annual in November; established 1975. Started as local crafts show for area artists to 1979. Purpose: to attract artists, craftspersons to Fountain Hills. Sponsored and supported by Fountain Hills Chamber of Commerce. Average statistics (all sections): 200 entrants, 15,000 attendance. Held in Fountain Hills for 3 days. Have demonstrations, entertainment, food, camping.

GLASS CONTEST: All Types; limit 3 per entrant (all sections). Also have painting, drawing, other crafts sections.

POTTERY CONTEST: All Types; limit 3 per entrant (all sections).

SCULPTURE CONTEST: All Types; limit 3 per entrant (all sections).

CRAFTS CONTEST: Any Medium; limit 3 per entrant (all sections).

AWARDS: $500 Best of Show Award (all sections). $100 First Prize each to glass, pottery, sculpture, general crafts.

JUDGING: By 3 art professionals.

ENTRY FEE: $5 per work. $75 for booth space (optional). Sale of work compulsory.

DEADLINES: Entry, event, November.

122

Newport News Fall Festival Juried Crafts Show
City of Newport News Department of Parks and Recreation
Kathy Harrell, Special Events Coordinator
2400 Washington Avenue
Newport News, Virginia 23601
U.S.A. Tel: (804) 247-8451

Entry August

International; entry open to all; annual in October; established 1974. Purpose: to promote personality of area by exposing public to traditional craftspersons. Sponsored and supported by City of Newport News Departments of Parks and Recreation. Average statistics: 120 entrants, 5 countries, 10 awards, 30,000 attendance, $300 sales per entrant. Have Craftsman's Market Show, A-frame and table hire.

POTTERY CONTEST: All Forms, original, handcrafted; limit 4 per entrant. Submit 1 35mm slide of 2D, 4 of 3D work for entry review. Entrants to participate in Craftsman's Market. No commercial crafts, commercially molded ceramics, items made from kits. Competition for some awards includes selected crafts. Also have general crafts sections.

STAINED GLASS CONTEST: All Forms. Requirements, restrictions same as for Pottery.

AWARDS: (Includes all sections): $500 Best of Show Awards. $100 each to best display, best demonstration, most authentic craft. $40 to best each media. Purchase Awards.

JUDGING: Not Specified. Not responsible for loss or damage.

ENTRY FEE: $10 jury fee. $25 display fee for 2 days.

DEADLINES: Entry, August. Acceptance, September. Event, October.

123

Swedish Days Outdoor Art Exhibit
Geneva Chamber of Commerce
Jean Gaines, Associate Director
5 North Third Street, P. O. Box 481
Geneva, Illinois 60134 U.S.A.
Tel: (312) 232-6060

Entry May

International; entry open to all; annual in June; established 1949. Purpose: to celebrate good hometown life. Held at Kane County Court House Lawn in Geneva for 2 days. Have crafts fair, exhibit and sale; music competition, children's carnival, fireworks, picnic supper, shows.

GLASS CONTEST: All Types, original. Submit minimum 3 slides or photos of work for entry review. No work produced from commercial kits. Also have fiber, graphics, painting, photography, pottery, and quilt sections.

POTTERY CONTEST: All Types. Requirements, restrictions same as for Glass.

SCULPTURE CONTEST: Ceramic. Requirements, restrictions same as for Glass. Competition includes fabric, metal.

AWARDS: First, Second Place Ribbons. Purchase Awards.

JUDGING: By jury.

ENTRY FEE: $25 per 10x10-foot display area.

DEADLINES: Entry, May. Judging, event, June.

124

Toledo Area Artists' Exhibition
Toledo Museum of Art
Robert Phillips, Curator of
Contemporary Art
P. O. Box 1013
Toledo, Ohio 43697 U.S.A. Tel: (419) 255-8000

Entry April

Regional; **entry open to 17 counties in Northwest Ohio and Southeast Michigan;** annual in June-July; established 1918. Sponsored and supported by Toledo Museum of Art, Toledo Federation of Art Societies. Held at Toledo Museum of Art for 1 month. Second contact: Toledo Federation of Art Societies, 2445 Monroe Street, Toledo, Ohio 43610.

GLASS CONTEST: All Types, original, ready for hanging if appropriate; limit 3 per entrant (all sections); set counts as 1. Completed in previous 2 years. No copies or work done under supervision. Competition for some awards includes jewelry, metalwork, textiles, woodwork, photography, fine arts.

POTTERY CONTEST: All Types Fired. Requirements, restrictions same as for Glass.

SCULPTURE CONTEST: All Types. Requirements, restrictions same as for Glass.

ENAMEL CONTEST: All Types. Requirements, restrictions same as for Glass.

MOSAIC TILE CONTEST: All Types Fired. Requirements, restrictions same as for Glass.

PORCELAIN CONTEST: All

Types Fired. Requirements, restrictions same as for Glass.

ELIGIBILITY: Open to Allen, Defiance, Fulton, Hancock, Henry, Lucas, Ottawa, Paulding, Putnam, Sandusky, Seneca, Van Wert, Williams, Wood, and Wyandot counties (Ohio); Lenawee, Monroe counties (Michigan).

AWARDS: Craft Club of Toledo Gold Medal to best craft. Roulet Medal to best sculpture (including wood, metal sculpture). *Including all sections:* $500 to best of show. 5 $250 First, 5 $175 Second, 5 $100 Third Prizes. Purchase Awards.

JUDGING: By 3 art professionals (purchase awards by Toledo Museum). Sponsor may photography entries for catalog, publicity. Not responsible for loss or damage.

SALES TERMS: Sales encouraged. 15% commission charge (excluding purchase awards).

ENTRY FEE: $10 plus $7.50 return shipping.

DEADLINES: Entry, notification, April. Event, June-July. Materials returned, August.

GRANTS (General)

Grants, Fellowships, Apprenticeships, and Assistantships primarily for CRAFTS RESEARCH, PRODUCTION, DEVELOPMENT and AID. Includes EMERGENCY ASSISTANCE, FACILITIES MAINTENANCE, MUSEUMS, and SCULPTURE. (Also see RESIDENCE GRANTS, SCHOLARSHIPS, FELLOWSHIPS.)

| 125 |

Change Inc. Emergency Assistance Grants
Susan Lewis, Secretary
Box 705, Cooper Station
New York, New York 10276 U.S.A.
Tel: (212) 473-3742
Entry dates continuous

National; **entry open to U.S. professionals;** continuous; established 1970. Purpose: to award emergency grants to professional artists in all field. Sponsored by Change Inc. Second contact: P. O. Box 480027, Los Angeles, California 90048.

CRAFT GRANTS: Emergency Assistance. $100-$500 to professional craftspersons in need of emergency assistance resulting from utility turn-off, eviction, unpaid medical bills, fire, illness. Submit detailed letter describing situation, proof of professional status, 2 recommendation letters from people in applicant's field, outstanding bills substantiating amount needed. Competition includes visual arts, photography, film, video.

JUDGING: By Board of Directors.

DEADLINES: Continuous.

| 126 |

National Endowment for the Arts (NEA) Crafts Fellowships and Grants to Individuals
2401 E Street N.W.
Washington, DC 20506 U.S.A.
Tel: (202) 634-6044
Entry dates vary

National; **entry open to professional U.S. citizens, residents;** most annual; established 1965. Sponsored by NEA (independent agency of the U.S. government) to encourage and assist U.S. cultural resources, make arts widely available, strengthen cultural organizations, preserve arts heritage, develop creative talent. Supported by annual appropriations from U.S. Congress, private donations. Average 3% of entries accepted. Address inquiries to programs *italicized* in parentheses.

CRAFTS FELLOWSHIP: Professional Creative Development *(Visual Arts Program)*. $12,500 fellowships to practicing professional craftspersons of exceptional talent and demonstrated ability, plus limited $4000 fellowships to emerging, promising artists for creative development, materials purchase, support to allow time for project work. Submit 10 35mm slides of recent work. Categories: Nonfunctional (works directed toward experimental aesthetic exploration), Functional (works in which function is of prime importance). Competition is biennial (odd years) and includes photography, video, sculpture (even years: conceptual, performance, new genres; printmaking, drawing, artists' books; painting). Application, April. Notification, 6-12 months later.

SCULPTURE FELLOWSHIP: Professional Creative Development *(Visual Arts Program)*. Awards, requirements, restrictions, deadlines same as for crafts.

CRAFTS GRANT: Folk Artisans *(Folk Arts Program)*. Up to 25 one-time-only $1000 Heritage Awards on nonmatching basis to nominated master folk artisan of demonstrated talent, previously unpaid for their contributions to arts and nation. Competition includes music. Application, May. Notification, December.

CRAFTS APPRENTICESHIP GRANT: Folk Arts Education *(Folk Arts Program)*. $1500 nonmatching grants to experienced folk artists wishing to study under a master artist

within their own tradition. Submit samples of master's work as well as of own work, evidence of master's willingness to teach. Not for school or on-going training programs. Competition includes music. Application, April. Notification, December.

ELIGIBILITY: U.S. citizens or permanent residents who are practicing professionals. Require project description, career summary, work samples, budget, supplementary documentation depending on program. Not for students pursuing higher education degrees, nonprofessionals engaged in arts-crafts as hobby, recipients of major NEA awards in previous 2 years. Final reports usually required after project completion.

JUDGING: Application review by Program Panel. Recommendation by National Council on the Arts. Final Acceptance by NEA chair. Based on quality of work as demonstrated by material submitted; record of professional activity and achievement; evidence that applicant's work reflects continued, serious, exceptional aesthetic investigation.

DEADLINES: Vary by Program. Application 6-12 months prior to notification.

127

National Endowment of the Arts (NEA) Crafts Grants to Organizations
2401 E Street N.W.
Washington, DC 20506 U.S.A.
Tel: (202) 634-6044

Entry dates vary

National; **entry open to U.S. nonprofit, tax-exempt organizations;** annual; established 1965. Sponsored by NEA (independent agency of the U.S. government) to encourage and assist U.S. cultural resources, make arts widely available, strengthen cultural organizations, preserve arts heritage, develop creative talent. Supported by annual appropriations from U.S. Congress, private donations. Address inquiries to programs *italicized* in parentheses.

CRAFTS GRANTS: Artists Organizations, Spaces *(Visual Arts Program).* Up to $20,000 on matching basis to organizations whose primary, ongoing purpose is to serve needs of, and enhance opportunities for individual artists and craftspersons, plus up to $10,000 on nonmatching basis for honoraria. Not for amateur, student or adult education groups; construction or renovation of facilities; real estate, maintenance cost; major equipment purchase; creation of new organizations. Categories: Exhibitions (contemporary works, including static and nonstatic pieces, sited temporary installations, other experimental, innovative activities), Services to the Field (financial, legal, technical), Working Facilities (technical assistance for experimentation, production of new work), Honoraria (paid directly to artists for use of their work in exhibitions or for their services in workshops, performances, other events). Application, June. Notification, April.

Art in Public Places *(Visual Arts Program).* Up to $50,000 (commissioned works), $25,000 (purchases), or $10,000 (public site planning, design) on matching basis to state, local government agencies, arts organizations (including education institutions, historical organizations, community art center, libraries) for commission or purchase of work to be installed permanently or temporarily at interior or exterior public sites (such as rivers, waterfronts, recreational facilities, parks, airports, roadsides, subways, buildings). Limited number of planning grants also available. Not for exhibitions; museum acquisitions; solely historical, commemorative, or memorial projects. Application, June, December. Notification, July of following year.

Arts Development *(Challenge Grants Program).* $50,000 to $1,500,-000 on minimum 1-to-3 matching basis to wide variety of arts organizations for long-term development of broad-based funding stimulating private sector investment in the arts. NEA funds released to grantees upon evidence of 1-to-1 matching funds, which must rise to minimum 3-to-1 ratio during grant term. Application, December. Notification, August.

Community Arts *(Expansions Arts Program).* Matching grants on basis of proven financial need (generally no more than 25% of organization's annual budget) to community arts groups rooted in and reflective of minority, inner-city, rural, tribal communities for workshops, classes, performances, exhibitions, and services through regional or national organizations. Not for pilot programs, festivals, competitions, pageants, outreach by major institutions, children's museums, capital construction, schools, social services agencies, arts service groups, consortia, human enrichment programs. Application, October, November. Notification, June, September.

Folk Arts Preservation, Presentation *(Folk Arts Program).* $5000 to $50,000 matching grants to organizations for media exhibits, distribution projects to document folk art work methods, repertoires, performance styles. Submit up to 10 photos showing technical competence, sensitivity to folklore documentation needs. Not for pure research, fine arts, historical presentation, start-up costs, construction, equipment, renovation. Competition includes music. Application, January, April, October. Notification, 6 months later.

Special Projects *(Inter-Arts Program).* $2500 to $50,000 on matching basis to presenting organizations, artists' colonies, national and regional service organizations for projects, programs that cross traditional disciplinary lines. Application dates vary by subprogram. Notification, 6 months later.

Visual Artists' Forums *(Visual Arts Program).* Up to $5000 on matching basis in any one fiscal year to wide range of organizations for lectures by visiting artists, seminars, symposia, conferences, workshops, demonstrations, publications, artist-in-residence programs.

ELIGIBILITY: Tax-exempt, non-profit organizations. Submit project description, dissemination plans, detailed budget, secured sources of matching grants, IRS certification of tax-exempt status, supplementary documentation depending on program. Application usually limited to 1 per year. Require final reports after program.

JUDGING: Application review by Program Panel. Recommendation by National Council on the Arts. Final awards by NEA chair. Review criteria vary by program, but all include demonstrated quality of previous work, merit of and ability to realize proposed project, potential contribution to national and NEA program goals, budget feasibility.

DEADLINES: Vary by program. Application, 6-12 months prior to notification.

| 128 |

National Endowment for the Arts (NEA) Crafts Museum Grants
2401 E Street N.W.
Washington, DC 20506 U.S.A.
Tel: (202) 634-6164

Entry dates vary

National; **entry open to U.S. museums;** annual; established 1965. Sponsored by NEA (independent agency of the U.S. government) to encourage and assist U.S. cultural resources, make arts widely available, strengthen cultural organizations, preserve arts heritage, develop creative talent. Supported by annual appropriations from U.S. Congress, private donations.

CRAFT MUSEUM GRANT: Educational Programs. Up to $25,000 on matching basis to museums, exhibition spaces without permanent collections to develop, strengthen arts-related educational programs, outreach projects. Application, December. Notification, June.

Permanent Collections Use. Up to $75,000 on matching basis to museums for greater use of permanent collections, including installation, temporary exhibitions, loans, preparation and publication of catalogs. Not for major structural modifications of buildings. Application, June. Notification, December.

Permanent Collection Catalog. Up to $75,000 on matching basis to museums for documentation and publication in catalogs of permanent collections, including scholarly handbooks. Application, June. Notification, December.

Special Exhibitions. Unlimited amounts on matching basis to museums to develop (up to $20,000 to borrow) exhibitions of artistic significance, including planning, organizing, shipping, insurance, catalogs, documentation, publicity, touring, educational programs, films, lecture series. Not for exhibitions of privately owned collections or works by curator, organizers, staff. Application, February. Notification, October.

Visiting Specialist Fellowships. Up to $15,000 on matching basis to museums to secure temporary consultation services of experts for specific projects. Applications, December. Notification, June.

ELIGIBILITY: Tax-exempt, non-profit organizations. Require project description, dissemination plans, detailed budget, secured sources of matching grants, IRS certification of tax-exempt status, supplementary documentation depending on program. Final reports normally required after program.

JUDGING: Application review by Program Panel. Recommendation by National Council on the Arts. Final by NEA chair. Review criteria vary by program, but all include demonstrated quality of previous work, merit of and ability to realize proposed project, potential contribution to national and NEA program goals, budget feasibility.

DEADLINES: Vary by program. Application, 6-12 months prior to notification.

129

Veterans Administration (VA) Art-in-Architecture Program
Lenore H. Jacobs, Coordinator
810 Vermont Avenue N.W.
Washington, DC 20420 U.S.A.
Tel: (202) 389-3420, 389-3398

Entry dates continuous

National; **entry open to U.S.;** continuous. Purpose: to provide VA Medical Centers, clinics, other facilities with art works as integral part of architectural design concept. Sponsored by Veterans Administration. Recognized by NEA.

CRAFTS GRANT: Commissioned for VA Facilities. Half percent of estimated construction cost of each VA facility (maximum $50,000) to U.S. artists for craftworks as integral part

of project's architectural design. Submit maximum 20 35mm slides, resume for entry review. Competition includes art, photo-murals, all other crafts.

JUDGING: Entry review by VA, project architects, art professionals appointed by NEA. Awards judging by Veteran Affairs Administrator.

DEADLINES: Application, open.

130

Bronfman Award for Excellence in the Crafts
Canadian Crafts Council
Peter Weinrich, Executive Director
46 Elgin Street, Suite 16
Ottawa, Ontario K1P 5K6 CANADA
Tel: (613) 235-8200

Entry August

National; **entry open to Canadian citizens;** annual; established 1977. Purpose: to reward excellence in craftsmanship over extended period of time. Sponsored by Canadian Crafts Council, Bronfman Foundation. Also sponsor various craft exhibitions, scholarships.

CRAFTS GRANT: For Body of Work. 1 $15,000 award presented annually to craftsperson demonstrating excellence in work; innovation, extension of traditional methods. Require nomination through Canadian Crafts Council member who is responsible for submitting 35mm slides, monochrome photos, curriculum vitae, evidence of citizenship, letter of agreement.

JUDGING: By jury consisting of Council, Foundation, expert representatives.

DEADLINES: Entry, August.

131

British Crafts Council Grants and Assistantships
12 Waterloo Place
London SW1Y 4AU, ENGLAND
Tel: 01-930 4811

Entry dates vary

National; **entry open to England, Wales.** Purpose: to assist craftspersons at various stages in their careers. Sponsored by British Crafts Council. Have loan scheme. Also sponsor conservation grants.

CRAFTS GRANTS: Equipment, Workshop Maintenance. Maximum 50% cost of equipment and-or financial assistance towards operational costs in first few months to craftspersons about to set up workshops or having run them for less than 2 years, for establishing workshop. Submit 35mm slides of work for entry review. Entrants not to be employed outside the workshop for more than 2 days a week.
Sabbatical, Project. Limited number of grants to craftspersons who have been working for minimum 7 years, for sabbatical leave to reassess work and-or undertake specific project. Submit 35mm slides of work for entry review.
Special Project: Grant or guarantee against loss for crafts projects of national significance to societies, organizations, individuals. Submit 35mm slides for entry review.

CRAFTS   ASSISTANTSHIP: Workshop Training. 1-year grants toward living wage during initial months of employment (renewable at a reduced rate) to trainees working under established craftspersons. Submit 35mm slides of work for entry review. Employer to provide comprehensive training and business experience.

Career Advancement. Limited number of 3-9 month assistance grants (including living expenses, payment to workshop) to art school graduates intending to set up workshop or pursuing careers as craftspersons for undertaking intensive training, gaining working experience in 1 or more established workshops. Submit 35mm slides of work for entry review.

JUDGING: By committee of craftspersons and others. Based on quality of work, technical ability, design content.

DEADLINES: Equipment, Workshop Maintenance, Workshop Assistant, Advanced Training grants: Entry, January, April, July, October. Sabbatical Project: Entry, January (biennial, even years). Special project: Entry, April, July, December.

GRANTS (Regional-State)

Grants, Fellowships, Apprenticeships limited to specific Region or State. Primarily for CRAFTS RESEARCH, PRODUCTION, DEVELOPMENT and AID. Includes CALIFORNIA, CONNECTICUT, FLORIDA, MASSACHUSETTS, MICHIGAN, MINNESOTA, NEVADA, NORTH CAROLINA, OHIO, RHODE ISLAND, SOUTHWEST AMERICAN INDIANS, and ONTARIO. (Also see RESIDENCE GRANTS, SCHOLARSHIPS, FELLOWSHIPS.)

132

Artists Foundation Fellowship Program
Dale Stewart, Manager

100 Boylston Street
Boston, Massachusetts 02116 U.S.A.
Tel: (617) 482-8100

Entry October

State; **entry open to Massachusetts independents, professionals;** annual; established 1975. Purpose: to recognize outstanding creative artists and craftspersons in Massachusetts; support future work of high merit. Sponsored and supported by Massachusetts Council on the Arts and Humanities. Average statistics (all sections): 4000 entries, 3500 entrants, 160 finalists, 75 awards. Have workshops.

CRAFTS FELLOWSHIP GRANT: All Media. $3500 grants to Massachusetts residents over age 18. Submit 10 prints or slides of work. Competition includes other crafts. Also have dance, film, music, photography, video sections.

JUDGING: By practicing, anonymous, out-of-state artists. Not responsible for loss or damage.

DEADLINES: Application, October.

| 133 |

Connecticut Commission on the Arts Project Grants
Financial Support Staff
340 Capitol Avenue
Hartford, Connecticut 06106 U.S.A.
Tel: (203) 566-7076

Entry June

State; **entry open to Connecticut residents of 2-years' standing;** annual in December; established 1970. Purpose: to promote artistic excellence, career development. Average statistics (all sections): 150 entrants, 25 awards. Held in Connecticut. Also sponsor technical funding support programs, Artists-in-Education, tour-

ing programs, grants for organizations.

CRAFTS GRANT: Special Project. $50,000 to be divided among approximately 25 entrants (joint entries accepted) for creation of new works, experimentation. Require Connecticut residence, public presentation of project. No avocational artists, full-time students, artists involved in academic research, grant recipients within past 3 years. Competition includes all visual art, crafts.

JUDGING: By panel. Based on artistic excellence, professional record, importance of project to career development, confirmation of public presentation.

DEADLINES: Entry, June. Grant, December.

| 134 |

Florida Division of Cultural Affairs Grant Program
Phil Werndli
Department of State
The Capitol
Tallahassee, Florida 32301 U.S.A.
Tel: (904) 487-2980

Entry dates continuous

State; **entry open to Florida;** continuous throughout year; established 1970. Purpose: to recognize, reward, encourage outstanding individuals in Florida. Sponsored by Florida Division of Cultural Affairs, NEA. Have artist resource files. Also sponsor grants to organizations, special programs.

CRAFTS   FELLOWSHIP GRANTS: Artistic Development, Special Project in Folk, Visual Arts. Limited number of $2500 grants to emerging craftspersons, $5000 to established craftspersons, for expenses directly related to production or presentation of work. Submit 7 35mm slides of work, 3 letters of recommendation, specific support materials (catalogs, press clippings, samples). Require Florida residency for duration of grant. Competition includes visual arts. Also have literature, film, radio, video, music, arts.

ELIGIBILITY: Open to Florida residents age 18 years and older. No degree-seeking students, persons in receipt of Division fellowships within past 5 years.

JUDGING: By review panel. Based on quality, creativity, artistic skill, professional achievements, peer evaluation.

DEADLINES: Continuous.

135

Inter-Arts of Marin Public Art Competitions
Kerry Vander Meer, Director
1000 Sir Francis Drake Blvd.
San Anselmo, California 94960
U.S.A. Tel: (415) 457-9744

Entry November

Regional; **entry open to Marin County, California;** annual; established 1979. Purpose: to increase interaction between artists and community, create public artworks. Sponsored and supported by San Francisco Foundation, Inter-Arts of Marin. Average statistics: 800 entries, 43 entrants, 3 awards. Held in Sausalito, California.

CRAFTS GRANT: **Commissioned for Public Places,** varying project, media. 1 grant (including all expenses) to Marin County craftsperson to design and execute project for public place. 2 $250 cash awards to 2 finalists. Submit maximum 20 slides of work completed within previous 3 years, resume for entry review. 3 finalists submit detailed models of proposal. Competition includes visual arts.

JUDGING: By 5 members elected by sponsoring agency and 2 advisors from Inter-Arts Board of Directors. Based on originality, permanence of materials, aesthetics, resistance to vandalism, low maintenance cost, site appropriateness, project budget (not to exceed $12,000).

DEADLINES: Application, November. Notification, January.

136

Massachusetts Artists Fellowship Program
The Artists Foundation
Susan R. Channing, Director
110 Broad Street
Boston, Massachusetts 02110 U.S.A.
Tel: (617) 482-8100

Entry February

State; **entry open to Massachusetts residents age 18 and over;** annual; established 1975. Purpose: to recognize and support outstanding creative artists; maintain Massachusetts as vital workplace for artists. Sponsored by Artists Foundation Inc. Supported by Massachusetts Council on the Arts. Average statistics (all sections): 4000 entries, 120 finalists. Also sponsor Artist-in-Residence Program, Artists Services Program (including workshops, Artweek Boston), research and development programs.

CLAY, GLASS, PLASTICS FELLOWSHIP GRANTS: **Unrestricted Use.** Several $5000 fellowships to Massachusetts residents. Submit maximum 10 35mm color slides (may include 1 view of 10 works or 2 more of fewer works) of work completed in previous 5 years in 9x12-inch clear acetate slide sheet. No project proposals required. Competition includes metal, fiber, leather, wood. Also have writing, film, video, music composition, choreography, visual arts, sculpture, photography sections.

ELIGIBILITY: Open to Massachusetts residents (6 months minimum) aged 18 and over; not enrolled in any undergraduate or graduate program. Only 1 fellowship may be held in any 5-year period.

JUDGING: By 3 professional out-of-state artists. Based on artistic excellence. Not responsible for loss or damage.

DEADLINES: Application, February.

137

Michigan Council of the Arts Grants and Apprenticeships
Office of Arts Services
1200 Sixth Avenue
Detroit, Michigan 48226 U.S.A.
Tel: (313) 256-3732

Entry Spring

State; **entry open to Michigan;** annual in Spring; established 1966. Purpose: to support, expand, encourage arts in Michigan. Sponsored by Michigan Council of the Arts. Supported by State of Michigan, NEA. Publish *Artist Update* (monthly). Also sponsor workshops; grants for organizations, folk ethnic programs (including mini-grants, consulting service, developmental arts grants, staffing grants, artists-in-schools, arts organization support, arts outreach), minority pilot programs (including touring, marketing, economic development, facilities and rentals, cultural preservation, planning).

CRAFTS GRANTS: Special Project, Advanced Training. Unspecified number of $4000 (maxi-

mum) grants awarded annually to professional Michigan craftspersons to complete works in progress, secure additional technical or professional experience, begin new works, develop individual careers.

Assistance: Unspecified number of $1000 (maximum) grants to Michigan craftspersons for technical, legal, other professional assistance.

CRAFTS APPRENTICESHIPS: Professional Training. Unspecified number of annual $3000 (maximum) grants to developing Michigan artists for study under established working craftspersons.

JUDGING: By Council members.

DEADLINES: Special Project Grants, Apprenticeships: Entry, awards, Spring. Assistance Grants: Entry, 6 weeks prior to program start.

138

Minnesota State Arts Board Individual Artists Program
John Maliga, Program Manager
432 Summit Avenue
Saint Paul, Minnesota 55102 U.S.A.
Tel: (612) 297-2603

Entry January

State; **entry open to Minnesota residents;** annual; established 1972. Purpose: to stimulate individual accomplishment, provide unique support for creative individuals, help defray costs of independent arts activities. Supported by State of Minnesota, NEA. Average statistics: 500 entries, 50 finalists. Also sponsor grants to organizations in Minnesota.

CRAFTS GRANTS: Special Project. $500-$5500 grants to Minnesota residents with limited experience to finance 2-year (maximum) original project (involving specific activity resulting in clearly defined work; workin-progress; advanced study (excluding degree programs). Submit list of number and types of materials used, description of work (written, videotaped, filmed or maximum 15 35mm slides) for entry review. Require credit line for grant support; final report within 60 days of end of project; financial records and other pertinent documents to be retained for 3 years from submission of final project report. Competition includes photography, film and video, 2D, literary arts. Also have performing arts.

JUDGING: By Preliminary Review Committee, Full Review Committee, Arts Board. Entry review based on eligibility, completeness. Awards judging based on quality of artistic activity, merit of proposed activity, explanation of amounts requested. Not responsible for loss or damage.

DEADLINES: Entry, January.

139

Nevada State Council on the Arts Grants and Assistance
Jaqueline Belmont, Executive Director
329 Flint Street
Reno, Nevada 89501 U.S.A.
Tel: (702) 784-6231

Entry dates vary

State; **entry open to Nevada;** continuous; established 1967. Purpose: to encourage excellence in the arts, make arts available to public, support programs of statewide significance. Sponsored by Nevada State Council on the Arts. Held in Nevada for 6 or 12 months. Have individualized technical assistance for project proposals. Also sponsor organizational support, arts services support; artists-in-residence program, information services. Second contact: Allied Arts Council, 420 South 7th Street, Las Vegas,

Nevada 89101; tel: (702) 385-7345.

CRAFTS GRANTS: Direct Assistance. Unspecified number of grants of $1000 maximum to individuals for specific 6-month projects related to Nevada. Require entrants provide 50% of total project cost.

Nevada Special Project. Unspecified number of annual grants ranging from $1001-$2500 to individuals for 12-month creative projects of exceptional merit related to Nevada. Projects lasting longer than 1 year are considered. Require entrants to provide 50% of total project costs, letters of invitation from sponsors.

ELIGIBILITY: Open to residents of Nevada (minimum 1 year).

JUDGING: Entry review by council members, professional advisors. Awards judging by full council.

DEADLINES: Direct Assistance: Entry, continuous. Awards within 45 days of application. Special Project: Entry, May. Awards, October-September.

140

North Carolina Arts Council Fellowships
Department of Cultural Resources
Jean W. McLaughlin, Coordinator
Raleigh, North Carolina 27611
U.S.A. Tel: (919) 733-2821

Entry May

Regional; **entry open to North Carolina Professionals;** biennial (even years); established 1964. Alternates with writing, composing choreography fellowships (odd years). Purpose: to encourage growth and evolution of arts in North Carolina. Sponsored by North Carolina Arts Council. Supported by North Carolina General Assembly and the NEA. Also sponsor artists-in-schools, folklife, documentation, management assistance and other grants, assistantships and scholarships available to organizations.

CRAFTS FELLOWSHIP GRANTS: Work Project, Supplies and Materials. 4 $5000 fellowships to professional craftspersons for specific career goals, supplies, materials. Require funds-report at end of grant period. Submit examples of work with application form. Competition includes fine arts, photography, film.

ELIGIBILITY: Open to professional craftspersons of 5 years' standing, resident of North Carolina for previous year.

DEADLINES: Application, May.

141

Ohio Arts Council Aid to Individual Artists
Denny Griffith, Coordinator
727 East Main Street
Columbus, Ohio 43206 U.S.A.
Tel: (614) 466-2613

Entry January

State; **entry open to Ohio;** annual in June; established 1978. Purpose: to provide direct, non-matching grants to craftspersons for creation of new work. Sponsored by Ohio Arts Council. Average statistics (all sections): 590 entries, 110 grants. Second contact: 50 West Broad Street, Columbus, Ohio 43215.

CRAFTS GRANTS: All Media. $500-$6000 to Ohio residents for planning, supplies, facilities-services, rental, research, presentation, reproduction, documentation, publication expenses for creating new work. Submit maximum 10 35mm slides of recent work; artists encouraged to submit 1-page description of direction,

focus, concepts to be employed; showcase works through exhibitions, publications. No students. Competition includes architecture-design, fine art, mixed media, creative writing, music, performing arts, photography, film, video.

JUDGING: Based on creative, technical excellence. Preference given to work advancing art.

DEADLINES: Application, January. Notification, June.

142

Rhode Island State Council on the Arts (RISCA) Grants
Daniel Lecht, Chair
312 Wickenden Street
Providence, Rhode Island 02903
U.S.A. Tel: (401) 277-3880

Entry April

State; **entry open to Rhode Island residents age 18 and over;** annual. Sponsored by RISCA (nonprofit organization). Have job listings, arts-related publication directory. Also sponsor Arts Management Certificate Programs, workshops, contests, Folk-Arts Programs, Artist-In-Education Program, Implementation Grants for small art organizations, Project Support Grants, Ticket Endowment.

CRAFTS-FOLK ART GRANTS: Individual Aid. Several $3000 (maximum) grants available to Rhode Island residents (excluding full-time students) for work in mixed media, crafts-folk arts. Competition includes visual arts, sculpture, literature, music, film, photography and choreography, video in alternate years.

ENTRY FEE: None.

DEADLINES: Entry, April.

| 143 |

SWAIA Indian Craftsmen Fellowships
Southwestern Association on Indian Affairs (SWAIA)
Moira McCardell, Executive Secretary
P. O. Box 1964
Santa Fe, New Mexico 87501 U.S.A.
Tel: (505) 983-5220

Entry April

Regional; **entry open to Southwest Professional American Indian Craftsmen;** annual in June; established 1980. Purpose: to provide a means for SWAIA to contribute to growth, development of American Indian Art. Sponsored and supported by SWAIA. Average statistics (all sections): 20 entrants, 3 awards. Also sponsor SWAIA Annual Indian Market and Competition.

CRAFTS GRANTS: Indian Career Advancement in All Crafts Media (including pottery). $500-$2500 (maximum $5000 in total annual grants) for 1 year or less to professional Indian craftsmen, U.S. citizens age 15-35, residents of New Mexico or Arizona, to support career advancement, purchase of materials. Submit maximum 10 35mm slides of recent work (include detailed views of surfaces) in 9x11-inch clear plastic sheet; current resume, biography; statement of purpose for entry review. Require submission of final report at end of support period including detailed 1-3-page statement indicating usefulness of grant, accomplishment; expenditures. Competition includes visual arts, writing.

JUDGING: By SWAIA Board members. Based on statement of interest, portfolio, slide review, financial need. Not responsible for loss or damage.

ENTRY FEE: None.

DEADLINES: Application, April. Awards, June.

| 144 |

Ontario Crafts Council Awards Program
346 Dundas Street West
Toronto, Ontario M5T 1G5 CANADA

Entry February

Provincial; **entry open to Ontario, Canada;** annual. Purpose: to widen craftspersons' horizons through study in their respective craft disciplines. Held in Toronto, Ontario. Also sponsor Provincial Exhibition, John Mather Award, Guild shop.

CRAFTS FELLOWSHIPS: Advanced Study. Several grants of maximum $3000 awarded to craftspersons, students for advanced study in the crafts fields. Grants greater than $1000 are awarded in 2 installments; the second after 2 months of completed study. Submit 2 letters of recommendation from recognized visual artists; copies of diplomas from educational institutions; maximum 20 slides of 15 examples of recent work in plastic display unit; statement of intent, detailed expenses. Competition includes all crafts.

CRAFTS GRANT: Exhibition Assistance. Maximum $1000 per year awarded several times annually to craftspersons to assist with costs pertaining to upcoming exhibition (including transportation, crating, materials). Submit 10 slides of current work, biography, letter confirming exhibition, details of additional funding sources.

ELIGIBILITY: Open to craftspersons residing in Ontario for 2 of previous 5 years. Grant: includes full-, part-time students in final year. Material Assistance: applicants must have completed training and 1 year as practicing craftsperson.

DEADLINES: Entry, February.

MINIATURE, SMALL WORKS

Miniature Crafts usually defined as being 10x10 inches maximum including frame (10x10x10 inches for sculpture), or with maximum framed perimeter of 44 inches, and 1/6 or less life size. Small Works are usually larger than Miniatures, ranging in size from 12x12 to 15x15 inches maximum including frame (12x12x12 to 15x15x15 inches for sculpture). However, these sizes may vary. Includes CERAMICS, ENAMEL, GLASS, SCULPTURE.

145

Country Art Festival
Mrs. Peter Milano, General Chair
2626 Yellow Creek Road
Akron, Ohio 44313 U.S.A. Tel: (216) 867-3830

Entry September

International; **entry open to non-students;** annual in September; established 1981. Formerly called BATH COUNTRY ART FESTIVAL. Purpose: to provide opportunity to increase knowledge, appreciate arts and crafts. Sponsored by Eastview School. Supported by private donations. Recognized by Akron Society of Artists. Average statistics (all sections): 5000 entries, 300 entrants, 21 awards, 3000 attendance, $32,000 total sales. Held at Eastview School in Bath for 4 days. Have jewelry, portfolio galleries; re-freshments. Tickets: $1-$1.50. Also sponsor local scholarships. Second contact: Diane Housely, Advisory Board, Country Art Festival, Eastview School, corner of North Revere and Spring Valley Roads, Bath, Ohio 44210.

ENAMELS CONTEST: **Miniature,** original, 10x10 inches maximum including frame; limit 10 miniatures plus 1 large piece (no size restrictions) per entrant. No student work, large works without miniature entries. Competition includes visual arts, scrimshaw, photography.

CERAMICS, GLASS, SCULPTURE EXHIBITIONS: All Forms, original, for sale, miniatures 10x10 inches maximum including frame; limit 10 miniatures plus 1 large piece (no size restrictions) per entrant. No student work, large works without miniature entries. Also have visual arts, photography, other crafts sections.

AWARDS: $1000 in Cash Awards. Merit Ribbons. Purchase Prizes. Only visual arts, photography, enamel, scrimshaw miniatures eligible for awards; subject to change to include all crafts media.

JUDGING: Entry review by 4 judges. Awards judging by 1 juror. Based on quality of execution, good taste. Sponsor may withhold awards; insures work during return. Not responsible for loss or damage.

SALES TERMS: Sales compulsory. 25% commission charge.

ENTRY FEE: $7 for juried miniature show. $2 for nonjuried entries.

DEADLINES: Entry, event, September.

146

Laramie Art Guild American National Miniature Show

Olive Cupal, Chair
Overland Trail Gallery
603-1/2 Ivinson Avenue
Laramie, Wyoming 82070 U.S.A.
Tel: (307) 742-5388

Entry September

International; entry open to all; annual in October; established 1975. Purpose: to recognize miniature art, artists, public interest in small-sized art. Sponsored and supported by Laramie Arts Guild, Wyoming Council for the Arts. Held in Laramie for 1 month. Average statistics (all sections): 300 entries, 125 entrants, 25 awards, 1000 attendance, $60 sales per entrant. Have workshops, field trips, demonstrations.

CRAFTS CONTEST: **Miniature, All Media,** original, 2D maximum 44x44 inches including framing, ready for hanging, 2 inches deep; 3D maximum 10x10x10 inches including base; limit 5 per entrant (all sections). No copies, photography. Competition includes arts, other crafts sections.

SCULPTURE CONTEST: **Miniature, All Media,** original, 10x10x10 inches maximum including pedestal; limit 5 per entrant (all sections). No copies.

AWARDS (all sections): $150 to best of show. $100 First, $50 Second Place Awards. Special Awards. Honorable Mentions. Ribbons.

JUDGING: By 3 recognized artists. Sponsors may photograph entries for news media, publicity. Not responsible for loss or damage.

SALES TERMS: Sales compulsory. 35% commission charge.

ENTRY FEE: $4 per work plus return postage.

DEADLINES: Entry, judging, September. Event, October. Materials returned, November.

147

Montana Miniature Art Society International Show

Elsie Jackson, Secretary-Treasurer
223 Fair Park Drive
Billings, Montana 59102 U.S.A.
Tel: (406) 656-8073

Entry March

International; **entry open to artists of legal age;** annual in May; established 1979. Purpose: to promote growth of miniature painting movement. Supported by Montana Miniature Society members. Recognized by Miniature Art Societies of Florida, New Jersey, Washington, D.C., Wyoming, New Mexico. Average statistics (all sections): 1000 entries, 4 countries. Held at Castle Gallery in Billings for 1 month. Second contact: Joan Christensen, 3123 Marguerite, Billings, Montana 59102; tel: (406) 656-8396.

ENAMELS CONTEST: **Miniature,** original, subject 1/6 or less of life size, 2D 10x10 inches maximum including frame; 3D 10x10x10 inches maximum including pedestal; ready for hanging; limit 3 per entrant (all sections). No jewelry, plastic shrinkwrap. Competition includes tapestry, scrimshaw, visual arts.

AWARDS: (Includes all sections): Best of Show. Collector's Choice Purchase Awards. Honorable Mention Ribbons. First, Second, Third Place Cash Awards. Ribbons. Special Awards.

JUDGING: Entry review by 4 judges. Awards judging by 1 judge. Sponsor insures up to $200 at exhibition. Not responsible for loss or damage.

SALES TERMS: Sales compulsory. 30% commission charge.

ENTRY FEE: $15 ($20 foreign). Sponsor pays return postage.

DEADLINES: Entry, March. Event, May. Materials returned, June.

| 148 |

New York University Small Works Competition
Robert J. Coad, Assistant Director
80 Washington Square East Galleries
New York, New York 10003 U.S.A.
Tel: (212) 598-3369

Entry December

International; entry open to all; annual in January-February; established 1977. Purpose: to provide exposure to artists. Sponsored by and held at New York University in New York City for 4 weeks. Average statistics (all sections): 4000 entries, 2200 entrants, 1 award, $4000 total sales.

CRAFTS CONTEST: Small Works in All Media, 12 inches maximum any dimension including matting, frame, base, ready for display; limit 3 per entrant. No works under glass; valued over $2000. Competition includes all 2D, 3D media.

AWARDS: $350 to best of show. $50 Juror's Awards. Honorable Mention.

JUDGING: By 1 prominent museum curator. Not responsible for loss or damage.

SALES TERMS: 20% commission charge.

ENTRY FEE: $5 per work plus return shipping.

DEADLINES: Entry, December. Event, January-February.

| 149 |

Purdue University Miniature Ceramic Exhibition (National Cone Box Show)
Purdue University Galleries
Mona Berg, Director
Department of Creative Arts
West Lafayette, Indiana 47906
U.S.A. Tel: (317) 494-3061

Entry September

National; entry open to U.S. artists; biennial (odd years) in November-December; established 1975. Sponsored by Purdue University Galleries. Supported by Edward Orton, Jr., Ceramic Foundation, Indiana Arts Commission. Average statistics: 650 entries, 300 entrants, 15 awards, 3000 attendance. Also sponsor Purdue University Small Print Exhibition.

CERAMICS CONTEST: Miniature, must fit into 2-7/8x2-7/8x6-inch Orton pyrometric cone box; limit 3 per entrant. Completed in previous 2 years.

AWARDS: 10-20 $100 Purchase Prizes.

JUDGING: By 2 artists-academics. Sponsor insures works at gallery and during return shipping; may photograph entries for publicity. Winning entries remain in sponsor's permanent collection.

SALES TERMS: Sales optional. No commission charge.

ENTRY FEE: $5.

DEADLINES: Entry, September. Judging, notification, October. Event, November-December.

150

Valencia Community College Annual Small Works Exhibition
Judith Page, Curator
P. O. Box 3028
Orlando, Florida 32802 U.S.A.
Tel: (305) 299-5000, ext. 72-298

Entry March

State; **entry open to Florida residents;** annual in April-May; established 1973. Purpose: to encourage, recognize local talented artists. Supported by and held at Valencia Community College in Orlando for 3 weeks. Average statistics: 250 entries, 150 entrants, 14 awards.

CRAFTS CONTEST: **Small Works,** 15 inches maximum any dimension including matting, framing, bases if appropriate; limit 2 per entrant. Submit actual works for entry review and awards judging.

AWARDS: $750 in Purchase Awards to works for sale only.

JUDGING: By 1 museum director or educator. Sponsor may photograph entries for publicity; insures work during exhibition.

ENTRY FEE: $5 plus return postage. No sales commission charge.

DEADLINES: Entry, judging, March. Event, April-May.

151

Zaner Gallery Small Works National Competition
John Haldoupis, Director
100 Alexander Street
Rochester, New York 14620 U.S.A.
Tel: (716) 232-7578

Entry August

National; **entry open to U.S. residents over age 18;** annual in November-December; established 1981. Average statistics: 3000 entries, 1800 entrants, 120 finalists, 13 award, 1000 attendance. Held at Zaner Gallery in Rochester for 1-2 months. Also sponsor National Watermedia Biennial, exhibitions.

SCULPTURE CONTEST: **Small Works,** original, 15 inches maximum any dimension (including base); prepared for exhibition; limit 2 per entrant. Completed in previous 2 years. Submit 2 35mm slides each work for entry review. Competition includes visual arts, all crafts.

MIXED MEDIA CONTEST: **Small Works,** original, 15 inches maximum any dimension including matting and framing, prepared for hanging; limit 2 per entrant. Produced in previous 2 years. Submit 1 35mm slide each work for entry review. Competition includes visual arts, all crafts.

AWARDS: (Includes all sections): $500 Zaner Corporation Purchase Award. 12 $50 Juror's Awards.

JUDGING: Entry review and awards judging by 1 art executive. Accepted slides remain in gallery for documentation. Sponsor may photograph entries for publicity, catalog. Not responsible for loss or damage.

SALES TERMS: Sales optional. 30% sales commission charge.

ENTRY FEE: $8 first, $10 second work plus return postage.

DEADLINES: Entry, August. Notification, September. Event, November-December. Materials returned, January.

POTTERY, SCULPTURE

*Pottery and Sculpture, including
INDIAN CRAFTS and MINIATURES.
Pottery usually defined as ceramic
containers. (Also see other
POTTERY, SCULPTURE
CATEGORIES.)*

152

Coca-Cola Bottling Company (CCBC) of Elizabethtown Art Show
Jan Schmidt, Chair
1201 North Dixie Highway
P. O. Box 647
Elizabethtown, Kentucky 42701
U.S.A. Tel: (502) 737-4000, ext. 222
Entry April

National; **entry open to U.S.;** annual in May; established 1972. Purpose: to encourage, promote crafts; educate, entertain. Sponsored and supported by CCBC of Elizabethtown (nonprofit organization). Average statistics (all sections): 600 entries, 500 entrants, 200 acceptances, 17 awards, 7000 attendance, $9000 in total sales. Held in Elizabethtown for 3 weeks. Have demonstrations, workshops, 3-week traveling exhibition, children's workshop, tours.

POTTERY CONTEST: All Types, original; limit 2 per Adult, 1 per Young People (all sections). Completed in previous 3 years. No kits, works assembled from purchased parts. Divisions: Adult, Young People (high school, junior high, elementary and under). Competition includes photography, visual arts, textiles, jewelry.

SCULPTURE CONTEST: All Types. Requirements, restrictions same as for Pottery.

AWARDS: (Includes all sections):

$3000 in Purchase Awards (prices set by artists). First, Second, Third Place Juror Awards. 25 Special Merit Awards (for traveling exhibition). First, Second, Third Place Public Vote Awards. Ribbons to purchase, special merit award winners. First, Second, Third Place Honorable Mention Ribbons to each division of young people.

JUDGING: By 1 renowned juror (Adult), special judge (Young People).

SALES TERMS: Sales optional. 20% commission charge.

ENTRY FEE: $7 per work ($3 young people) plus $4 handling fee. Entrants pay return postage.

DEADLINES: Entry, April. Judging, event, May.

153

Lodi Art Center Annual Show
Bill Chapman and Donna Korphage, Directors
14-1/2 West Pine Street
P. O. Box 45
Lodi, California 95241 U.S.A.
Tel: (209) 368-4925
Entry April

International; entry open to all; annual in May; established 1960. Purpose: to bring art to public; enable artists to exhibit, sell works, compete for awards. Sponsored by Lodi Art Center. Supported by local individuals, organizations. Average 600 entries (all sections). Held at Barengo Vineyards in Acampo, California for 4 days. Have free wine tasting. Also sponsor monthly artists demonstrations.

POTTERY CONTEST: All Types, minimum 8 inches any dimension (including attached base); maximum 75lbs. per section, 300lbs. total, 75lbs. optional display stand; unlimited entry. Require hand-delivery. No unassembled items. Also have painting, graphics sections.

SCULPTURE   CONTEST: All Types, original, minimum 15 inches any dimension (including attached base); maximum 75lbs. per section, 300lbs. total, 75lbs. optional display stand; unlimited entry. Require hand-delivery. No soft sculpture, unassembled items. Competition includes fine art.

MIXED MEDIA: All Types, original, 6x6 feet maximum, glassed, framed, ready for hanging; unlimited entry. Other requirements, restrictions same as for Sculpture. Competition includes fine art.

AWARDS: $100 Awards of Excellence (includes all sections). $75 First, $50 Second, $25 Third, 2 Honorable Mentions each to pottery, sculpture, mixed media. Special Purchase Awards totaling $5025.

JUDGING: By 3 judges. Sponsor reserves right to refuse works based on handling facilities. Not responsible for loss or damage.

SALES TERMS: 25% commission charge (includes special purchase awards).

ENTRY FEE: $3.50 per work.

DEADLINES: Entry, April. Judging, event, May.

| 154 |

SWAIA Annual Indian Market and Competition
Southwestern Association on Indian Affairs
Mora McCardell, Executive Secretary
P. O. Box 1964
Santa Fe, New Mexico 87501 U.S.A.
Tel: (505) 983-5220

Entry August

Regional; **entry open to Arizona, New Mexico Indians;** annual in August; established 1922 (Market), now includes competition. Sponsored and supported by Southwestern Association on Indian Affairs. Average statistics (all sections): 400 entrants, 500 entries, 490 awards, 70,000 attendance. Held in Santa Fe for 2 days. Have up to $300 in awards to entrants dressed in best traditional tribal apparel. Also sponsor Indian Artists, Craftsmen and Writers Fellowships.

POTTERY   CONTEST: Indian Crafted, Traditional, sole property of artist, handmade, native materials, native firing; limit 5 per entrant (3 per category). Completed in previous 2 years. Entrants provide and attend sales displays. Categories: Unslipped, Undecorated, Incised, Carved, Painted Designs on Burnished Black or Red Surface (Santa Clara, San Ildefonso style), Painted Designs on Matte or Semi-Matte surface (Hopi, Zia, Acoma style). Competition for some awards includes jewelry, textiles, student.
Nontraditional   Pottery: New Forms, Innovations, includes wheel-thrown, stoneware, kiln fired, nontraditional techniques. Other requirements, restrictions same as for Pottery (traditional).
Miniature: Traditional, Nontraditional, Figures, Sgraffito, 3 inches height or diameter. Other requirements, restrictions same as for Pottery (traditional).

SCULPTURE-CARVING   CONTEST: Indian Crafted, ceramic, stone, miniature, other. Miniature should be 3 inches maximum. Other requirements, restrictions same as for Pottery. Competition includes metal, wood, graphic arts, jewelry, textile, student.

AWARDS: $500 Best, 150 $60 First,

$40 Second, $20 Third Prizes to sculpture-carving (includes stone, metal, wood, other), pottery. $100 Awards to each category-section. *Includes all sections:* $1000 Best of Show Award. Up to $300 Special Awards to individuals. Ribbons.

JUDGING: By approximately 15 judges. Sponsor may withhold awards. Not responsible for loss or damage.

SALES TERMS: Sales compulsory. No commission charge.

ENTRY FEE: $65 for 8x6-foot exhibit booth (3 per booth).

DEADLINES: Entry, judging, event August.

| 155 |

Fletcher Brownbuilt Pottery Award
Mr. E. P. Fuller, Competition Organizer
Cain Road
Penrose
Auckland 6, N2, NEW ZEALAND
Tel: 09-595-019

Entry May

International; entry open to all; annual in June; established 1977. Purpose: to encourage excellence in ceramics in New Zealand. Sponsored by Fletcher Brownbuilt. Supported by Fletcher Brownbuilt, Auckland Studio Potters. Recognized by Fletcher Challenge. Average statistics: 200 entries, 200 entrants, 8 countries, 7 awards. Held at Auckland War Memorial Museum for 2 weeks. Second contact: Linda Carswell, Fletcher Brownbuilt, Private Bag, Auckland, New Zealand.

POTTERY CONTEST: All Forms, original; limit 1 per entrant. No work produced under supervision.

AWARDS: NZ $3000 to best in show. 6 Certificates of Merit.

JUDGING: By 1 internationally renowned judge. Based on excellence. Sponsor keeps winning entry; may photograph entries; insures all work.

SALES TERMS: Sales compulsory. 20% commission charge.

ENTRY FEE: None.

DEADLINES: Entry, May. Event, June.

RESIDENCE GRANTS, SCHOLARSHIPS, FELLOWSHIPS
Resident Grants, Scholarships, and Fellowships primarily for CRAFTS RESIDENCE STUDY, RESEARCH, TEACHING, and PRODUCTION. Includes CERAMICS, CLAY, GLASS, SCULPTURE. (Also see GRANTS, SCHOLARSHIPS, FELLOWSHIPS.)

| 156 |

American-Scandinavian Foundation(ASF) Awards for Study in Scandinavia
Exchange Division
127 East 73rd Street
New York, New York 10021 U.S.A.
Tel: (212) 879-9779

Entry October

National; **entry open to U.S. graduate students;** annual from summer to summer; established 1980. Purpose: to promote advance study in Scandinavian countries for outstanding men and women. Sponsored and supported by ASF, founded 1910 for advancement of U.S.-Scandinavian cultural relations. Publish *Scandinavian Review* (quarterly). Also sponsor George C. Marshall Fund for study in Denmark; Alice and Corrin Strong Fund for Creative-Performing Arts, Literature; PEN Translation Prizes; exchange, travel programs; educational services; language classes; exhibitions.

CRAFTS RESIDENCE FELLOW-SHIPS: Advanced Foreign Study, Research. Unspecified number of $500 (short-term) to $5500 (academic year) fellowships for advanced study in Scandinavia (Denmark, Finland, Iceland, Norway, Sweden). Submit focused study plan, evidence of its feasibility (including admission to Scandinavian institution, information on availability of research materials), approval of academic authorities, 3 reference letters, curriculum vitae, work samples (photos, slides, portfolios, research proposals), academic records from all post-secondary institutions attended, bibliography, other support materials. Not for dependent support, English-language or introductory studies. Applicants considered for Fulbright-Hays Travel Grants for academic year.

ELIGIBILITY: Open to U.S. first-year (or higher) graduate students (including those planning programs emphasizing participation in Scandinavian university courses and lectures as integral part of U.S. post-graduate degree) with appropriate language competence and evidence of confirmed affiliation with, or invitation by, Scandinavian institution.

JUDGING: By ASF. Criteria include significance, feasibility of study plan; qualifications; appropriateness of study in Scandinavia; financial need. Younger scholars preferred if equally qualified. Award amounts subject to ASF adjustment, alteration, withdrawal; may be withheld. Not responsible for loss or damage of support materials.

ENTRY FEE: $10 service fee.

DEADLINES: Application, October. Support materials, November. Notification, March for following summer-summer academic year.

| 157 |

Artists for Environment Foundation Artists-in-Residence Program
Kenneth N. Salins, Director
Box 44
Walpack Center, New Jersey 07881
U.S.A. Tel: (201) 948-3630

Entry November

National; **entry open to U.S. craftspersons;** biannual in Fall and Spring; established 1971. Purpose: to provide opportunity for professional artists, craftspersons to work unencumbered, within national park setting; promote natural environment as source of inspiration. Sponsored by Department of Interior National Park Service, Union of Independent Colleges of Art. Supported by NEA, New Jersey State Council on the Arts. Average statistics (all sections): 80 entrants, 2 grants. Held at Delaware Water Gap National Recreation Area at Walpack Center, for 3 months. Have art gallery. Also sponsor 1-semester college landscape painting program for students from prominent U.S. art colleges, 8-week summer art program in cooperation with Maryland Institute College of Art.

CRAFTS RESIDENCE GRANTS: Professional Work. 2 3-month grants of unspecified value, including house with paid utilities and studio space, to craftspersons for opportunity to work without financial concerns. Submit resume, statement of purpose, samples of recent work (6 35mm slides in 8x11-inch clear plastic sheet) for review. Competition includes visual arts, photography.

JUDGING: By review committee. Sponsor keeps slides of accepted applicants. Not responsible for loss or damage.

ENTRY FEE: None. Entrant pays return postage.

DEADLINES: Application, November. Acceptance, February. Residencies, Fall, Spring.

158

Arts at Menucha Summer Workshop Scholarships
The Creative Arts Community
Bernice McCormick, President
P. O. Box 4958
Portland, Oregon 97208 U.S.A.
Tel: (503) 281-6814

Entry July

International; **entry open to age 21 and over;** annual in August; established 1965. Purpose: to promote awareness of, sensitivity to, appreciation for fine arts as cultural arts. Sponsored by creative arts community. Supported by corporations and individuals. Recognized by Oregon Arts Commission. Average statistics (all sections): 65 entrants, 3 countries. Held at Menucha Retreat and Conference Center in Corbett, Oregon for 2 weeks. Have recreational and sports facilities. Also sponsor weekend workshops throughout the year. Second contact: Jackie West, 2200 N.E. Gile Terrace, Portland, Oregon 97212.

CERAMICS RESIDENCE SCHOLARSHIP: Summer Workshop. Several partial scholarships up to $250 to craftspersons for 1 or 2 weeks tuition, art supplies, board, domitory accommodation at Menucha Retreat and Conference Center on Corbett. Entrants may work in more than 1 area. Competition includes weaving, sculpture, photojournalism, visual and performing arts, poetry.

JUDGING: Not specified.

ENTRY FEE: $50 deposit ($500 tuition fee for 2 weeks, $270 for 1 week, additional fees for private or semi-private accommodations).

DEADLINES: Application, July. Event, August.

159

Bunting Fellowship Program
Mary Ingraham Bunting Institute of Radcliffe College
10 Garden Street
Cambridge, Massachusetts 02138
U.S.A. Tel: (617) 495-8212

Entry October

National; **entry open to U.S. women;** annual in July-June. Purpose: to provide women the opportunity to complete substantial projects in their fields, to advance their careers. Sponsored by and held at Mary Ingraham Bunting Institute of Radcliffe College. Supported by Harvard and other Northeastern Universities. Also sponsor science fellowships, nontenured faculty fellowships.

CRAFTS RESIDENCE FELLOWSHIP: Independent Study. Unspecified number of $14,500 fellowships to women for completion of special project advancing their careers and contributing to their fields. Require residence in Boston for duration of fellowship. Competition includes academics, writers, visual artists.

ELIGIBILITY: Open to U.S. women with doctorates of 2-years' standing, or equivalent professional experience (for nonacademics).

JUDGING: By committee of faculty members from colleges, universities in Northeast. Based on the difference completion of the project will make to applicant's life, contribution to her field.

DEADLINES: Entry, October. Notification, May. Fellowship, July-June.

160

Cummington Community of the Arts Artist-in-Residence Scholarships
David Thomson, Director
Potash Hill Road
Cummington, Massachusetts 01026
U.S.A. Tel: (413) 634-2172

Entry dates continuous

International; entry open to all; continuous; established 1923. Formerly called THE MUSIC BOX (1923-30), PLAYHOUSE IN THE HILLS (1930-53), CUMMINGTON SCHOOL OF THE ARTS (1953-68). Purpose: to stimulate artistic growth by providing living and studio space to artists recently committed to the arts or disadvantaged by race, sex, age, economic status. Sponsored and supported by Cummington Community of the Arts. Supported by NEA, Massachusetts Council on the Arts and Humanities. Average 75 artists (all sections). Held on 150-acre site in Cummington in the Berkshire Mountains. Have individual living accommodations, kitchen, dining hall, library, darkrooms, kiln, studios, workshops, galleries, concert shed. Publish *Cummington Journal.* Also sponsor children's summer program.

CRAFTS RESIDENCE SCHOLARSHIPS: Studio Work. Several partial tuition abatements (each month) for 1-7 months to craftspersons with financial difficulties. Require interview. Submit 10-12 slides of work, resume, work plan, complete financial statement (including past 2 year's income, tax forms, savings, holdings, projected income, expenses). Competition includes film, video, photography, visual and performing arts.

JUDGING: By professional artists appointed by Board of Trustees. Based on work, interview.

DEADLINES: Application, 2 months before desired residency (continuous).

161

Fulbright-Hays Grants
Institute of International Education (IIE)
Theresa Granza, Manager
809 United Nations Plaza
New York, New York 10017 U.S.A.
Tel: (212) 883-8265

Entry November

National; entry open to U.S.; annual in April-June; established 1946 by legislation authorizing use of foreign currencies accruing to U.S. abroad for educational exchanges. Named after Senator J. William Fulbright. Purpose: to increase mutual understanding between U.S. and other nations through foreign study. Sponsored by IIE (founded to promote peace, understanding through educational, cultural exchanges in all academic fields), U.S. International Communication Agency (USICA). Supported by annual appropriations from U.S. Congress, other governments. Average 3300 entrants (all sections). Also sponsor grants to visiting scholars, American scholars-professionals, predoctoral fellowships, teacher exchanges, Hubert H. Humphrey North-South Fellowship Program (study-internships), Faculty Research Abroad Program, Doctoral Dissertation Research Abroad Program, Group Projects Abroad, Fulbright Awards for University Teaching and Advanced Research Abroad. Second contact: USICA, 1776 Pennsylvania Avenue N.W., Washington, D.C. 20547.

CRAFTS RESIDENCE GRANTS: Foreign Study. Round-trip transportation, language and orientation course, tuition, books, health-accident insurance, single-person maintenance for 6-12 months, study in 1 foreign country (doctoral candidates may receive higher stipends). Competition includes all media.

ELIGIBILITY: Open to U.S. citizens with majority of high school, college education in the U.S.; B.A. or equivalent (or 4 years professional experience-study in proposed creative art field). Require host country language proficiency, certificate of good health, study plan, project proposal, reasons for choosing particular country, statement of what contribution foreign experience will make to professional development, work samples, possible interview.

JUDGING: Professional juries and binational commissions in field of expertise prepare nominations to Fulbright agencies abroad; U.S. Board of Foreign Scholarship.

DEADLINES: Application, November. Judging, November-December. Preliminary notification, January. Awards, April-June.

162

Fulbright Awards for University Teaching and Advanced Research Abroad
Council for International Exchange Scholars (CIES)
Suite 300
Eleven Dupont Circle

Washington, DC 20036 U.S.A.
Tel: (202) 833-4950

Entry June, July

National; **entry open to U.S.;** annual for academic year; established 1946 by legislation authorizing use of foreign currencies accruing to U.S. abroad for educational exchanges. Named after Senator J. William Fulbright. Purpose: to increase mutual understanding between U.S. and other nations through foreign study, teaching. Sponsored and administered by CIES and U.S. International Communication Agency (USICA). Supported by annual appropriations from U.S. Congress, other governments. Average statistics (all grants): 2500 entrants, 1000 semifinalists, 500 awards, 100 countries. Also sponsor Fulbright-Hays Grants, other grants for teacher-scholar exchanges, research abroad. Second contact: USICA, 1776 Pennsylvania Avenue N.W., Washington, D.C. 20547.

CRAFTS RESIDENCE GRANTS: University Teaching, Advanced Research. Stipend (in lieu of salary), round-trip transportation, other allowances for 1 academic year or less for university teaching and-or postdoctoral research abroad. Applicant must rank countries and opening of major interest from Fulbright list. Competition includes all media.

ELIGIBILITY: Open to U.S. citizens, scholars, creative artists, professionals, institutions. Require demonstrated training-expertise in appropriate subject, language (academic degrees, university teaching, publications, etc.); doctorate, if specified by host country (for teaching); doctorate or recognized professional standing by faculty rank, publications, exhibition record (for research); project presentation; other documentation.

JUDGING: 50 discipline-area committees and binational commissions assist CIES in preparing nominations to Fulbright agencies abroad and U.S. Board of Foreign Scholarship.

DEADLINES: Application, June (American Republics, Australia, New Zealand), July (Africa, Asia, Europe). Judging, September-December. Notification, January-April. Awards given 12-18 months following notification, usually September-October to June-July academic terms of host institution.

163

Glen Echo Park Creative Education Residency Program
Diane Kellogg
Glen Echo Park
Glen Echo, Maryland 20812 U.S.A.
Tel: (301) 992-6229

Entry November

International; **entry open to qualified professional groups, individuals;** annual in January; established 1971. Purpose: to support development of human growth and potential; provide high quality cultural programming in informal atmosphere; create resource center of of practical and liberal knowledge and skills for the public. Sponsored and supported by National Park Service. Average statistics (all sections); 4 sessions of 100 classes each year, 700 students each term. Held at Glen Echo Park. Have art gallery, antique carousel, dance and sculpture studios, tours. Also sponsor children's theater, weekend festivals, musical and dance events, courses and workshops offered in multi-use classrooms.

CRAFTS TEACHING RESIDENCY: All Media. 9 2-3-year teaching residencies (including salary, rent-free facilities, maintenance and administrative support) to qualified professional groups or individuals to operate cultural, environmental, and-or educational programs for individuals or special groups at Glen Echo Park. Programs may include services, products, studio demonstrations, workshops, lecture courses, displays; and should involve public participation. Salary paid directly from student tuition fees. Submit resume, background information, photographs of work, detailed proposal for each course or workshop. Require entrant participation in festivals and other programs offered at Glen Echo Park. Competition includes visual arts, consumer interest programs, photography, music, writing, theater, dance, adventure programs.

JUDGING: Based on extent to which use of facility will maximize public benefit; program compliments existing programs; professional qualifications. Sponsor retains $6 from each student's fees.

ENTRY FEE: None.

DEADLINES: Entry, November. Notification, December. Residency, January.

164

Haystack Mountain Residence Grants
Haystack Mountain School of Crafts
Howard M.Evans, Director
Deer Isle, Maine 04627 U.S.A.

Entry March

International; **entry open to age 18 and over;** annual for Summer. Purpose: to provide artists with sustained exhilaration, respect for individual uniqueness, regard for potential of personal capacity. Sponsored by and held at Haystack Mountain School of Crafts in Deer Isle. Average statistics: maximum 65 residents, 10 day students. Have courses, workshops in crafts, photography; undergraduate, graduate course credits available.

CRAFTS RESIDENCE GRANTS: Studio-Coursework in Clay, Glass (flat, stained). Free tuition ($100 per week) for up to 6 weeks, room and board to candidates qualifying as technical assistants. Require 1-year graduate specialization or equivalent. Competition includes blacksmithing, fiber crafts, metals, wood, fine arts, graphics, photography.

JUDGING: Partly based on need; consider geographical range, maintenance of men-women ratio and age differential.

ENTRY FEE: $15.

DEADLINES: Application, March. Residence, Summer.

| 165 |

Institute of American Indian Arts Residence Scholarships
Ramona M. Tse Pe, Admissions Director
Cerrillos Road
Santa Fe, New Mexico 87501 U.S.A.
Tel: (505) 988-6493

Entry March

National; **entry open to native American students;** annual. Purpose: to assist native Americans develop leadership, promote self-determination, increase employment opportunities in professional fields. Sponsored by Bureau of Indian Affairs. Held at Institute of American Indian Arts in Santa Fe. Have liberal arts program, placement services. Second contact: Mary E. Ross, Education Specialist, U.S. Department of the Interior, Bureau of Indian Affairs, Washington, D.C. 20245.

CRAFTS RESIDENCE SCHO-

LARSHIPS: Study of Ceramics, Glass Blowing, Sculpture. Limited number of renewable yearly scholarships (including on-campus room and board, tuition, limited classroom material, $60 miscellaneous expenses) to full-time, unmarried, native American students for study at Institute of American Indian Arts. Require student pay transportation costs, personal expenses, laboratory fees. Submit certificate of degree of Indian blood, letter of acceptance into accredited degree program, grades or transcripts from previous semester. Competition includes photography, film, visual and performing arts, other crafts.

ELIGIBILITY: Open to full-time, unmarried students with at least 1/4 degree blood quantum American Indian, Eskimo, Aleut, of tribes federally recognized and served by Bureau of Indian Community, enrolled or accepted for enrollment in accredited college or university leading to bachelor degree, demonstrating financial need.

JUDGING: By Bureau of Indian Affairs Area Agency.

DEADLINES: Application, March.

| 166 |

MacDowell Colony Residence Fellowships
Christopher Barnes, General Director
100 High Street
Petersborough, New Hampshire 03458 U.S.A. Tel: (603) 924-3886

Entry quarterly

International; **entry open to professionals;** quarterly; established 1907 by American composer Edward MacDowell. Purpose: to help professional artists pursue work under optimal conditions. Sponsored by and held at MacDowell Colony in Petersborough.

Supported by NEA, small endowment, private donors. Average statistics (all sections): 650 entrants, 5 countries, 175 residents. Have 30 isolated studios, 3 residence halls, pianos, graphics workshops, library, main hall, on 45 acres of fields, woods. Publish *MacDowell Colony Newsletter* (triannual). Also sponsor Edward MacDowell Medal (presented annually in August to major artist), MacDowell Corporate Award (annually to individual in corporate life who exemplifies patronage of the arts). Second contact: Charles Edwards, Director of Development, MacDowell Colony, 163 East 81st Street, New York, New York 10028.

CRAFTS RESIDENCE GRANTS: Professional Work. 5-8-week grants to professional artists for working, living accommodation and solitude (no instruction). Submit 5 color slides of work completed in previous 3 years (sculptures may include 1 8x10-inch monochrome photo of any work represented on slides), resume of art schools attended, 3 references. Competition includes film, writing, photography, arts.

JUDGING: By professional artists. Based on talent and references; number of accepted applicants; financial need for room, board, private studio (1 residence per year).

ENTRY FEE: $5 (filing fee). Accepted residents asked to make contributions if able.

DEADLINES: Entry, January (for June-August), April (September-November), July (December-February), October (March-May).

| 167 |

Montalvo Artist-in-Residence Program
Montalvo Center for the Arts
Harriet Leman, Publicity Director
P. O. Box 158
Saratoga, California 95070 U.S.A.
Tel: (408) 867-3586

Entry dates continuous

International; entry open to all; continuous for 1-3 months; established 1948. Named after Garcia Ordonez de Montalvo, 16th century Spanish novelist. Sponsored by Montalvo Association (private, nonprofit corporation). Supported by Montalvo Center for the Arts Air Committee, trust endowment investment income. Held at Montalvo, 19-room, Mediterranean-style villa on 175-acre estate of late James D. Phelan, U.S. senator and San Francisco mayor. 5 artists (all sections) accepted at any one time. Have exhibition gallery, lectures, classes, workshops, readings, seminars, competitions, field trips, art sales, visiting artists, arboretum, indoor-outdoor theaters for plays, pavilion for recitals, concerts, library. Also sponsor Montalvo Summer Music Festival.

CRAFTS RESIDENCE GRANTS: Creative Project. Limited funds available (up to $75 per month for single; $90 for married couple) for 1-3-month residency at Montalvo Villa, plus extension of 3 months (if needed and agreeable), including apartment, linens, laundry room, utilities except phone, (no equipment, food, materials), to artists unable to pay residency cost, to work on new projects or complete projects already started. Submit samples, resume, 1-page publicity summary, work proposal, 3 recommendations from professionals in field, personal photo. Provide own equipment, food, materials. No children, pets, overnight guests. Competition includes architecture, visual arts, music, photography, writing.

JUDGING: By board of Trustees.

ENTRY FEE: $30 (cleaning-breakage deposit).

DEADLINES: Application, 6 months prior to desired residency.

| 168 |

New York State Summer School of the Arts Visual Arts Scholarships
New York State Education Department
Charles J. Trupia, Executive Director
NYSSA, Room 679 EBA
Albany, New York 12234 U.S.A.
Tel: (518) 474-8773

Entry January

State; **entry open to New York high school students age 14-17;** annual in July-August; established 1976. Purpose: provide intensive training in professional atmosphere to talented high school students. Sponsored by Division of Humanities and Arts, New York State Education Department, Chautauqua Institution. Held at State University College at Fredonia, New York for 4 weeks. Have room, board, facilities, art supplies, lectures, screenings. Also sponsor scholarships in schools of film or media, visual arts, choral studies, dance, theater, orchestral studies.

CRAFTS RESIDENCE SCHOLARSHIPS: Summer Training in Ceramics, Sculpture. $75-$650 to New York high school students for summer school giving exposure to variety of crafts, art disciplines and techniques, and study under direction of nationally known artists. Submit portfolio containing 8-10 works. Competition includes fine, commercial arts, other crafts.

JUDGING: Based on ability, need.

DEADLINES: Application, January. Judging, February-March. Residence, July-August.

| 169 |

Oregon School of Arts and Crafts Residency Program
Sharon Marcus, Curriculum Director
8245 S.W. Barnes Road
Portland, Oregon 97225 U.S.A.
Tel: (503) 297-5544

Entry May

International; **entry open to postgraduates;** annual in September-July; established 1979. Purpose: to assist promising craftspersons develop professional careers. Supported by NEA. Average statistics (all sections): 200 entries, 5 awards. Held in Portland for 11 months. Have 6 studios period.

CLAY RESIDENCE GRANTS: Studio Work. 11-month residency including small monthly stipend, studio, access to equipment, classes, workshops, lectures, to postgraduate artisans for study at Oregon School of Arts and Crafts in Portland. Submit maximum 10 slides of work for entry review. Competition includes metal, wood, fabrics, book-arts, drawing and design.

JUDGING: By faculty review committee. Based on entire submission.

DEADLINES: Application, May. Event, September-July following year.

| 170 |

United States and Japan Exchange Fellowship Program
Japan-United States Friendship Commission
Francis B. Tenny, Executive Director
1875 Connecticut Avenue N.W., Suite 709

Washington, DC 20009 U.S.A.
Tel: (202) 673-5295

Entry March, September

National; **entry open to mid-career U.S. artists;** semiannual beginning in April, October; established 1977. Purpose: to aid education and culture at highest level; enhance reciprocal people-to-people understanding; support close friendship and mutuality of interests between U.S. and Japan. Sponsored by Japan-United States Friendship Commission; NEA (U.S.); Agency for Cultural Affairs (Japan). Also sponsor Book Translation Awards, American Performing Arts Tours in Japan, Japanese Cultural Performances in U.S. Second contact: Nippon Press Center Building, 201 Uchisaiwai-cho, 2 chome, Chiyoda-ku, Tokyo; tel: 508-2380.

CRAFTS RESIDENCE GRANTS: Work, Study in Japan. 5 fellowships of $1600 monthly stipends plus round-trip transportation, overseas travel fare for spouse and children to age 18, baggage allowance and additional expenses for language training, interpreter, etc. to creative and practicing craftspersons well established in field, for 6-9 consecutive months, to observe Japanese traditional and contemporary artistic developments. Require completed training, written report at conclusion of residency. No applicant working or residing in Japan at time of application; no historians, scholars, art critics, students, groups. Competition includes visual arts, dance, design, journalism, literature, music composition, photography, theater, writing.

JUDGING: Entry review by private citizen advisory panels of experts in respective fields. American selection committee chooses semifinalists. Final awards judging by Japanese awards committee. Priority to projects that involve crafts or craftspersons not well known in Japan, exchanges not viable on self-supporting basis, and arts characteristic of contemporary or historical national traditions.

DEADLINES: Application, March, September. Notification, April, October.

171

Crafts Council of Australia Fellowship
Crafts Council Centre
Richard Heathcote, Executive Assistant
100 George Street, The Rocks
Sydney, N.S.W. 2000, AUSTRALIA
Tel: (02) 241-1701

Entry September

International; **entry open to English speakers age 25 and over;** annual; established 1978. Purpose: to support craftspersons and related professionals having made significant impacts in their fields. Sponsored by the Crafts Council of Australia (founded 1971, funded by Australian federal government), other Australian art galleries, institutions. Average 40 applicants. Publish *Crafts Australia* (quarterly journal). Also sponsor Crafts Resources Productions (produces crafts films, slide kits, books, leaflets), National Crafts Trade Fair, Crafts Council of Australia Gallery, lectures, exhibitions, other educational activities.

CRAFTS RESIDENCE FELLOWSHIP: Research, Work in Australia. 1 A$16,500 per annum stipend, return airfare (for overseas fellows), domestic Australian airfare, additional assistance (materials, equipment, space, research assistant), for 6-12-month stay and consideration of 12-month extension to craftsperson who has made significant contribution to his-her field. Submit detailed work proposal, outline of necessary resources, educational qualifications, photo, slides, names of previous awards, scholarships, exhibitions, publications, other activities. Require written report at conclusion of fellowship. Competition includes writing, other related fields.

JUDGING: Not specified.

ENTRY FEE: None.

DEADLINES: Entry, September.

SCHOLARSHIPS, FELLOWSHIPS

Scholarships, Fellowships, and Grants primarily for CRAFTS STUDY and RESEARCH. Includes CERAMICS, CLAY, GLASS, POTTERY, SCULPTURE, ENAMELING, MOSAIC, and MUSEUM OPERATIONS, EARLY AMERICAN CRAFTS. (Also see RESIDENCE GRANTS.)

172

Historic Deerfield Summer Fellowship Program in Early American History and the Decorative Arts
J. Ritchie Garrison, Director of Education
Historic Deerfield, Inc.
Deerfield, Massachusetts 01342
U.S.A. Tel: (413) 774-5581

Entry date not specified

International; **entry open to college undergraduates;** annual in Summer; established 1956. Purpose: to encourage careers in museum profession, historic preservation, American studies,

American history and art. Sponsored by and held at Historic Deerfield, Inc. Also sponsor programs of local interest.

CRAFTS FELLOWSHIP: Study of Early American Decorative Arts. 10 full ($2000) and partial ($800) fellowships to students for tuition in early American History and Decorative Arts at Historic Deerfield.

JUDGING: By committee of Historic Deerfield staff and trustees.

DEADLINES: Entry, not specified. Fellowship, Summer.

173

Kearney State College Special Activities Grants Scholarships
Kearney State College Art Department
Jerry Austin, Committee Chair
Kearney, Nebraska 68847 U.S.A.
Tel: (308) 236-4221

Entry March

State; **entry open to Nebraska high school graduates;** annual for academic year. Purpose: to recruit outstanding high school artists. Sponsored by and held at Kearney State College. Average 50 entrants (all sections).

CRAFTS SCHOLARSHIPS: Freshman Year Study in Ceramics. 25 $200 tuition waivers to Nebraska students entering freshman year for art study at Kearney State College. Submit slides or photographs of representative selection of works in portfolio, 3 reference letters. Competition includes fiber, sculpture, arts, other crafts.

JUDGING: By 5 faculty artists. Based on craftsmanship, technique, concept, originality, artistic merit.

DEADLINES: Application, March. Scholarships for academic year.

174

Blossom-Kent Art Tuition Scholarships

Kent State University
School of Art
Kent, Ohio 44242 U.S.A. Tel: (216) 672-2192

Entry May

National; **entry open to students, craftspersons;** annual in June-July; established 1967. Purpose: to provide intensive education in the visual arts through working with nationally recognized visiting artists and resident faculty. Sponsored by Kent State University. Supported by Kent State University, NEA, Ohio Arts Council. Recognized by National Association of Schools of Art. Held at Kent State University for 1 year. Also sponsor music, theater events.

CERAMICS, GLASS SCHOLARSHIPS: Graduate, Undergraduate Study. 5-15 tuition wavers ($366 undergraduate, $403.50 graduate) to students, craftspersons for intensive training at Kent State University. Require award winners enroll for 6 semester-hours credit. Submit portfolio of 12 slides or photographs; brief description of art background, current projects, interest, direction. Competition includes painting, drawing, graphics, illustration, jewelry, metals.

SCULPTURE SCHOLARSHIPS: Graduate, Undergraduate Study. Requirements same as for Ceramics.

ELIGIBILITY: Open to graduates, undergraduates currently enrolled in art schools, departments; practicing craftspersons.

JUDGING: By resident faculty. Based on merit.

DEADLINES: Application, notification, May. Enrollment, June-July.

175

Memphis Academy of Arts Portfolio Awards

Carol A. DeForest, Admissions Director
Overton Park
Memphis, Tennessee 38112 U.S.A.
Tel: (901) 726-4085 ext. 6

Entry March

International; entry open to all; annual for academic year. Purpose: to give financial aid to students otherwise unable to attend school. Sponsored and supported by and held at Memphis Academy of Arts. Recognized by NASAD. Average statistics (all sections): 650 entries, 65 entrants, 2 countries. Also sponsor Work-Study Program.

CRAFTS SCHOLARSHIPS: Clay Study. 1 full tuition scholarship to best portfolio, 10-15 partial tuition scholarships from $200-$2000 to students demonstrating financial need to help defray cost of tuition, fees, supplies, living expenses at Memphis Academy of Arts. Submit actual portfolio or 10-20 35mm slides. Competition includes fiber, metalsmithing, visual arts.

JUDGING: By Academy financial aid office and computer assessment.

DEADLINES: Entry, March. Scholarships, academic year.

176

North Country Community College Craft Management Scholarships

Nina Holland, Director
20 Winona Avenue
Saranac Lake, New York 12953
U.S.A. Tel: (518) 891-2915

Entry date not specified

International; **entry open to students over age 17;** annual in September; established 1978. Purpose: to aid students wishing to design, produce, or sell quality crafts. Sponsored by and held at North Country Community College in Saranac Lake for 2 years. Also sponsor internships for advanced students.

CRAFTS SCHOLARSHIPS: Pottery Study. $750 scholarship to promising crafts management student to help defray cost of education at North Country Community College. Competition includes other crafts.

DEADLINES: Grant commencement, September.

177

Pauly D'Orlando Memorial Art Scholarship
Religious Art Guild
Barbara M. Hutchins
Unitarian Universalist Association
25 Beacon
Boston, Massachusetts 02108 U.S.A.
Tel: (617) 742-2100

Entry October

International; **entry open to students sponsored by, or members of, Unitarian Universalist Society;** annual for academic year; established 1981. Named after Pauly D'Orlando, enamelist. Purpose: to aid art students to further study in their major. Sponsored and administered by Religious Art Guild. Supported by First Unitarian Church of New Orleans. Recognized by Unitarian Universalist Association. Also sponsor Vincent Brown Silliman Music Award, Dorothy Rosenberg Poetry Award, "tribute award." Second contact: Rev. Edwin A. Lane, 3 Church Street, Cambridge, Massachusetts 02138.

CRAFTS SCHOLARSHIP: Enameling Study. One 1-year $725 scholarship to student for tuition fees, art supplies (nonrenewable). Paid directly to selected school of art. Submit short essay outlining background, needs, goals; statement of tuition fees; minimum 3 slides or photographs of original work; recommendation letter from Unitarian minister, officer or sponsor. Competition includes drawing, painting, printmaking.

ELIGIBILITY: Open to students sponsored by, or members (minimum 1 year) of Unitarian Universalist Society. Applicant not to be in receipt of other awards.

JUDGING: Based on entire package of submissions.

DEADLINES: Application, April to November. Notification, February.

178

Seideneck Scholarship
Monterey Peninsula Museum of Art
Thomas J. Logan, Director
559 Pacific Street
Monterey, California 93940 U.S.A.

Entry date continuous

Regional; **entry open to Monterey Peninsula students;** continuous throughout year; established 1974. Purpose: to enable art students to become familiar with museum operations and practical approach to art. Sponsored by and held at Monterey Peninsula Museum of Art for 1 semester.

CRAFTS SCHOLARSHIPS: Study of Museum Operations. Several 1 semester scholarships available to undergraduates majoring in crafts for study of craft applications and museum operations at Monterey Peninsula Museum of Art. Competition includes arts.

JUDGING: By museum director.

DEADLINES: Entry, event, continuous.

| 179 |

Thousand Islands Museum Craft School Scholarships
Patricia Brown, Director
314 John Street
Clayton, Ohio 13624 U.S.A.
Tel: (315) 686-4123

Entry dates not specified

International; entry open to all; annual in summer; established 1966. Purpose: to preserve, promote knowledge of arts and crafts. Sponsored by Thousand Islands Museum, Shipyard Museum in Clayton, Jefferson Community College. Supported by Thousand Islands Antique Show and Sale, membership. Recognized by New York Council on the Arts, Empire State Alliance, Handweavers Guild of America. Held in Clayton for 1-2 weeks. Have textile library, permanent collection, educational programs.

CRAFTS SCHOLARSHIP: Study of Pottery, Sculpture, Stained Glass, Enameling. Scholarships available for students to attend 1- and 2-week workshops at Thousand Islands Museum Craft School. Competition includes painting, graphics, photography, other crafts.

DEADLINES: Not specified.

| 180 |

Virginia Museum Fellowships
Virginia Museum of Fine Arts
Boulevard & Grove Avenue
Richmond, Virginia 23221 U.S.A.
Tel: (804) 257-0824

Entry March

State; **entry open to Virginia;** annual; established 1978. Purpose: to provide financial aid for education and experience in the arts. Sponsored by Virginia Museum of Fine Arts. Supported by Women's Council of the Virginia Museum, Virginia Commission for the Arts, NEA.

CRAFTS FELLOWSHIPS: Study in All Media.
Student Scholarships. Up to $2000 to students who attend or will attend recognized undergraduate art schools. Paid over 10-12 months. Submit work samples (1 original, 10 slides; if 3D, 1 additional detail slide per item), 3 professional recommendations, most recent academic transcript. Require monthly reports and work (assigned) aiding the museum. Competition includes architecture, art history, design, film, fine arts, photography, video.
Graduate Student Fellowships. Up to $4000 to students who attend or will attend graduate school at recognized colleges or universities. Requirements same as for Student Scholarships.

CRAFTS GRANTS: Professional Work in All Media.
Virginia Museum Professional Grants. Up to $2500 to professional artists to aid in work or assist in project benefiting Virginians. Paid over 10-12 months. Requirements same as for Fellowships.
Virginia Commission for the Arts Professional Grants. 4 $8000 stipends to professionals for work on project. Paid in lump sum. Requirements same as for Fellowships.

ELIGIBILITY: Born in, or resident of Virginia for 5 of last 10 years.

JUDGING: Entry review and awards judging by board members, artists. Finalists interviewed at museum. Based on artistic merit, financial need. Partial awards at judges' discretion. May be terminated at any time for lack of diligence, sincerity, failure to submit monthly reports. Not responsible for loss or damage.

DEADLINES: Application, March. Notification, May.

181

Austro-American Society Scholarship Program for Art Students
Federal Ministry for Science and Research
Postfach 104
Minoritenplatz 5
1014 Wien, AUSTRIA

Entry March

International; **entry open to students age 19-35;** annual in June. Purpose: to provide scholarships to pursue regular course of study at Australian Art Academy. Have foreign student advisory service. Also sponsor scholarships in arts, agriculture; scholarships for postgraduate training courses in medicine, commerce and industry; minority group scholarships.

CRAFTS SCHOLARSHIP: All Media Study. 50 9-month full scholarships (including tuition fees), renewable for 3 academic years to crafts students for study at Austrian Art Academy. Administered in monthly stipends of AS5000 (undergraduates), AS5500 (postgraduates). Require entrants have sufficient command of German language; take qualifying test. Competition includes fine and commercial arts.

ELIGIBILITY: Students age 19-35, having completed minimum 6 semesters at Austrian or foreign art academy or university.

JUDGING: Entry review by Scholarship Commissions at various acade-

mies. Awards judging by Federal Ministry of Science and Research.

DEADLINES: Entry,   March. Awards, June.

182

Northern Arts Craft Fellowship and Residency
Barbara Taylor, Crafts Officer
10 Osborne Terrace
Jesmond, Newcastle-upon-Tyne
ENGLAND Tel: (0632) 816334

Entry June

International; entry open to all; annual in September; established 1978. Supported by Sunderland and Newcastle-upon-Tyne Polytechnics. Held in Northern England for 2 years. Publish *Arts Newsletter* (monthly), *Craft Quarterly.*

CRAFTS FELLOWSHIP: Advanced Study. $6000 per year to outstanding craftsperson for further study of crafts in Northern Arts region. Submit slides. Require residency in Northern Arts region for duration of fellowship.

CRAFTS RESIDENCY: Advanced Study. $4000 per year (including living accommodation). Requirements, restrictions same as for Fellowship.

JUDGING: By Northern Arts crafts advisory panel, host organization. Based on slides, interviews.

DEADLINES: Entry, June. Award commencement, September.

183

International Center for the Teaching of Mosaic (CISIM) Scholarships
Lawyer Giovanni Amadei, Chair
Azienda Autonoma Soggiorno e Turismo
Via San Vitale, 2

48100 Ravenna, ITALY Tel: (0544) 35755

Entry April

International; **entry open to non-Italian nonprofessionals, age 14-50;** annual in June-September; established 1966. Purpose: to encourage cultural exchange, spread knowledge of art and technical methods in mosaic making. Sponsored by CISIM. Supported by Tourist Office of Ravenna. Recognized by Academy of Fine Arts. Have field trips.

MOSAIC SCHOLARSHIP: Summer Study in Ravenna. Small number of 100,000 L grants (given at end of course) available to students to cover fees for 15-day summer course at CISIM. Submit curriculum vitae, other relevant information.

ELIGIBILTY: Open to nonprofessional, non-Italian mosaic artists without diplomas from mosaic institutes.

JUDGING: Preference to those supported by declarations from individuals, institutes that confirm interest in mosaic.

ENTRY FEE: 100,000 L (beginner section); 130,000 L (advanced section).

DEADLINES: Application, April. Courses, June-September.

SCULPTURE

Sculpture in all Clay and Glass media (including composition, plaster, stone). Includes HARNESS RACING and HUMOR. (Also see other SCULPTURE CATEGORIES.)

| 184 |

Harness Tracks of America Annual Art Competition and Auction
Stanley F. Bergstein, Executive Vice-President
35 Airport Road
Morristown, New Jersey 07960
U.S.A. Tel: (201) 285-9090

Entry August

International; entry open to all; annual in October; established 1976. Purpose: to encourage and create high quality, professional art reflecting the sport of harness racing. Sponsored and supported by Harness Tracks of America. Average statistics (all sections): 430 entries, 18 awards, 600 attendance, $39,000 total sales, $600 sales per entrant. Held in Lexington, Kentucky for a week during Grand Circuit Meeting at Red Mile. Publish *Horseman and Fair World, Harness Horse.* Second contact: Sara Short, United States Trotting Association, 750 Michigan Avenue, Columbus, Ohio 43215.

SCULPTURE CONTEST: Harness Racing Theme, Plaster, Composition; unlimited entry. Submit slides for entry review. Competition includes bronze and wood sculpture, other visual arts. Also have painting, print, graphics sections.

AWARDS: (Includes wood, bronze): $750 First, $375 Second, $225 Third, $150 Fourth Prize. 2 Special Excellence Awards.

JUDGING: Entry review by jury. Awards judging by guest juror. Based on quality, technical accuracy, potential saleability, promotional utility. Sponsor may photograph winning entries, exhibit first 5 winners for 1 year.

SALES TERMS: Works are auctioned. 30% commission charge.

ENTRY FEE: Not specified.

DEADLINES: Entry, August. Judging, event, October.

185

Ridge Art Association Annual Fine Arts Competition
210 Cypress Gardens Blvd.
Winter Haven, Florida 33880 U.S.A.
Tel: (813) 294-3551, ext. 279

Entry January

National; **entry open to U.S.;** annual in January-February; established 1961. Sponsored by and held at Ridge Art Association in Winter Haven for 2 weeks. Also sponsor gallery shows, annual outdoor sidewalk show. Second contact: Joyce Hetzer, 663 Avenue 1, N.W., Winter Haven, Florida 33880; tel: (813) 294-1412.

SCULPTURE   CONTEST: All Forms, original, hanging pieces 72 inches wide maximum; framed and ready for display; limit 3 per entrant. Completed in previous 2 years. No commercial work. Competition includes visual arts, photography, other crafts.

MIXED MEDIA CONTEST: All Forms. Requirements, restrictions same as for Sculpture.

AWARDS: (Includes all sections): $1000 to best of show. $500, $300 Second, $200 Third Place Awards. 3 $100 Merit Awards.

JUDGING: By 1 art professional. Sponsor may withhold awards; photograph entries for publicity. Not responsible for loss or damage.

SALES TERMS: 33-1/3% commission charge.

ENTRY FEE: $20.

DEADLINES: Entry, judging, January. Event, January-February.

186

Gabrovo International Biennial of Cartoon and Satirical Sculpture
House of Humor and Satire
Stefan Furtounov, Director
P. O. Box 104
5300 Gabrovo, BULGARIA Tel: (066) 2-72-28

Entry January

International; entry open to all; biennial (odd years) in May-September; established 1973. Purpose: to stimulate development of humor and satire in cartoon and sculpture, review achievements of past 2 years. Sponsored by House of Humor and Satire in Gabrovo, Bulgarian Artists and Journalists Unions, National Commission to UNESCO in Bulgaria, Editorial Boards of 4 newspapers. Supported and held at House of Humour and Satire in Gabrovo for 5 months. Average statistics (all sections): 2000 entries, 600 entrants, 50 countries. Publish *Apropos* magazine. Also sponsor Hitar Petar (Artful Peter) Prize for Humor and Satire in Literature, Painting; International Photo Jokes Competition.

SCULPTURE CONTEST: Humorous, Satirical; limit 2 per entrant. Made of durable materials. First-time entrants submit biographical data, self-cartoon portrait, photograph. Competition includes all crafts. Also have cartoon section.

AWARDS: (Includes all sections): Golden Aesop Sculpture, 1500 levs Grand Prize. Gabrovo Necklace (gold), 750 levs to best sculpture. 2 Gabrovo Necklaces (silver), 500 levs to second; 3 250 lev Prizes to third. 10 100 lev Prizes. Special Prizes. 40 entrants invited for 4-day stay at Gabrovo during festival.

JUDGING: By 15-person international jury. Sponsor covers exhibition expenses. All entries become part of permanent collections.

ENTRY FEE: None.

DEADLINES: Entry, January. Judging, May. Event, May-September.

187

Canadian Agricultural International Woodcarving Exhibition
Ross T. Farr, Agricultural Manager
Exhibition Place
Toronto, Ontario M6K 3C3 CANADA
Tel: (416) 593-7551

Entry July

International; entry open to all; annual in August-September; established 1977. Purpose: to promote interest in, appreciation of woodcarving; unite professionals and amateurs. Supported by Record Marples Inc., Canadian Carver, National Wood Carvers Association of America, Ontario Woodcarver's Association, manufacturers. Average statistics (all sections): 1800 entries, 300 entrants, 8 countries. Held at Canadian National Exhibition for 3 weeks. Have agricultural, educational exhibits, entertainment, security.

SCULPTURE CONTEST: Stonecarving, original, handcrafted, maximum 44lbs., in the round; unlimited entry. No carving duplicated by machinery. Divisions: Canadian (realistic, abstract), International.

AWARDS: C$100 plus Henry Taylor "Silver Plated Carving Tool" and $100 Gift Certificate, Canadian National Exhibition Gold Medal to best stonecarving. Stanley Tools Golden Hammer Award of Merit to second. $75 First, $50 Second, $25 Third Place Awards to each category.

JUDGING: By 1 stonecarving expert. Sponsor may withhold awards. Not responsible for loss or damage.

ENTRY FEE: None. Entrant pays return postage.

DEADLINES: Entry, July. Materials, August. Event, August-September.

SCULPTURE, GENERAL CRAFTS

Sculpture and General Crafts including CERAMICS, ENAMEL, GLASS, PORCELAIN, POTTERY. (Also see other SCULPTURE, CRAFTS CATEGORIES.)

188

Art on the Green Juried Show
Citizens Council for the Arts
Sue S. Flammia
P. O. Box 901
Coeur d'Arlene, Idaho 83814 U.S.A.
Tel: (208) 667-3561

Entry April

International; entry open to all; annual in August; established 1968. Purpose: to celebrate arts through displays, demonstrations, performances. Sponsored and supported by Citizens Council for the Arts. Held at North Idaho College, Coeur d'Arlene for 3 days. Have arts and crafts booths, Clothesline Sales, mini-booths for high-school students or younger, Children's Art Corner, demonstrations, entertainment, food booths.

SCULPTURE CONTEST: All Media, original, maximum 5 feet high, 150lbs., ready for display; limit 2 per entrant (all sections). Produced in previous 2 years. No copies, unfired ceramics, plaster. Competition includes visual arts, photography, other crafts sections.

CRAFTS CONTEST: All Media, original, 48 inches maximum outside dimensions, framed, ready for display (or hanging if appropriate); limit 2 per entrant (all sections). Produced in previous 2 years. No copies, commercial kits, unfired ceramics, plaster. Also have visual arts, photography, other crafts sections.

AWARDS: (Includes all sections): $250 North Idaho Presidents Purchase Award. $250 Community Purchase Award. $175 Ralph E. Hommberg Memorial Award. $200 Best Decorated Booth Award.

JUDGING: By 3-person jury. May withhold awards; not responsible for loss or damage.

SALES TERMS: Sales compulsory. Overpriced items rejected. 20% commission charge.

ENTRY FEE: $3 per work.

DEADLINES: Entry, April. Judging, event, August.

189

Broward Art Guild Anniversary Exhibition
3450 North Andrews Avenue
Fort Lauderdale, Florida 33309
U.S.A. Tel: (305) 546-0121

Entry April

Regional; **entry open to residents in tri-county area (Broward, Dale, Palm Beach) in Florida;** annual in May-June. Sponsored by Broward Art Guild, Landmark Bank. Held at Broward Art Gallery in Fort Lauderdale for 1 month. Have gallery, school. Also sponsor shows, exhibitions, festivals, educational programs and classes, symposiums, poster and photography contests.

SCULPTURE CONTEST: All Forms (including nonfunctional ceramics), original, 6 feet maximum any dimension; limit 2 per entrant (all sections). Produced in previous 2 years. Require hand-delivery. No overtly obscene work. Competition includes visual arts, photography, other crafts.

CRAFTS CONTEST: Constructions, Mixed Media. Requirements, restrictions same as for Sculpture.

AWARDS: (Includes all sections): $500 to best in show. 4-7 $100 Merit Awards.

JUDGING: By 1 academic. Not responsible for loss or damage.

SALES TERMS: Sales optional. 20% commission charge.

ENTRY FEE: $10 for 1 work, $15 for 2.

DEADLINES: Entry, April. Event, May-June.

190

Falkirk Annual Juried Art Exhibition
San Rafael Recreation Department
Consuela Underwood, Director
1408 Mission Avenue
San Rafael, California 94901 U.S.A.
Tel: (415) 456-1112

Entry February

County; **entry open to residents of Marin County, California;** annual in March-May; established 1974. Sponsored by San Rafael Recreation Department. Average statistics (all sections): 300 entries, 1000 attendance.

Held at Falkirk Community Cultural Center in San Rafael for 6 weeks.

SCULPTURE CONTEST: All Media, portable by 1 person; limit 2 per entrant. Completed in previous year. Competition includes visual arts, all crafts.

CRAFTS CONTEST: Assemblage, 42-inches wide maximum including frame, ready for hanging (if appropriate); limit 2 per entrant. Completed in previous year. Competition includes visual arts, all crafts.

AWARDS: (Includes all sections): $250 Purchase Award. $150 Best of Show Award. 2 $75 Merit Awards. Honorable Mentions.

JUDGING: Entry review and awards judging by 1 art expert. Sponsor insures works for duration of exhibition.

SALES TERMS: 30% commission charge.

ENTRY FEE: $3 per work.

DEADLINES: Entry, February. Acceptance, March. Event, March-May.

191

Great Lakes Regional Art Exhibition
Valley Art Center
Jay D. Moore, President
155 Bell Street
Chagrin Fall, Ohio 44022 U.S.A.
Tel: (216) 247-7507

Entry June

Regional; **entry open to U.S. residents of Great Lakes Area;** annual in September-October; established 1982. Purpose: to pay tribute to supporters of Valley Art Center, provide recognition to Cleveland as the "Sleeping Giant of the Visual Arts." Sponsored by Valley Art Center (founded 1935),

Higbee Company. Average statistics (all sections): 3000 entries, 1500 entrants, 25 awards, 40,000 attendance. Held at Higbee Company Department Store Auditorium in Cleveland, Ohio for 3 weeks.

SCULPTURE CONTEST: All Types, original, 30x36x80 inches maximum (wxdxh); limit 2 per entrant (all sections). Submit 2-3 35mm slides for entry review. No glass slides. Competition includes fiberwork, precious metals, graphics, pastels, photography, painting, water media.

CRAFTS CONTEST: Glass, Enamel, Porcelain, original, 2D 44x44 inches maximum including frame, appurtenances; 3D 30x36x80 inches (wxdxh). Other requirements, restrictions same as for Sculpture.

ELIGIBILITY: Open to residents of Minnesota, Wisconsin, Michigan, Illinois, Ohio, Pennsylvania, New York west of and including Syracuse.

AWARDS: $1000 First, $700 Second, $300 Third Prize, Honorable Mentions to sculpture, crafts, (includes precious metals, graphics, fiberwork, photography, pastel). *Including all sections:* $2000 to best of show. 3 $1500, 4 $1000 Purchase Awards. $1000 People's Choice Award.

JUDGING: Entry review by 1 juror per section. Awards judging by 5 jurors. Sponsors may photograph entries for publicity. Not responsible for loss or damage.

SALES TERMS: Sales optional. 15% commission charge.

ENTRY FEE: $10 per work plus return postage.

DEADLINES: Entry, June. Judging, event, September-October.

192

Meridian Museum of Art Bi-State Competition
Dan W. Griffin, Director
P. O. Box 5773
Meridian, Mississippi 39301 U.S.A.
Tel: (601) 693-1501

Entry December

Regional; **entry open to Mississippi, Alabama;** annual in February; established 1973. Purpose: to provide quality exhibition for local artists. Sponsored by Meridian Museum. Supported by local commerce and industry. Average statistics (all sections): 300 entries, 100 entrants, 9 awards, 1000 attendance, $2500 sales. Held at Meridian Museum of Art for 1 month. Second contact: 25th Avenue at 7th Street, Meridian, Mississippi 39301.

SCULPTURE CONTEST: All Media, original, maximum 5 feet any dimension, 175lbs.; limit 3 per entrant (all sections). May submit slides for entry review. Require hand-collection. Competition includes photography, visual arts, other crafts.

CRAFTS CONTEST: All Media, original, 2D works ready for hanging; limit 3 per entrant (all sections). May submit slides for entry review. Require hand-collection. Competition includes photography, visual arts, other crafts.

MIXED MEDIA CONTEST: All Media. Requirements, restrictions same as for Crafts.

AWARDS: $750 Museum Purchase Award. 3 $300 Purchase Awards. Merit Awards.

JUDGING: By 1 art professional. Sponsor may photograph entries for catalog, publicity; not responsible for loss or damage.

SALES TERMS: Sales compulsory. 20% commission charge.

ENTRY FEE: $10.

DEADLINES: Entry, December. Materials, January. Event, February.

193

Paula Insel Annual Art Exhibition
Galerie Paula Insel
987 Third Avenue
New York, New York 10022 U.S.A.
Tel: (212) 355-5740

Entry July

International; entry open to all; annual in September; established 1955. Sponsored by Galerie Paula Insel, United Mutal Banks. Average 100 entrants. Held at varying locations for 2 weeks. Also sponsor Paula Insel Puerto Rican Art Exhibition (March), 20 bank shows, "This Is My City" annual event.

SCULPTURE CONTEST: All Types; entry limit not specified.

CRAFTS CONTEST: Ceramics (may include other media); entry limit not specified. Competition includes all visual arts.

AWARDS: Merchandise Prizes. Ribbons.

JUDGING: By critics. Not responsible for loss or damage.

SALES TERMS: Sales compulsory. 40% commission charge.

ENTRY FEE: $8 per work plus return postage.

DEADLINES: Entry, July. Judging, event, September.

194

Paula Insel Puerto Rican Art Exhibition
Galerie Paula Insel
39 Los Meros
Box 7271
Playa Ponce, Puerto Rico 00731
U.S.A. Tel: (809) 844-8478

Entry January

International; entry open to all; annual in March; established 1975. Sponsored by Galerie Paula Insel. Average statistics (all sections): 40 entries, 10 entrants. Held at airports for 2 weeks. Also sponsor Paula Insel Art Exhibition (September), bank shows, "This Is My Life" annual event.

SCULPTURE CONTEST: All Types; entry limit not specified.

CRAFTS CONTEST: Ceramics (may include other media); entry limit not specified. Competition includes all visual arts.

AWARDS: Merchandise Prizes.

JUDGING: Not specified. Not responsible for loss or damage.

SALES TERMS: Sales compulsory. 40% commission charge.

ENTRY FEE: $8 per work plus return postage.

DEADLINES: Entry, January. Judging, event, March.

195

Portrait of the Forks of the Delaware Exhibition
Easton Community Art League
39 North 5th Street
Easton, Pennsylvania 18042 U.S.A.

Entry October

International; entry open to age 18 and over; annual in December. Sponsored by Community Art League of Easton. Supported by City of Easton, Pennsylvania Council on the Arts. Have music. Also sponsor Center Square Art Fair.

SCULPTURE CONTEST: All Media, original, maximum 24x24x36 inches, thematic; limit 2 per entrant. Completed in last 5 years. Require hand-delivery, entrants provide display stand. Submit explanation of craft for entry review. Competition includes textiles, jewelry, woodcrafts, fine and commercial arts, photography.

CRAFTS CONTEST: All Types (including pottery, stained glass), original, thematic, 36x36 inches maximum, ready for hanging if appropriate. Other requirements, restrictions same as for Sculpture.

AWARDS: Not specified.

JUDGING: By 3 artists. Not responsible for loss or damage.

ENTRY FEE: Not specified.

DEADLINES: Entry, October. Event, December.

196

Temple Emanu-El Brotherhood Art Festival
8500 Hillcrest Road
Dallas, Texas 75225 U.S.A.
Tel: (214) 368-3613

Entry January

National; entry open to U.S.; annual in April; established 1962. Festival has become creditable forum for introduction of new and maturing art talent. Sponsored and supported by Temple Emanu-El Brotherhood. Average statistics: 400 entries, 150 entrants, $32,000 total sales. Held at Emanu-El Temple in Dallas for 2 weeks.

SCULPTURE CONTEST: All Media, 36x48 inches maximum, ready for hanging if appropriate; unlimited entry. Submit slides only, biographical sketch for entry review and awards judging. Also have visual arts, photography sections.

CRAFTS CONTEST: All Media (including ceramics). No jewelry. Competition includes arts, other crafts. Other requirements, restrictions same as for Sculpture.

AWARDS: First, Second, Third Place Awards each to sculpture, crafts.

JUDGING: By 3 judges.

SALES TERMS: Sales compulsory. 40% commission charge.

ENTRY FEE: None.

DEADLINES: Entry, January. Judging, event, April.

STUDENT, AMATEUR, YOUTH

Student, Amateur, Children, Youth contests and exhibitions, including CERAMICS, CLAY, ENAMEL, GLASS, PLASTIC, POTTERY, SCULPTURE, STONE, and GENERAL CRAFTS. Amateur usually defined as made entirely for fun and pleasure, with no commercial purpose or profit in mind, by persons not engaged in crafts as their main source of income at the time of production; and which has not been sold, commissioned, sponsored, or subsidized. However, these definitions may vary. (Also see OTHER CATEGORIES.)

197

Anacortes Arts and Crafts Festival Nonprofessional Competition
Barbara Jackson, Director
414 Commercial Avenue
P. O. Box 6
Anacortes, Washington 98221 U.S.A.
Tel: (206) 293-6211

Entry July

Regional; **entry open to Anacortes-area amateurs;** annual in August; established 1961. Sponsored and supported by Anacortes Arts and Crafts Festival (nonprofit). Average statistics (all sections): 125 screened booths, 20,000 attendance. Have booth exhibits. Also sponsor Skagit Artist Invitational, Professional & Amateur Photography Competition. Second contact: Anacortes Chamber of Commerce, 14th and Commercial, Anacortes, Washington 98221; tel: (205) 293-2832.

CRAFTS-SCULPTURE CONTEST: All Media, ready for hanging if appropriate; limit 2 per entrant per medium. No classwork, copies, kits. Also have visual arts, photography.

ELIGIBILITY: Open to residents of Whatcom, Skagit, Snohomish, San Juan, Island counties.

AWARDS: $25 First, $15 Second, $5 Third Place Awards to sculpture, crafts.

JUDGING: By local artists. Not responsible for loss or damage.

SALES TERMS: Sales optional. 20% commission charge.

ENTRY FEE: $4 per medium plus return postage.

DEADLINES: Entry, July. Event, August.

198

Arkansas Industrial Arts Association Student Project Competition

Kenneth Jordan, Professor of Industrial Education
Box K-UCA
University of Central Arkansas
Conway, Arkansas 72032 U.S.A.
Tel: (501) 450-3144

Entry date not specified

State; **entry open to Arkansas secondary school students;** annual in May; established 1950. Sponsored and supported by Arkansas Industrial Arts Association. Average statistics (all sections): 200 entries, 20 awards. Held for 1 day.

PLASTICS CONTEST: Student Project; limit 1 per entrant. Completed in present school year in regular classroom periods (maximum 1 class hour daily). Divisions: State Level (Senior High Unit Shop, Senior High General Shop), District Level (Junior High), Local Level.

ELIGIBILITY: Active members of local Industrial Arts Student Association. Senior High Unit Shop: Grades 9-12, entries made in unit shop where more than 1 semester devoted to area of entry. Senior High General Shop: Grades 9-12, entries from general shop program, maximum 12 laboratory weeks (60 hours) in area of entry. Junior High Division: Grades 7-9.

AWARDS: First, Second, Third Place Awards to each category, division. Awards at local level at discretion of local association.

JUDGING: By 10 judges selected by executive committee.

ENTRY FEE: $1.

DEADLINES: Entry, not specified. Event, May.

199

Arts NW Student Juried Fine Art Show

Diane Berge, President
1500 Western Avenue
Seattle, Washington 98101 U.S.A.
Tel: (206) 682-4435

Entry October

International; **entry open to U.S., Canadian, Mexican art students;** annual in December; established 1981. Purpose: to encourage development of visual artists through exhibition and sale of work . Sponsored by Arts NW (founded 1978). Held in Seattle for 1 month.

CERAMICS CONTEST: 3-Dimensional; limit 3 per entrant (all sections), set counts as 1. Submit 4-5 35mm slides for awards judging. No work done under supervision. Competition includes visual arts, photography, fiber, metal design, collage.

SCULPTURE CONTEST: 3-Dimensional. Requirements, restrictions same as for Ceramics.

AWARDS: $500 in Cash Prizes (includes all sections).

JUDGING: By 3 professionals. Based on merit. Sponsor temporarily retains slides for publicity; insures work during exhibition.

SALES TERMS: Sales optional. 35% commission charge.

ENTRY FEE: $10.

DEADLINES: Entry, October. Judging, November. Event, December.

200

Interlochen National Youth Art Competition

Interlochen Center for the Arts

Interlochen, Michigan 49643 U.S.A.
Tel: (616) 276-9221

Entry February

National; **entry open to students in grades 7-12, resident in U.S.;** annual in May-August. Held at Interlochen Center for the Arts for 3 months.

CRAFTS CONTEST: All Media, 2D 44x44 inches maximum including framing under plexiglass, or matting, suitable for installation; 3D 60 inches maximum including base; limit 6 per entrant. Submit 35mm slides, photographs (3D minimum 2 from different angles) for entry review and awards judging. No glass. Divisions: Grades 7-9, 10-12.

AWARDS: $200 First, $100 Second, $50 Third Place Award to each division. Interlochen Arts Academy and National Musical Camp Scholarship Awards.

JUDGING: Sponsor may photograph entries for publicity; insures work during exhibition. Not responsible for loss or damage.

ENTRY FEE: $5.

DEADLINES: Entry, February. Judging, April. Event, May-August.

201

Marietta College Crafts National Exhibition
Arthur Howard Winer, Director
Marietta College Art Department
Marietta, Ohio 45750 U.S.A.
Tel: (614) 373-4643, ext. 275

Entry September

National; **entry open to U.S. amateur, students;** annual in November; established 1972. Formerly called MARIETTA COLLEGE CRAFTS REGIONAL EXHIBITION (1972-73). Purpose: to display and reward artists throughout U.S. Sponsored and supported by Marietta College. Average statistics (all sections): 2840 entries, 1100 entrants, $5500 in awards. Held at Marietta College for 1 month. Also sponsor Marietta National Painting and Sculpture Exhibition.

SCULPTURE CONTEST: All Media (including ceramics, glass, plastics, stone), original, ready for mounting on masonry or concrete; limit 3 per entrant (set counts as 1). Submit 1 35mm slide (4 for 3D) per entry. No molds, supervised class work. Competition includes visual arts, photography.

CRAFTS CONTEST: All Media (including ceramics, glass, enamel, plastics). Requirements, restrictions same as for Sculpture.

MIXED MEDIA CONTEST: All Types. Requirements, restrictions same as for Sculpture.

AWARDS: (Includes all sections): $2500 Judges' Awards. $1000 Judges' Awards of Craftsmanship. $1500 in Purchase Prizes. The Hand and the Spirit Crafts Gallery Award.

JUDGING: By 3 national judges. Based on merit. Purchase Prizes selected by Marietta College art department. Sponsor insures during exhibition only. Not responsible for in-transit loss or damage.

SALES TERMS: Sales optional. 25% commission charge (including purchase prizes).

ENTRY FEE: $15 plus return postage.

DEADLINES: Entry, judging, September. Notification, October. Event, November.

<hr>

202

Oxnard Multicultural Festival Youth Competition
Bedford Pinkard, Chair
1500 Colonia Road #16
Oxnard , California 93030 U.S.A.
Tel: (805) 486-4311, ext. 610 or 616

Entry April

Regional; **entry open to Oxnard-area high school students;** established 1977. Purpose: to recognize talents of young artists, offer them opportunity to display work. Sponsored by Union Oil Company of California, City of Oxnard Parks and Recreation Department. Held at Oxnard Community Center Complex for 2 days. Also sponsor arts and crafts exhibit. Second contact: Cheryl Collart, 800 Hobson Way, Oxnard, California 93030; tel: (805) 486-4311, ext. 614.

CERAMICS CONTEST: All Forms; limit 2 per category. No excessively fragile entries. Require hand-delivery. Divisions: One (grades 7-9), Two (grades 10-12). Also have visual arts sections.

AWARDS: $75 First, $50 Second, $25 Third Prize to each division.

JUDGING: By panel of judges from art community. Winning entries displayed at Carnegie Cultural Center for 1 month.

ENTRY FEE: None.

DEADLINES: Entry, event, April. Materials returned, May.

203

Rockport National Amateur Art Festival
Rockport Chamber of Commerce
Sumner G. Ropper, Executive Director
P. O. Box 67
Rockport, Massachusetts 01966
U.S.A. Tel: (617) 546-6575

Entry September

International; **entry open to U.S., Canadian amateurs;** annual in October; established 1939. Purpose: to promote art, especially amateur. Sponsored and supported by Rockport Chamber of Commerce. Average statistics (all sections): 140 entries, 8000 attendance. Held at Rockport Art Association for 4 days. Have demonstrations by professionals.

CERAMICS CONTEST: All Types, 34x40 inches maximum including frame; limit 1 per entrant. Competition includes painting, drawing, graphics.

SCULPTURE CONTEST: Clay. Requirements, restrictions same as for Ceramics.

AWARDS: Prizes and Certificates to best of show, first, second, third places (includes all sections). Prizes, Certificates, $25 Popular Vote Award. Honorable Mentions to ceramics, sculpture.

JUDGING: By professional artists. Not responsible for loss or damage.

ENTRY FEE: $3 plus $7.50 handling. No sales.

DEADLINES: Entry, September. Event, October.

204

Scholastic Art Awards
Scholastic, Inc.
50 West 44th Street
New York, New York 10036 U.S.A.
Tel: (212) 944-7700, ext. 606

Entry January

International; **entry open to U.S., Canadian students under age 20;** annual in January; established 1928. Purpose: to recognize and encourage student achievements in creative art. Sponsored and supported by Scholastic Inc., Armstrong World Industries, Strathmore Paper Company. Average 200,000 entries (all sections). Publish classroom magazines, instructional material.

POTTERY CONTEST: Kiln-Fired Clay Articles (such as bowls, vases, bottles, etc.), original, maximum 24 inches any dimension, 25lbs., glazed or unglazed. No copies. Divisions: Grades 7-9, 10-12. Competition for some awards, scholarships includes other media. Also have art, photography, other crafts.

SCULPTURE CONTEST: All Types, in round or relief, original, maximum 24 inches any dimension, 25lbs. (including base), modeled, carved, cast, or assembled. No fragile entries, assisted work. Competition includes fine arts, other crafts.

DESIGN CONTEST: 2- and 3-Dimensional (includes all media), utilitarian, non-utilitarian objects, maximum 24 inches any dimension, 10lbs.

CRAFT PORTFOLIO CONTEST: All Types, original, 24x31 inches maximum, hard-covered, contents mounted or matted on white; limit 8 samples or representations of work (3 to be drawings, 5 to be photos or slides of 3D work). No colored mats, frames, glass, copies from photographs, magazines, book illustrations. Competition includes fine art, other crafts.

ELIGIBILITY: Open to students in grades 7-12 (under age 20), enrolled in public or private schools; approved by school art department. Scholarship entrants to be in upper half of class graduating in January, June of award year; to meet entrance requirements of cooperating schools and colleges; to demonstrate financial need.

AWARDS: *Regional Honors:* Gold Achievement Keys, Certificates of Merit. $100 Armstrong Awards each to best craft (all sections), sculpture "Blue Ribbon" finalists chosen from winners of Golden Keys to compete nationally. *National Awards:* Gold Medal Plaques, Cash Awards. 100 Scholastic Art Award Scholarships to top seniors. 5 $4000 Strathmore Paper Scholarships to senior portfolios. 30 National Awards to sculpture, 20 to pottery.

JUDGING: By educators and artists recommended by Advisory Committee of Art Educators. Juried on regional and national levels. Based on quality, school record. Sponsor may photograph entries. Not responsible for loss or damage.

ENTRY FEE: None.

DEADLINES: Entry, January. Materials returned, September (portfolios, May).

205

Texas State Arts and Crafts Fair Young Artist Competition
Texas Arts and Crafts Foundation
Audie Hamilton, Executive Director
P. O. Box 1527
Kerrville, Texas 78028 U.S.A.
Tel: (512) 896-5711

Entry November

State; **entry open to Texas residents under age 21 (Arts and Crafts Fair open to all);** annual in May-June; established 1972. Fair established as project of Texas Tourist Development Agency. Purpose: to showcase talented young artists. Sponsored by Texas Arts and Crafts Foundation. Average statistics (all sections): 400 entrants, 245 finalists, 53 awards, 40,-

000 attendance. Held at Schreiner College campus in Kerrville for 2 weekends. Have State Fair events, food, lodging facilities. Tickets: $2-$4. Also sponsor workshops.

CRAFTS CONTEST: All Media (including pottery, sculpture), original; limit 2 media per entrant. Submit 3 35mm slides per medium for entry review; resume, legal proof of age, residency. No manufactured, mass-produced or molded items, work done under instruction. Competition includes fine arts, other crafts.

CRAFTS FAIR: All Media, original. Entrants provide and attend sales displays. Submit slides for entry review.

AWARDS: 1 $500 college scholarship for following academic year to best young artists. 3 (including 1 to scholarship winner) free booth spaces at State Fair (includes overnight accommodation, meals at Schreiner College). 50 Excellence Certificates in State Fair sections.

JUDGING: Entry review by 3 jurors. Sponsor retains slides. Not responsible for loss or damage.

ENTRY FEE: None. $135 for 8x10-foot exhibit booth at art fair.

DEADLINES: Entry, November. Notification, January. Event, May-June.

206
Very Special Arts Festival Program
National Committee-Arts for the Handicapped (NCAH)
Ralph Nappi, Associate Director
1825 Connecticut Avenue, Suite 417
Washington, DC 20009 U.S.A.
Tel: (202) 332-6960

Entry dates continuous

International; **entry open to children and youth;** continuous; established 1975. Purpose: to provide noncompetitive forum for disabled and nondisabled children and youth to share accomplishments in arts; integrate disabled students into mainstream cultural activity. Various sponsors. Supported by Bureau of Education for the Handicapped, Kennedy Foundation, Alliance for Arts Education, private sponsors. Recognized by American Federation of Teachers, U.S. Office of Education's Division of Arts and Humanities. Held at locations throughout the U.S. Have technical assistance and training, program development, research and evaluation, demonstration activities. Publish various documents, newsletters, papers, reports, guidebooks, etc. Second contact: NCAH, 1701 K Street N.W., Suite 905, Washington, D.C. 20006; tel: (202) 223-8007.

CRAFT ARTS EXHIBITIONS: All Types, year-round arts program incorporating inservice training of personnel and culminating in festival featuring wide variety of arts experiences for disabled and nondisabled children. Also have music, drama, dance programs.

ENTRY FEE: None.

DEADLINES: Continuous.

207
Young Arkansas Artists Competitive Exhibition
The Arkansas Art Center
Townsend Wolfe, Director
MacArthur Park, P. O. Box 2137
Little Rock, Arkansas 72203 U.S.A.

Entry March

State; **entry open to Arkansas pre- and grade school students;** annual in April-May; established 1958. Purpose: to encourage young Arkansas artists. Sponsored by Arkansas Art Center. Supported by Arkansas Art Center, Arkansas Arts Council, National Art Education Association. Average 300 accepted entries. Held at Arkansas Art Center for 5 weeks. Also sponsor Toys Designed by Artists Exhibition; Delta Art Exhibition; print, drawing, crafts exhibitions. Have open house day, traveling exhibition for 1 year.

CRAFTS-SCULPTURE EXHIBITION: All Forms; limit 12 entries per school. 2D matted works eligible for traveling exhibition. Require submission through school. Competition includes fine arts, all crafts.

JUDGING: By panel of Arkansas art teachers, members of National Art Education Association.

ENTRY FEE: None. Entrant pays return postage.

DEADLINES: Entry, March. Event, April-May.

WORKSHOPS
Workshops throughout U.S., Canada, England. Includes CERAMICS, CLAY, ENAMELING, GLASS, GLAZING, PLASTER, PORCELAIN, POTTERY, RAKU, SCULPTURE, and GENERAL CRAFTS.

208

Elizabeth Nields Clay Workshop
Box 300 R.D. 1
Otego, New York 13825 U.S.A.
Tel: (607) 783-2476

Entry dates not specified

International; entry open to all; an-

nual in August; established 1974. **Workshop** covering glazing (available as 1-day study, $10), wheel, functional pieces, sculpture open to beginning, experienced potters and sculptors. Recognized by Hofstra University (credit may be arranged in some cases). Held in Otego for 1 month. Fee: $510 tuition and materials. $380 room and board. Also have 8-session course available for Gilbertsville area, $70; 5-session children's courses, $28.

209

Farmington Valley Arts Center (FVAC) Workshops
P. O. Box 220
Avon, Connecticut 06001 U.S.A.
Tel: (203) 678-1867

Entry Spring,Summer

Regional; **entry open to FVAC members;** annual in Spring, Summer; established 1978. **Workshops** in pottery open to beginning, advanced potters. Sponsored by and held at FVAC for 2-8-day sessions through Spring and Summer. Fees: $30-$70 plus materials fee and $15 annual membership. Also sponsor children's art classes, art fair.

210

Indiana Central University Crafts Workshops
Gerald G. Boyce
Office of Academic Services
1400 East Hanna Avenue
Indianapolis, Indiana 46227 U.S.A.
Tel: (317) 788-3253

Entry July

International; entry open to all; annual in June-July. **Workshops** in uses of electric kiln available on credit, non-credit basis. Sponsored by and held at Indiana Central University for 3 weeks (5-day sessions). Fee: $100.

211

Miami University CraftSummer Workshops
Peter Dahoda, Director
130 Upham Hall
Oxford, Ohio 45056 U.S.A. Tel: (513) 529-5645, 529-7128

Entry June, July

International; entry open to all; annual in Summer. **Workshops** in enameling, handmade tile, glassblowing, porcelain open to beginning, advanced craftspersons on credit, non-credit basis. Sponsored by and held at Miami University for 1- and 2-week sessions in June, July. Fee: $100. Also sponsor Gifted Youth Art Workshop.

212

New Jersey Arts Foundation Summer Arts Institute
Jacqueline E. Rubel, Executive Director
Levin Theater, Mason Gross School of the Arts
Douglass Campus, Rutgers University
New Brunswick, New Jersey 08903 U.S.A. Tel: (201) 247-8795, 932-8467

Entry May

International; **entry open to high school students;** annual in July-August; established 1980. **Workshops** in crafts open to state and nationally recognized 10th-, 11th-, 12th-grade students. Formerly called INTERNATIONAL FOLK FESTIVAL. Sponsored by New Jersey Arts Foundation. Held at Rutgers University in New Jersey for 2 months. Fee: None. Also sponsor workshops in other crafts, fine arts, performing arts, photography, film, and writing.

213

Oxbow Workshops
The School of the Art Institute of Chicago at Oxbow
Krystin Grenon, Administrative Director
Saugatuck, Michigan 49453 U.S.A. Tel: (312) 443-3703

Entry dates continuous

International; **entry open to advanced students over age 18;** annual in July-August. **Workshops** in ceramics, plaster, sculpture open to experienced craftspersons, advanced students; college credit available. Sponsored by the School of the Art Institute of Chicago at Oxbow. Supported by NEA, Michigan Council of the Arts, Illinois Arts Council. Held at Oxbow in Saugatuck for 1-3-week sessions. Have housing, meal facilities. Fees: $200-$375 per week based on residency, length of session. Also have classes in fine arts, photography.

214

Pipe Sculpture Workshop East-West
Jerry L. Caplan, Director
5812 Fifth Avenue
Pittsburgh, Pennsylvania 15232 U.S.A. Tel: (412) 661-0179

Entry May, June

International; entry open to all; annual in June-July; established 1973. **Workshops** in extruded clay form sculpture (clay pipe cylinders). Sponsored by and held at Logan Clay Company in Logan, Ohio (June), and Mission Clay Company in Fremont, California (July). Average 15-20 participants. Submit slides for jurying. Entry fee: $165.

| 215 |

Pittsburgh Center for the Arts Workshops
1047 Shady Avenue
Pittsburgh, Pennsylvania 15232
U.S.A. Tel: (412) 361-0455

Entry dates continuous

Regional; **entry open to all (require membership in Pittsburgh Center for the Arts);** continuous throughout year. **Workshops** in ceramics, porcelain, raku, stained glass open to beginning, advanced craftspersons. Sponsored by and held at Pittsburgh Center for the Arts for sessions of varying duration. Entry fee: $70 (includes membership).

| 216 |

Quadna Mountain Resort Summer Arts Study Center
University of Minnesota
320 Westbrook Hall
77 Pleasant Street S.E.
Minneapolis, Minnesota 55455
U.S.A. Tel: (612) 373-4947

Entry dates not specified

International; entry open to all; annual in Summer. **Workshops** in ceramics, glassmaking open to beginning, experienced students; some workshops available for credit. Sponsored by University of Minnesota. Held at Quadna Mountain Resort in Minnesota for 9 1-week sessions. Have camping, motel, recreation facilities. Entry fee: $105. Some workshops require additional materials fee. Also have classes in visual arts, photography, writing, other crafts.

| 217 |

The Waumbek Center Crafts Workshops
Meg Senuta, Executive Director
U.S. Rt. 2, P. O. Box 38
Jefferson, New Hampshire 03583
U.S.A. Tel: (603) 586-4350

Entry dates not specified

International; entry open to all; annual in July-August. **Workshops** in sculpture (clay, stone carving, mixed media), clay (hand-building) open to beginning, advanced adults and children. Supported by NEA, New Hampshire Commission on Arts. Sponsored by and held at Waumbek Center for Arts for 6 weeks (1-7-day sessions). Have kiln. Entry fee: $36-$75 ($9 children). Some classes require materials fee. Also sponsor crafts fair, lectures, classes in fine arts, theater, music, other crafts.

| 218 |

Westchester Art Workshop
Wayne Kartzinel
Westchester County Center
White Plains, New York 10607
U.S.A. Tel: (914) 682-2481

Entry dates vary

International; entry open to all; continuous through academic year; established 1926. **Workshops,** extended courses in ceramics, stained glass, enameling, sculpture open to beginning, advanced adults and children on credit, non-credit basis. Sponsored by and held at Westchester Art Workshop for varying periods. Entry fee: $37 (resident), $93 (non-resident) for mini-semester; $65 (resident), $187 (non-resident) for teen classes, Spring semester; $30-$45 for special workshops. Also have classes in fine arts, photography, other crafts. Also sponsor biennial crafts fair.

219

Artsperience Canadore College Craft Workshops
Keith Campbell, Program Consultant
P. O. Box 5001
North Bay, Ontario P1B 8K9
CANADA
Entry June

International; entry open to all; annual in July; established 1978. **Workshops** in pottery, glazing, stained glass open to individuals, families. Sponsored by and held at Canadore College for 1 month (5-day sessions). Supported by Canada Council, Ministry of Culture, Art Gallery of Ontario. Fees: $40-$50 plus materials fee. Also have classes in fine arts, photography, dance, writing, other crafts.

220

Mohawk College Creative Arts Weekend Workshops
Box 2034
Hamilton, Ontario L8N 3T2 CANADA
Tel: (416) 389-4461
Entry dates vary

International; entry open to all; continuous throughout year; established 1972. **Workshops** in ceramics, cloisonne open to adults, teens. Sponsored by and held at Mohawk College for 1-3-day sessions. Fee: $30-$50 for instruction, materials. Also sponsor classes in fine arts, other crafts; Mactaquac Craft Festival.

221

Rozynska Pottery Summer Workshops
Stanley Rozynski
Way's Mills, RR1
Ayer's Cliff, J0B 1C0 Tel: (819) 838-4321
Entry dates vary

International; entry open to all; annual in Summer; established 1966. **Workshops** in various pottery methods including throwing, glazing, decorating, firing open to beginning, advanced potters. Sponsored by and held at Rozynska Pottery for 5 2-week sessions. Average 11 potters each session. Entry fee: $475 for registration, instruction, accommodation.

222

A Pottery Course in Kent
John Solly
36 London Road
Maidstone, Kent ME16 8QL, ENGLAND Tel: 0622-54623
Entry dates vary

International; entry open to all; annual in Spring or Summer; established 1960. **Workshops** in hand-building, wheel-throwing, various glaze and decorative techniques open to beginning, experienced students. Sponsored by John Solly. Held in Kent for 11 1-week sessions. Recognized by Craftsmen Potters Association of Great Britain. Entry fee: £50.

223

Ridge Pottery Course
Ridge Pottery
Douglas Phillips, Pottery Director
Queen Carmel, Near Yeovil
Somerset BA22 7NF, ENGLAND
Tel: (0935) 850753
Entry dates not specified

International; entry open to all; annual in June-September; established 1977. **Workshop** facilities open to potters of all standards. Course covers clay preparation, throwing, high-low temperature firing, porcelain, saltglaze. Sponsored by and held at Ridge Pottery in Queen Carmel for 10 5-1/2-day sessions. Average 12 students per session. Entry fee: £58 (including materials) per session.

CRAFTS FAIRS, FESTIVALS (Ceramics)

Crafts Fairs, Festivals, Shows, Sales accepting CERAMICS (listed alphabetically by state). Attendance usually required.

224

Boynton's Great American Love Affair Art Festival

City of Boynton Beach Recreation & Park Department
Eleanor Jean Krusell, Supervisor
120 North East Second Avenue
P. O. Box 232
Boynton Beach, Florida 33435
U.S.A. Tel: (305) 734-8111, ext. 432

Entry February

International; **entry open to professional craftspersons, local students;** annual in March; established 1974. Formerly BOYNTON BEACH ANNUAL FESTIVAL OF THE ARTS to 1981. Sponsored by Boynton Beach City and Chamber of Commerce. Average statistics (all sections): 150 entrants, 10,000 attendance. Held at Boynton Beach Civic Center for 5 days. Have performing artists, art auction. Second contact: Jim Patterson, Boynton Beach Chamber of Commerce.

CRAFTS FAIR: Ceramics, original. Require entrant attendance. Submit 2 slides of work, 1 of display area for entry review. No casts, molds. Competition includes fine arts, photography, other crafts.

AWARDS: $300 Best of Show Award and Ribbon (includes all sections). $100 First, $50 Second, $25 Third Place Awards. Honorable Mention Ribbons.

JUDGING: By 3 judges. Not responsible for loss or damage.

ENTRY FEE: $30 for 8x12-foot exhibit space.

DEADLINES: Entry, February. Judging, event, March.

225

Marco Island Art League Show

Elizabeth Denniston, President
1025 Winterberry
P. O. Box 745
Marco Island, Florida 33937 U.S.A.

Entry October

National; **entry open to U.S.;** annual in February; established 1971. Purpose: to promote art awareness on Marco Island. Sponsored by Art League of Marco Island. Average statistics (all sections): 1200 entries, 100 (maximum) entrants, 12,000 attendance. Held on Marco Island for 1 day. Also sponsor workshops, lectures, demonstrations.

CRAFTS FAIR: Ceramics (including clay, glass), original. Entrants provide sales displays. Submit 3 slides for entry review. No agents, commercial dealers. Competition for some awards includes fine and commercial arts, photography.

AWARDS: $100 Best of Show, $50 First Awards. $25 Merit Awards.

JUDGING: By 3 professionals. Not responsible for loss or damage.

ENTRY FEE: $5 jury fee plus $40 for 10x5-foot exhibition space. No sales commission charge.

DEADLINES: Entry, October. Notification, November. Event, February.

226

Fort Dodge Art in the Park
Fort Dodge Area Fine Arts Council
Visual Arts Committee
Blanden Memorial Art Gallery
920 Third Avenue South
Fort Dodge, Iowa 50501 U.S.A.
Tel: (515) 573-2801, 573-2316

Entry July

International; entry open to all; annual in August; established 1974. Purpose: to give exposure to artists, educate public; encourage community support of arts. Sponsored by Fort Dodge Area Fine Arts Council; Fort Dodge Department of Parks, Recreation, Forestry; Riverfront Commission. Supported by local business, organizations. Average statistics (all sections): 90 entrants maximum, 21 awards, 10,000 attendance. Held at Alson Park in Fort Dodge for 1 day. Have entertainment, food service, demonstrations. Also sponsor Artists-in-Schools, drama, puppet presentations.

CRAFTS FAIR: Ceramics. Entrants provide and attend sales displays. Submit 5 slides or photos of work for entry review. Competition includes visual arts, photography.

AWARDS: $8000 in Purchase Awards.

JUDGING: Entry review by screening board. Awards judging by 3-5 art professionals. Based on originality, creativity. Not responsible for loss or damage.

ENTRY FEE: $15. No sales commission charge.

DEADLINES: Entry, July, Event, August.

227

Boston Mills All Ceramics Fair
Don Getz, Director
P. O. Box 173
Peninsula, Ohio 44264 U.S.A.
Tel: (216) 657-2807

Entry March

International; entry open to all; annual in September; established 1982. Formerly called ARTISAN FAIR. Purpose: to promote exposure and sale of high quality ceramic art. Sponsored by Akron Beacon Journal Charity Fund, Junior Womens Club of Akron. Supported by Boston Mills Ski Resort. Recognized by Ohio Arts Council. Average statistics: 600 entrants, 150 finalists, 12 awards. 20,000 attendance, $150,000 total sales. Held at Boston Mills Ski Resort in Peninsula for 3 days. Tickets: $3 adult, $2 senior citizens. Also sponsor Boston Mills Art Festival (annual in July), Boston Mills Artists Workshops.

CRAFTS FAIR: Ceramics (including pottery, sculpture, jewelry, wall hangings), original. Require hand-delivery. Entrants provide and attend sales displays. Submit 4 35mm slides for entry review. No mass-produced work.

AWARDS: $500 to best of show. 11 Awards totaling $1700. Exclusive ceramics exhibition at Boston Mills Art Festival for all winners.

JUDGING: By panel of 2 ceramics professionals. Based on originality, professionalism. Sponsor may photograph winning entries.

SALES TERMS: Sales compulsory. No commission charge.

ENTRY FEE: $8 jury fee. $50-$100 booth fee.

DEADLINES: Entry, March. Event, September.

228

Shadyside Summer Arts Festival

Ed D'Allessandro
P. O. Box 10187
Pittsburgh, Pennsylvania 15232
U.S.A. Tel: (412) 681-2809

Entry May

International; entry open to all; annual in August; established 1971. Sponsored by Shadyside Chamber of Commerce. Average statistics (all sections): 180 entrants, 200,000 attendance. Held on Walnut Street in Pittsburgh for 3 days. Have participant demonstrations, security. Second contact: Stylegate, 5508 Walnut Street, Pittsburgh, Pennsylvania 15232.

CRAFTS FAIR: Ceramics (including pottery), handcrafted, original design. Entrants provide and attend sales displays. Submit 5 slides for entry review. No molded greenware, commercial slip-cast molds, leaded glazes on utilitarian ware. Competition includes commercial arts, photography, other crafts.

AWARDS: (Includes all sections): Best of Show, First, Second, Third, Fourth, Fifth Prizes. Best Booth Award.

JUDGING: By 6 category experts.

SALES TERMS: Sales compulsory.

ENTRY FEE: $5 handling fee. $145 (per entrant) for 10x6-foot booth.

DEADLINES: Entry, May. Event, August.

229

Toronto Outdoor Art Exhibition

Beth Salney, Coordinator
Penthouse One
1442 Lawrence Avenue West
Toronto, Ontario M6L 1B5 CANADA
Tel: (416) 241-4419

Entry January

International; entry open to all; annual in July; established 1961. Purpose: to celebrate, display works of Canada's finest artists. Sponsored by Toronto Outdoor Art Exhibition Committee. Supported by Ontario Arts Council, Bronfman Family Foundation. Recognized by Visual Arts Ontario. Average statistics (all sections): 15,000 entries, 500 entrants, 4 countries, 14 awards, 100,000 attendance, 20 sales per entrant. Held at Nathan Philips Square in Toronto for 3 days. Have food, press booth. Also sponsor scholarship program, press luncheon with special prizes. Second contact: Ken Jarvis, Treasurer, Four Season's Hotel, 1100 Eglington Avenue East, Don Mills, Toronto, Ontario, Canada.

CRAFTS FAIR: Ceramics (including glass, pottery). Entrants provide and attend sales displays. Submit 5 slides or photographs of recent work for entry review. No large quantities of reproductions. Divisions: Open, Student (includes all media). Competition for some awards includes art, photography,other crafts.

AWARDS: $300 to best ceramic. $250 to best crafts (includes all crafts). *Includes all sections:* $1500 Jack Reppen Memorial Award to best of show. $1000 City of Toronto Purchase Award. $200 to best student.

JUDGING: Entry review by jury. Awards judging by 3 professionals.

SALES TERMS: Sales optional. No commission charge.

ENTRY FEE: $50 ($25 student) for 10-foot exhibit space (per entrant if shared).

DEADLINES: Entry, January. Event, July.

CRAFTS FAIRS, FESTIVALS (Ceramics, Glass, Enamel)

Crafts Fairs, Festivals, Shows, Sales accepting CERAMICS, GLASS, ENAMEL (listed alphabetically by state). Attendance usually required.

230

Fine Art Museum of the South Outdoor Arts and Crafts Fair
Greta Massing
P. O. Box 8404
Mobile, Alabama 36608 U.S.A.
Tel: (205) 343-2667

Entry September

National; **entry open to U.S.;** annual in September; established 1964. Purpose: to offer community opportunity to acquire fine original works. Sponsored by Fine Arts Museum of the South. Average statistics (all sections): 200 entrants, 20 awards, 40,000 attendance, $85,000 total sales. Held at Fine Arts Museum at Langan Park in Mobile for 2 days. Have entertainment, food, children's activities. Tickets: 50¢.

CRAFTS FAIR: Ceramics, Blown Glass, original. Entrants attend sales displays. Submit slides for entry review. No art supplies, copies, molds, kits. Competition includes visual arts, photography, mixed media, other crafts.

AWARDS: (Includes all sections): $3000 in Purchase Prize Awards. 5 $2000 Distinction Awards. 10 Merit Award Ribbons.

JUDGING: By jury. Sponsor may combine, divide awards.

ENTRY FEE: $5 jury fee plus $35 exhibition fee.

DEADLINES: Event, September.

231

Metrozoo Festival of the Arts
Zoological Society of Florida
12400 S. W. 152nd Street
Miami, Florida 33177 U.S.A.
Tel: (305) 255-5551

Entry January

International; entry open to all; annual in February. Sponsored by Zoological Society of Florida. Held at Metrozoo in Miami for 2 days.

CRAFTS FAIR: Ceramics, Glass, Enamel, original. Submit 3 slides, description for entry review. No work using products or by-products derived from hides, teeth, bones of any animals.

AWARDS: $300 Gold, $250 Silver, $150 Bronze Awards to ceramic-glass-enamel, and sculpture.

JUDGING: Not responsible for loss or damage.

ENTRY FEE: $5 plus $60 for 15x10x8-foot (wxdxh) exhibition space.

DEADLINES: Entry, January. Judging, event, February.

232

Park Forest Art Fair
Park Forest Art Center
Eugene R. Dooley
410 Lakewood Blvd.
Park Forest, Illinois 60466 U.S.A.

Entry June

International; **entry open to age 18 and over;** annual in September; established 1955. Sponsored by Park Forest

Art Center, Park Forest Plaza Merchants' Association. Average 180 entrants (all sections). Held at Park Forest Shopping Plaza for 2 days.

CRAFTS FAIR: Ceramics, Glass, original, glass to be hand-blown or molded; unlimited entry (no group entries). Entrants provide and attend sales diplays. Submit 5 slides for entry review. Competition includes visual arts, photography, other crafts.

AWARDS: $600 First, $400 Second, $200 Third, $100 Fourth Prizes. $100 Municipal Art League Award. $1600 in Purchase Awards.

JUDGING: Entry review and awards judging by jury. Not responsible for loss or damage.

SALES TERMS: Sales compulsory. No commission charge.

ENTRY FEE: $5 plus $20 for 12-foot (minimum) booth space.

DEADLINES: Entry, June. Judging, event, September.

233

Lafayesta
Lafayette Art Center
Sharon Theobold, Executive Director
101 South 9th Street
Lafayette, Indiana 47901 U.S.A.
Tel: (317) 742-1128

Entry June

National; **entry open to U.S.;** annual in September; established 1974. Formerly called FIESTA, INTERNATIONAL FESTIVAL OF ARTS, AND CRAFTS to 1980. Purpose: to expose area residents to outstanding artists. Sponsored and supported by Lafayette Art Center. Held at Indiana Veterans Home in West Lafayette for 2 days. Have ethnic food, children's arts and crafts area, demonstrations, entertainment, tables, chairs for hire.

Tickets: $1-$5. Also sponsor Tippecanoe Biennial.

CRAFTS FAIR: Ceramics, Glass. Entrants provide and attend sales displays. Submit 4 35mm slides for entry review. No kits, copies, molds, manufactured items. Competition includes photography, visual arts, other crafts.

AWARDS: (Includes all sections): $5000 in Excellence, Merit, Purchase, Commission Awards.

JUDGING: Entry review by jury headed by University Art Coordinator. Awards judging by 2 art professionals. Not responsible for loss or damage.

ENTRY FEE: $30 (refundable) for 8x10-foot exhibit booth (2 artists maximum per booth).

DEADLINES: Entry, June. Acceptance, July. Event, September.

234

Floral City Arts and Crafts Festival
City of Monroe
Eileen Biggs, Administrative Director
City Hall
120 East First Street
Monroe, Michigan 48161 U.S.A.
Tel: (313) 243-0700, ext. 258

Entry June

International; entry open to all; annual in July; established 1980. Sponsored and supported by City of Monroe, Downtown Retail committee, private donations. Average statistics (all sections): 100 entrants, (200 maximum), 25 awards, 30,000 attendance. Held at Loranger Square in downtown Monroe for 2 days. Have entertainment, parade, music, dancing, food.

CRAFTS FAIR: Ceramics, Stained

Glass (including hand-built, slip-cast). Entrants provide and attend sales displays. Also have photography, visual arts, other crafts sections.

AWARDS: Ribbons to best of show (includes all sections). Ribbons to each section.

JUDGING: By 2 judges with arts backgrounds. Not responsible for loss or damage.

ENTRY FEE: $8 for 4x8-foot display easel, $15 for booth space.

DEADLINES Entry, June. Event, July.

235

New Mexico Arts and Crafts Fair
Peggy Winkwirth, Secretary
2745 San Mateo N.E., Suite G
Albuquerque, New Mexico 87110
U.S.A. Tel: (505) 884-9043

Entry February

State; **entry open to New Mexico residents age 18 and over;** annual in June; established 1965. Purpose: to encourage professional artists to display and sell arts and crafts of New Mexico. Sponsored and supported by New Mexico Arts and Crafts Fair, nonprofit organization. Average statistics (all sections): 2000 entries, 750 entrants, 225 finalists, 10 awards, 100,000 attendance. Held at New Mexico Fairground in Albuquerque for 3 days. Have working demonstrations, youth exhibits, entertainment, food. Tickets: $1.50.

CRAFTS FAIR: Ceramics, Glass (including stoneware, porcelain, raku; etched, blown and stained glass; jewelry), original, limited editions. Entrants attend sales displays. Submit 3 small work samples per media or category (1 may be multiple piece) or color slides of large work for entry review.

No copies, kits, student work, hobby crafts. Competition includes visual arts, photography, other crafts.

AWARDS: Not specified.

JUDGING: By 10 crafts judges from Southeastern U.S.

SALES TERMS: Sales compulsory. No commission charge.

ENTRY FEE: $9 per subsection for 8x8-foot booth space. $85 single booth, 1 exhibitor ($130 2 exhibitors); $170 2 booths, 2 exhibitors ($195 3 exhibitors). Collaborators count as 1 exhibitor.

DEADLINES: Entry, judging, February. Event, June.

236

New World Festival of the Arts
Claire Grieves, Co-Chair
P. O. Box 246
Manteo, North Carolina 27954
U.S.A. Tel: (919) 473-2133

Entry June

National; **entry open to U.S., Puerto Rico;** annual in August; established 1982. Purpose: to provide artists with opportunity to show and sell creative work, increase awareness of current trends in visual arts. Sponsored by Town of Manteo. Supported by North Carolina Arts Council, business. Recognized by Sea and Sounds Art Council, Manteo. Average 100 entrants. Held on waterfront of Manteo for 2 days.

CRAFTS FAIR: Ceramics, Glass; limit 150 entrants (all sections). Entrants provide and attend sales displays. Submit 3 35mm slides (for carousel projection) for entry review. Competition includes fiber, jewelry, leather, metalsmithing, woodcrafts, fine and commercial arts, photography.

AWARDS: $5000 in Cash and Patron Purchase Awards.

JUDGING: Entry review and awards judging by 2 national judges each. Not responsible for loss or damage.

SALES TERMS: Sales compulsory. No commission charge.

ENTRY FEE: $50 for minimum 10x10x8-foot exhibition space.

DEADLINES: Entry, June. Event, August.

237

Cincinnati Summerfair
Linda Deatrick, Executive Director
Department GG
P. O. Box 3277
Cincinnati, Ohio 45201 U.S.A.
Tel: (513) 421-3535

Entry February

International; entry open to all; annual in June; established 1968. Purpose: to provide opportunity for artists to display quality, original work. Sponsored by Summerfair, Inc. Average statistics (all sections): 450 entrants, 200 exhibitors (maximum), 35 finalists, 50,000 attendance, $1500 sales per entrant. Held at Riverfront Stadium in Cincinnati for 2 days. Have musical entertainment, advertising program, refreshments. Tickets: $2.50. Also sponsor Poster Competition.

CRAFTS FAIR: Ceramics, Glass, original; limit 1 category per entrant. Entrants provide and attend sales displays. Submit 5 slides, brief description for entry review. No commercially produced entries, kits. Also have visual art, other crafts.

AWARDS: $200 First, $150 Second, $75 Third Prize.

JUDGING: By committee member and 4 art experts. Sponsor may photography entries for publicity. Not responsible for loss or damage.

ENTRY FEE: $10 jury fee. $40 (refundable) for 10x10-foot booth space (maximum 2 exhibitors per booth) plus $40 for canopy (optional).

DEADLINES: Entry, February. Judging, event, June.

238

Northeast Craftworks
Hadassah
Jeania C. Karmiel, Chair
Box 1515
Kingston, Pennsylvania 18704 U.S.A.
Tel: (717) 696-2248

Entry January

National; entry open to U.S.; annual in March; established 1981. Purpose: to raise funds for Hadassah, a Jewish Women's Organization. Sponsored by Hadassah. Average statistics: 500 entrants, 3 awards, 2000 attendance, $25,000 total sales, $500 sale per entrant. Held in Wilkes-Barre in Pennsylvania for 2 days. Tickets: $5 for Saturday preview, $1.50 for Sunday. Have electrical connection for exhibitors.

CRAFTS FAIR: Ceramics, Glass, original. Completed in previous 2 years. Submit 3 slides or 8x10-inch color prints, with brief description for entry review and awards judging.

AWARDS: Special Recognition Awards.

JUDGING: By 3 academics.

SALES TERMS: Sales compulsory. 10% commission charge.

ENTRY FEE: $5 jury fee plus $50 for 8x10-foot booth space.

DEADLINES: Entry, January. Event, March.

| 239 |

Oshkosh Public Museum Art Fair
Brenda Hauber, Registrar
1331 Algoma Blvd.
Oshkosh, Wisconsin 54901 U.S.A.
Tel: (414) 424-0452
Entry July

International; entry open to all; annual in July; established 1960. Purpose: to encourage creativity, expression in visual arts. Sponsored by Oshkosh Public Museum. Supported by local donations. Average statistics (all sections): 200 entrants, $3000 in awards, 20,000 attendance, $300 sales per entrant. Held on Oshkosh Museum grounds for 1 day. Have food, demonstrations, children's workshops.

CRAFTS FAIR: Ceramics, Glass, original. Entrants provide and attend sales displays. Competition includes photography, visual arts, other crafts.

AWARDS: $3000 in Cash and Purchase Awards (includes all sections).

JUDGING: By 1 or more qualified individuals. Sponsor displays winning entries in museum gallery for 1 month.

ENTRY FEE: $25 for 15-foot exhibit space. No sales commission charge.

DEADLINES: Entry, Event, July.

| 240 |

Winnebagoland Art Fair
Oshkosh Fine Arts Association
Mary L. Hinds, General Chair
617 South Westfield
Oshkosh, Wisconsin 54901 U.S.A.
Tel: (414) 233-4685
Entry June

Regional; **entry open to Midwest U.S.;** annual in June; established 1957. Sponsored and supported by Oshkosh Fine Arts Association. Average statistics (all sections): 200 entrants, $3000 in awards, 15,000 attendance, $50,000 sales. Held in Oshkosh for 1 day. Second contact: Nancy Marks, 1522 Ohio, Oshkosh, Wisconsin 54901; tel: (414) 235-1736.

CRAFTS FAIR: Ceramics, Glass, Enamel, original. Submit 5 slides or photos of work for entry review. No molds. Competition includes fine arts, photography, other crafts.

AWARDS: $150 to best of show; $2500 in Purchase Awards (includes all sections). $75 First, $50 Second, $25 Third Place Award. $10 Honorable Mentions (includes woodcrafts).

JUDGING: By 1 judge. Not responsible for loss or damage.

SALES TERMS: Sales compulsory. No commission charge.

ENTRY FEE: $20 for 10x20-foot exhibit space.

DEADLINES: Entry, event, June.

CRAFTS FAIRS, FESTIVALS (Ceramics, Glass, Pottery, Sculpture, Enamel)

Crafts Fairs, Festivals, Shows, Sales accepting CERAMICS, GLASS, POTTERY, SCULPTURE, ENAMEL, CHINA, MOSAIC, PLASTIC, STONE (listed alphabetically by state). Attendance usually required.

241

Fine Arts Museum of the South Arts and Crafts Fair

Greta Massing, Chair
P. O. Box 8426
Mobile, Alabama 36608 U.S.A.
Tel: (205) 343-2667

Entry June

International; entry open to all; annual in September; established 1964. Purpose: to offer community exposure to artists and craftspersons. Sponsored by Fine Arts Museum of the South, Art Patrons League. Average statistics: 200 entrants (maximum), 19 awards, 50,000 attendance, $85,000 total sales. Held at Fine Arts Museum of the South in Mobile for 2 days. Have security.

CRAFTS FAIR: Ceramics, Blown Glass, Sculpture (including mixed media); unlimited entry. Entrants provide and attend sales displays. Submit 3 35mm slides per category, 1 photo or diagram of display, written description of work. No china painting, bottle sagging, items made from commercial kits, molds, patterns. Competition includes art, photography, other crafts.

AWARDS: (Includes all sections): $2500 in Purchase Prizes. 5 $200 Awards of Distinction. 10 $50 Merit Awards.

JUDGING: Entry review by 1 judge. Awards judging by 2 jurors. Not responsible for loss or damage.

SALES TERMS: 75% of displayed work to be for sale.

ENTRY FEE: $5 jury fee. $45 for 12x8-foot exhibit space.

DEADLINES: Entry, June. Acceptance, July. Event, September.

242

Affaire in the Gardens Fine Art and Crafts Fair

Beverly Hills Recreation and Parks Department
Michele Merrill
450 North Crescent Drive
Beverly Hills, California 90210 U.S.A.
Tel: (213) 550-4864

Entry February, July

International; **entry open to professionals;** biannual in April, September; established 1974. Purpose: to establish appreciation of fine arts and crafts in Beverly Hills and vicinity. Sponsored by Beverly Hills Recreation and Parks Department. Average statistics (all sections): 200 entrants, 3 countries, 50 awards, 30,000 attendance. Held at Beverly Gardens Park in Beverly Hills for 1 weekend. Have music, entertainment, international foods.

CRAFTS FAIR: Ceramics, Stained Glass, Sculpture (including other hard media), original. Entrants provide and attend sales displays. Submit 5 photos minimum (slides accepted) of current work, 1 photo of complete display, portrait for entry review; 8x10- or 5x7-inch monochrome press photos of entrant demonstrating craft, resume for publicity. Competition for some awards includes visual arts, photography, other crafts.

AWARDS: (Includes all sections): $500 Vernors Purchase Award. $100 Mayors Award. $100 Best of Show. *Each category:* $100 First Place Prize. First, Second, Third Place Ribbons. 2 Honorable Mentions.

JUDGING: Entry review by jury. Awards judging by professional in each category. Based on quality, originality. Not responsible for loss or damage.

ENTRY FEE: $5 plus $70 (refundable) for 9x12-foot display area.

DEADLINES: Entry, February, July. Acceptance, March, August. Judging, event, April, September.

| 243 |

Westwood Sidewalk Art and Craft Show

Western Los Angeles Regional Chamber of Commerce
Wayne Erickson, General Manager
10880 Wilshire Blvd.
Los Angeles, California 90024 U.S.A.
Tel: (213) 475-4577

Entry February, July

International; entry open to all; semiannual in May, October; established 1969. Sponsored by Western Los Angeles Regional Chamber of Commerce. Average statistics (all sections): 600 entrants, 2 countries, 40 awards, 125,000 attendance. Held in 3 Los Angeles locations for 2 days.

CRAFTS FAIR: Ceramics, Stained Glass, Sculpture. Entrants attend sales displays. Submit minimum 3 photos of current work, picture or drawing of complete exhibit for entry review. No imports, manufactured items. Competition for some awards includes photography, visual arts, other crafts.

AWARDS: $150 First, $100 Second, $50 Third Place Awards each to sculpture (all media), ceramics. 4 $150 First Place Awards to diverse media (including stained glass).

JUDGING: By museum exhibitors. Based on quality and originality. Not responsible for loss or damage.

ENTRY FEE: $95-$200 for 12x3-foot booth space, according to location (may be shared).

DEADLINES: Entry, February, July. Judging, events, May, October.

| 244 |

Tarpon Springs Art and Crafts Festival

Tarpon Springs Chamber of Commerce
Scottie Gemmell
914 South Pinellas Avenue
Tarpon Springs, Florida 33589
U.S.A. Tel: (813) 937-6109

Entry February

International; entry open to all; annual in April; established 1975. Sponsored by Tarpon Springs Chamber of Commerce. Average statistics: 200 entrants, 2 participating countries, 37 awards, 50,000 attendance. Held at Craig Park in Tarpon Springs for 2 days. Have performing arts, food, refreshments. Second contact: Kay Cotton, 112 South Pinellas Avenue, Tarpon Springs, Florida 33589.

CRAFTS FAIR: Ceramics, Glass, Sculpture, original. Entrants provide and attend sales displays. Submit 3 35mm slides of work per category, 1 of display stand. No commercial molds, displays, art supplies. Competition includes visual arts, photography, other crafts.

AWARDS: (Includes all sections): $1000 Best of Show Award. $375 Cash Awards each to ceramics, crafts, sculpture (all media). 30 $100 Awards of Distinction. $4000 in Purchase Awards.

JUDGING: By noted authorities and recognized judges. Sponsor may withhold awards.

ENTRY FEE: $5 jury fee plus $45 (refundable) for 10x12-foot booth space.

DEADLINES: Entry, February. Judging, event, April.

| 245 |

Wichita Art Museum Art and Book Fair
Friends' Alliance of the Wichita Art Museum
619 Stackman Drive
Wichita, Kansas 67203 U.S.A.
Tel: (316) 268-4621

Entry December

International; entry open to all; annual in May; established 1959. Purpose: to encourage active interest in creative art. Sponsored by Friends' Alliance of Wichita Art Museum. Held at Wichita Art Museum for 2 days. Have sales rental gallery, library. Also sponsor exhibits of local artists; films, lectures, docent programs.

CRAFTS FAIR: Ceramics, Leaded Glass, Pottery, China Painting, Other Media. Entrants provide and attend sales displays. Submit 3 slides for entry review. No commercial displays. Competition includes visual arts, photography, other crafts.

AWARDS: 12 $150 Cash Prizes (includes all sections).

JUDGING: By 3 judges. Sponsor keeps slides. Not responsible for loss or damage.

ENTRY FEE: $50 for 10x10-foot outdoor, or 8x10-foot indoor booth space (limit 1 space per entrant).

DEADLINES: Entry, December. Acceptance, February. Event, May.

| 246 |

Cincinnati Crafts Affair
Ohio Designer Craftsmen Enterprises
JoAnn H. Stevens, Executive Director
1981 Riverside Drive
Columbus, Ohio 43221 U.S.A.
Tel: (614) 486-7119

Entry July

National; entry open to U.S.; annual in November; established 1979. Sponsored by Ohio Designer Craftsmen Enterprises, Craft Guild of Greater Cincinnati. Supported by Ohio Arts Council. Average statistics: 100 entrants, 8500 attendance, $120,000 total sales. Held at Cincinnati Music Hall in Cincinnati for 3 days. Tickets: $2.50. Also sponsor Cleveland Designer Craftsmen Show, Winter Fair, juried exhibitions, shop, wholesale marketing program.

CRAFTS FAIR: Ceramics, Glass, Sculpture, Enamel, Mixed Media, original; limit 2 categories per booth. Entrants provide and attend sales displays. Submit 4 slides per category for entry review. No commercial molds, manufactured items. Competition includes fiber, graphics, leather, metal, wood, photography.

AWARDS: 5 $100 Awards (includes all sections).

JUDGING: By 1 juror. Based on design, craftsmanship, general display. Sponsor may photograph, publish slides. Not responsible for loss or damage.

SALES TERMS: Sales compulsory. No commission charge.

ENTRY FEE $5 per category plus $115 for 8x10-foot exhibit space ($30 extra for end-of-aisle). Married couples, business partners may share 1 space.

DEADLINES: Entry, July. Acceptance, August. Event, November.

247

Cleveland Designer Craftsmen Fair

Ohio Designer Craftsmen Enterprises
JoAnn H. Stevens, Executive
Director
1981 Riverside Drive
Columbus, Ohio 43221 U.S.A.
Tel: (614) 486-7119

Entry July

National; **entry open to U.S.;** annual in November; established 1980. Sponsored by Ohio Designer Craftsmen Enterprises. Supported by Ohio Arts Council. Average statistics: 100 entrants, $70,000 total sales. Held at Cleveland Masonic Hall in Ohio for 3 days. Tickets: $2.50. Have Winter Fair Exhibition. Also sponsor Cincinnati Craft Affair.

CRAFTS FAIR: Ceramics, Glass, Sculpture, Enamel, original; limit 2 categories per booth. Entrants provide and attend sales displays. Submit 4 slides per category for entry review. No commercial molds, manufactured items. Competition includes fiber, leather, graphics, metal, wood, photography.

AWARDS: $500 in Cash Prizes.

JUDGING: By 1 juror. Based on design, craftsmanship, general display. Sponsor may photograph entries. Not responsible for loss or damage.

SALES: Sales compulsory. No commission charge.

ENTRY FEE: $5 jury fee per category. $115 for 9x7-foot exhibit space. Married couples, business partners may share 1 space.

DEADLINES: Entry, July. Acceptance, August. Event, November.

248

Murrells Inlet Outdoor Arts and Crafts Festival

Wilma D. Martin, Executive Director
P. O. Box 231
Murrells Inlet, South Carolina 29576
U.S.A. Tel: (803) 651-7555,
651-3490

Entry March

International; entry open to all; annual in Spring; established 1973. Purpose: to provide outlet for artists in show-and-sale atmosphere. Sponsored by Murrells Inlet Outdoor Arts and Crafts Festival, Inc. Supported by Georgetown County Arts Council, Myrtle Beach Chamber of Commerce, local businesses. Recognized by South Carolina Arts Commission, Parks, Recreation & Tourism. Average statistics (all sections): 188 entrants, 2 countries, 200,000 attendance. Held in Magnolia Park in Murrells Inlet for 3 days. Tickets: $1 adults, 75¢ children. Have participant demonstrations.

CRAFTS FAIR: Ceramics, Glass, Mosaic, Other, original; 3 minimum per entrant (collaborators count as 1). Produced recently. Entrants provide and attend sales displays. Submit 2 slides or photos for entry review. No molds, patterns, kits, commercially manufactured jewelry, dealers, groups, reproductions. Competition includes visual arts, photography, other crafts.

AWARDS: $250 Purchase Awards. (Includes all sections): $100 First, $50 Second, $25 Third Place Awards, Honorable Mention Awards each to sculpture, crafts.

JUDGING: By professionals. Not responsible for loss or damage.

SALES TERMS: Sales compulsory. No commission charge

ENTRY FEE: $48 for 10x10-foot exhibition booth.

DEADLINES: Entry, March. Event, Spring.

| 249 |

El Paso Festival International Marketplace

El Paso Arts Alliance
Mary Anne Hedderson, Director
333 East Missouri
El Paso, Texas 79901 U.S.A.
Tel: (915) 533-1700

Entry April

Regional; **entry open to Southwest U.S.;** annual in July; established 1981. Purpose: to display creative efforts of artists and craftspersons; develop new markets for their works. Sponsored by El Paso Arts Alliance, City Arts Resources Department. Supported by City and County of El Paso, Texas Commission on the Arts. Average 150,000 attendance (all sections). Held at El Paso Civic Center for 5 days. Have demonstrations, exhibits, films, entertainment, food, shops. Tickets: $1. Publish *Artbeat* (bimonthly). Second contact: City Arts Resources Department, III Civic Center Plaza, El Paso, Texas 79901.

CRAFTS FAIR: Ceramics, Glass, Sculpture, Enamel, Plastics, Stone, Mixed Media, original. Entrants provide and attend sales displays. Submit 3-5 35mm slides for entry review. No moldware. Competition includes painting, other crafts.

ELIGIBILITY: Open to Arizona, Colorado, New Mexico, Oklahoma, Texas, Utah.

AWARDS: $1000 in Crafts Prizes. $500 in General Prizes. Purchase Prizes (includes all sections).

JUDGING: By panel of nationally know judges. Based on merit. Sponsor may photograph entries for publicity. Not responsible for loss or damage.

SALES TERMS: Sales compulsory. 15% commission charge (includes purchase prizes).

ENTRY FEE: $5 plus $50 for 10x10-foot exhibit booth.

DEADLINES: Entry, April. Event, July.

| 250 |

Waynesboro Fall Festival Art Show

Waynesboro Fall Foliage Festival Inc.
Jean Mehler
P. O. Box 626
Waynesboro, Virginia 22980 U.S.A.
Tel: (703) 949-8491, 949-8513

Entry September

National; **entry open to U.S.;** annual in October; established 1972. Purpose: to acquaint visitors with benefits and quality of life available to local residents. Sponsored by Waynesboro Fall Foliage Festival Inc. Average statistics (all sections): 180 entrants, 25 awards, 10,000 attendance, $30,000 total sales. Held in downtown Waynesboro for 2 days. Have dancing, entertainment, antique and gem show, band concerts, marathon race, bike tours. Second contact: T. Kevin Gaw, Box 396, Waynesboro, Virginia 22980; tel: (703) 943-2811.

CRAFTS FAIR: Ceramics, Stained Glass, Pottery, Sculpture, Enamel. Entrants provide and attend sales displays. Submit 3 photos, slides of work for entry review. No mass-produced items, commercial molds, greenware, bisque, toys, imports, kits, dealers. Competition for some awards includes visual arts, photography, other crafts.

AWARDS: (Includes all sections):

$500 Best of Show Award. $6000 in Purchase Prizes. 10 $50 Judge's Awards. $125 First, $75 Second Prize each to ceramics-pottery, sculpture (all media), other media (all sections).

JUDGING: By 1 professional judge. Not responsible for loss or damage.

ENTRY FEE: $25 for 7x11-foot exhibit space.

DEADLINES: Entry, September. Event, October.

251

Art Fair USA
Wisconsin Festivals, Inc.
Dennis R. Hill, Director
3233 South Villa Circle
West Allis, Wisconsin 53227 U.S.A.
Tel: (414) 321-4566

Entry March, September

National; **entry open to U.S. artists age 18 and over;** biannual in April, November; established 1968. Average statistics (all sections): 200 entrants, 15,000 attendance, $80,000 total sales. Held at Wisconsin State Fair Park for 2 days. Have entertainment, demonstrations. Tickets: $1.50 (children under 12 free). Also sponsor nonjuried Crafts Fair USA, Holiday Craft and Gift Show.

CRAFTS FAIR: Ceramics, Glass, Sculpture, Enamel (including blown, stained glass), original. Entrants provide and attend sales displays. Submit 5 slides or photos, resume for entry review. Competition includes visual arts, photography, other crafts.

AWARDS: $1000 in Cash Awards.

JUDGING: By 2 professors.

SALES TERMS: Sales compulsory. No commission charge.

ENTRY FEE: $75 for 10x10-foot exhibit space (refundable).

DEADLINES: Entry, March, September. Event, April, November.

252

John Michael Kohler Arts Center Outdoor Arts Festival
Mary Jo Ballschmider, Manager
608 New York Avenue
P. O. Box 489
Sheboygan, Wisconsin 53081 U.S.A.
Tel: (414) 458-6144

Entry May

International; **entry open to artists age 18 and over;** annual in July; established 1970. Purpose: to provide educational-cultural experiences; sales outlet for artists. Sponsored by John Michael Kohler Arts Center. Average statistics (all sections): 135 entrants (maximum), 11 awards, 23,000 attendance. Held in John Michael Kohler Arts Center in Sheboygan for 2 days. Have entertainment, children's workshops, exhibitions, sales gallery, food service. Also sponsor exhibitions, classes, workshops, performing arts programs.

CRAFTS FAIR: Ceramics, Glass, Sculpture, original; unlimited entry. Entrants provide and attend sales displays. Submit 5 35mm slides of minimum 3 works (include 1 slide of each medium, 1 of display unit) for entry review; resume for publicity. No kits, commercial molds, copies. Competition includes photography, visual arts, other crafts.

AWARDS: $1200 in Cash Awards (includes all sections).

JUDGING: By professional artist-educator. Based on entire presentation.

SALES TERMS: Sales compulsory. No commission charge.

ENTRY FEE: $25 (refundable) for 10x12-foot booth space (1 artist per space).

DEADLINES: Entry, May. Event, July.

CRAFTS FAIRS, FESTIVALS (Ceramics, Pottery, Sculpture, General Crafts, Mixed Media)

Crafts Fairs, Festivals, Shows, Sales accepting CERAMICS, POTTERY, SCULPTURE, GENERAL CRAFTS, MIXED MEDIA (listed alphabetically by state). Attendance usually required.

253

Eastern Shore Art Association (ESAA) Outdoor Art Show
Ruth McMillan, Registrar
P. O. Box 443
Fairhope, Alabama 36532 U.S.A.
Tel: (205) 928-2228, 928-5188

Entry March

National; **entry open to U.S.;** annual in March; established 1971. Formerly called FAIRHOPE ARTS AND CRAFTS to 1971. Purpose: to promote artists; interest in art. Average statistics (all sections): 150 entrants (maximum), 30 winners.Held in Fairhope for 3 days. Have Eastern Shore Art Academy (quarterly classes), workshops, lectures, films.

CRAFTS FAIR: Pottery, Sculpture, **Mixed Media,** original. Entrants provide and attend sales displays. No copies, items made from commercial molds, kits, patterns. Competition includes visual arts, photography, other crafts.

AWARDS: Cash Prizes and Ribbons.

JUDGING: By 2 college faculty members. Not responsible for loss or damage.

SALES TERMS: Sales compulsory. No commission charge.

ENTRY FEE: $40 for 10x10-foot exhibit.

DEADLINES: Entry, event, March.

254

Sacramento Potters Group Pot Show
John Hunter, Chair
8329 Marina Greens Way
Sacramento, California 95826 U.S.A.
Tel: (916) 381-2935

Entry May

Regional; **entry open to Sacramento Valley;** annual in June; established 1976. Purpose: to promote pottery as a hobby. Sponsored and supported by Sacramento Potters Group. Average statistics: 30 entrants, 30 entries, 10 awards. Held at Country Club Plaza Shopping Center in Sacramento for 2 days. Publish *Seconds* (newsletter). Second contact: John Reiger, 5301 Harte Way, Sacramento, California 95822.

CRAFTS FAIR: Pottery, original, handcrafted. Entrants provide and attend sales display. Submit 2 photos, slides for entry review. No molds.

AWARDS: Awards to best of show, wheel work, handbuilt, display. Judge's Award. Potter's Choice Award. Cash, Merchandise Awards.

JUDGING: By 1 juror. Sponsor may photograph entries for publicity. Not responsible for loss or damage.

ENTRY FEE: $45 for 10x15-foot exhibit space. No sales commission charge.

DEADLINES: Entry, May. Event, June.

255

Affair on the Square Sidewalk Art Show
Chattahoochee Valley Art Association
William B. Gay, Director
112 Hines Street
P. O. Box 921
LaGrange, Georgia 30241 U.S.A.
Tel: (404) 882-3267

Entry April

International; **entry open to professional artists;** annual in May; established 1963. Sponsored by Chattahoochee Valley Art Association. Held outdoors in LaGrange for 2 days. Have auditorium in case of rain. Also sponsor LaGrange National Competition, Harvest Heyday Arts and Crafts Show.

CRAFTS FAIR: Pottery, General Crafts; 4 works per entrant. Entrants provide and attend sales displays. Competition for some awards includes photography, visual arts, other crafts.

AWARDS: Up to $1000 in Purchase Awards (all sections). $75 Merit Award and Blue Ribbon to best, each section. One exhibitor chosen for 1-person show at Gallery (all sections). 10 Honorable Mention Ribbons.

JUDGING: By art professional. Not responsible for loss or damage.

ENTRY FEE: $25 (individual), $40 (group) for maximum 10 linear feet (5x5- or 5x10-foot hanging panel) or

equivalent table space. No sales commission charge.

DEADLINES: Entry, April. Event, judging, May.

256

Riverbend Mall Arts and Crafts Fair
Nancy L. Smith, Marketing Director
Riverbend Mall
Riverbend Drive and Turner McCall Blvd.
Rome, Georgia 30161 U.S.A.
Tel: (404) 295-4828

Entry June

Regional; **entry open to Southeast U.S.;** annual in July; established 1976. Purpose: to encourage quality craftspersons to exhibit and attract public to mall. Sponsored by Riverbend Mall Merchant Association. Average statistics: 80 entrants, 14,000 attendance. Held at Riverbend Mall for 2 days. Have pegboard, table rentals, participant demonstrations.

CRAFTS FAIR: Ceramics, Pottery, original. Entrants provide and attend sales displays. Submit slides, photos for entry review. Categories: Ceramics, Pottery, Miscellaneous Crafts. Competition for some awards includes other crafts. Also have visual arts, photography sections.

AWARDS: $100 Best of Show Award (includes all crafts). $50 First, $25 Second, $10 Third Place to each category. Ribbons.

JUDGING: By 1 art professional. Not responsible for loss or damage.

ENTRY FEE: $35 for 15x8-foot exhibit space. No sales commission charge.

DEADLINES: Entry, June. Event, July.

257

Allentown Outdoor Art Festival
Allentown Village Society
Chair of Entries
P. O. Box 1566
Ellicott Station
Buffalo, New York 14205 U.S.A.
Tel: (716) 881-4269

Entry March

International; entry open to all; annual in June; established 1958. Purpose: to promote arts, crafts, community. Sponsored by Allentown Village Society (nonprofit). Average statistics (all sections): 480 entrants, 25 states and provinces, 500 entrants maximum, 36 awards, 250,000 attendance. Held in Allentown Village in Buffalo for 2 days. Also sponsor poster competition.

CRAFTS FAIR: Ceramics, Pottery, original, handcrafted. May use commercial items if incidental to original creation. Entrants provide and attend sales displays. Submit 2 or 4 35mm slides per media for entry review. No greenware, kits, molds. Divisions: Abstract, Realistic. Competition for some awards includes visual arts, photography, other crafts.

CREATIVE HARD CRAFTS FAIR: All Types (including glass). No divisions; novelty crafts, kits, molds. Other requirements, restrictions same as for Crafts Fair.

AWARDS: $1000 Best of Show Award (includes all sections). $150 First, $100 Second, $50 Third Award to pottery, ceramics (each division), hard creative crafts.

JUDGING: Entry review and awards judging by jury. Based on points system. Not responsible for loss or damage.

ENTRY FEE: $5, plus $50 for 15-foot exhibit space (limit 1 space per exhibitor).

DEADLINES: Entry, March. Event, awards, June.

258

Center Square Art Fair
Community Art League, Inc., of Easton
Pam LaDuca, Coordinator
39 North Fifth Avenue
Easton, Pennsylvania 18042 U.S.A.
Tel: (215) 253-1487

Entry September

International; entry open to all; annual in September; established 1966. Purpose: to provide competition, opportunity to display, sell original artwork in festival environment. Sponsored by Community Art League, Downtown Improvement Group of Easton. Average statistics (all sections): 100 entrants, 21 winners. Held at Center Square in Easton for 1 day. Have parking, exhibition screens, art raffle drawings, music. Also sponsor Portrait of the Forks of the Delaware Exhibition, gallery shows, art classes. Second contact: Downtown Improvement Group, 157 S. Fourth Street, Easton, Pennsylvania 18042; tel: (215) 258-2881.

CRAFTS FAIR: Pottery, original. Entrants provide and attend sales displays. No copies, greenware. Divisions: Adult, Youth. Competition includes visual arts, photography, other crafts.

AWARDS: (Includes all sections): $700 in Awards. Best of Show, First, Second, Third Prizes to crafts. Honorable Mention Ribbons.

JUDGING: By 3 jurors. Not responsible for loss or damage.

ENTRY FEE: $10 ($5 youth) for 10

linear feet. No sales commission charge.

DEADLINES: Entry, August. Event, September.

259

Tullahoma Fine Art and Crafts Festival
Tullahoma Fine Arts Center
Lucy F. Hollis
401 South Jackson Street
Tullahoma, Tennessee 37388 U.S.A.
Tel: (615) 455-1234

Entry May

International; entry open to all; annual in May; established 1969. Sponsored by Tullahoma Fine Arts Center. Supported by local businesses. Average statistics (all sections): 150 entrants, 10,000 attendance. Held in Tullahoma for 2 days. Tickets: 50¢. Also sponsor annual Christmas Boutique, monthly classes, workshops.

CRAFTS FAIR: Ceramics, Pottery, Sculpture, original, handcrafted. Completed in previous 3 years. Entrants provide sales displays. Submit 1 or 2 pieces for jurying. No copies eligible for prizes (except purchase awards). Competition includes fine art, photography, other crafts.

AWARDS: $100 to best of show. $25 to best designed booth. $300 in other Cash Prizes. $3500 in Purchase Prizes. Ribbons to first, second, third place. Gift Certificates.

JUDGING: By jury. Not responsible for loss or damage.

ENTRY FEE: $30 for each 15x15-foot exhibit space. No sales commission charge.

DEADLINES: Entry, event, May.

260

Norfolk Granby Mall Art Show
Downtown Norfolk Development Corporation
Robbie Levine, Associate Director
Suite 101
201 Granby Mall
Norfolk, Virginia 23510 U.S.A.
Tel: (804) 623-1757

Entry May

International; entry open to all; annual in June; established 1980. Purpose: to support arts and cultural events of Norfolk. Sponsored by Downtown Norfolk Development Corporation. Average statistics (all sections): 125 entrants, 13 awards. Held in downtown Norfolk Granby Mall for 3 days.

CRAFTS FAIR: Ceramics, Pottery, original. Entrants provide and attend sales displays. Competition includes arts, photography, other crafts.

AWARDS: $5000 in Purchase Awards. $600 Best of Show Award. 10 $100 Excellence Awards. $100 Special Artist's Choice Award. Ribbons.

JUDGING: By 2 jurors.

ENTRY FEE: $30 for 6x8-foot space. $50 for 2 spaces. No sales commission charge.

DEADLINES: Entry, May. Event, June.

261

Virginia Beach Boardwalk Art Show
Virginia Beach Art Center
Joseph White, Chair
1711 Arctic Avenue
Virginia Beach, Virginia 23451
U.S.A. Tel: (804) 428-9294

Entry February

National; **entry open to U.S.;** annual in June; established 1955. Sponsored by Virginia Beach Arts Center. Average statistics (all sections): 900 entrants, 23 awards, 100,000 attendance, $350,000 total sales. Held on Virginia Beach Boardwalk for 5 days. Have previous 2 years' award-winners special exhibit. Also sponsor Virginia Beach Neptune Show

CRAFTS FAIR: Ceramics, Pottery, original; unlimited entry (2-person team counts as 1). Entrants provide and attend sales displays. Submit 3 35mm slides for entry review. No commercial reproductions, kits, previous award-winners. Competition includes visual arts, sculpture, photography, other crafts.

AWARDS: (Includes all sections): $2000 Best in Show Purchase Award. $1000 Distinction Award. 8 $200 Excellence Awards. 10 $100 Merit Awards. 3 $100 Special Awards.

JUDGING: Entry review by crafts experts. Awards judging by 3 qualified, nationally recognized judges. Not responsible for loss or damage.

ENTRY FEE: $10 plus $50 (refundable) for 7x8x6-foot (hxwxd) exhibit space (maximum 2 spaces per entrant). No sales commission charge.

DEADLINES: Entry, February. Judging, event, June.

CRAFTS FAIRS, FESTIVALS (Ceramics, Sculpture, General Crafts, Mixed Media)

Crafts Fairs, Festivals, Shows, Sales accepting CERAMICS, SCULPTURE, GENERAL CRAFTS, MIXED MEDIA

(listed alphabetically by state). Attendance usually required.

$\boxed{262}$

Cocoa Village Art Festival
Sue Nesbit, Chair
P. O. Box 1967
Cocoa, Florida 32922 U.S.A.
Tel: (305) 636-3131, 452-8468

Entry August

International; entry open to all; annual in October; established 1973. Sponsored by Cocoa Village Autumn Art Festival. Average 300 entrants (all sections). Held in Cocoa Village for 2 days.

CRAFTS FAIR: Ceramics, Sculpture, General Crafts, original, handcrafted; minimum 6 pieces per category per entrant. Produced in previous 2 years. Entrants provide and attend sales displays. Submit maximum 4 35mm slides per category, representative of work for entry review. No commercial molds, dough art, kits. Competition for some awards includes visual arts. Also have photography, student sections.

AWARDS: $400 Best of Category, 4 $100 Merit Awards each to ceramics, creative crafts (all media), sculpture (includes visual arts, all crafts). $3000 in Purchase Awards. $200 Best Display Award (includes all sections). *Student section:* $50 Best of Show Award. 2 $25 Merit Awards each to K-6, 7-9, 10-12 grades.

JUDGING: By panel of 2 jurors. Sponsor may withhold awards. Not responsible for loss or damage.

ENTRY FEE: $40 per category for 6x12-foot exhibit space (refundable). Student section: free, no advanced registration.

DEADLINES: Entry, August. Acceptance, September. Event, October.

263

Exponova Art Exhibition and Competition
Nova University
3501 University Drive
Coral Springs, Florida 33065 U.S.A.
Tel: (305) 753-3300

Entry March

International; entry open to all; annual in April. Sponsored by Nova University. Held on grounds of Hilton Inn in Coral Springs for 2 days. Have evening entertainment.

CRAFTS FAIR: Ceramics, Sculpture, original, presented for display. Entrants provide and attend sales displays. Submit 4 35mm slides (including 1 of display) for entry review. No commercial displays, shared spaces. Competition includes visual art, photography, other crafts.

AWARDS: $750 Best of Show Award. 5 $250 Merit Awards.

JUDGING: By museum personnel, professional artists. Not responsible for loss or damage.

ENTRY FEE: $5 jury fee plus $45 booth fee. No sales commission charge.

DEADLINES: Entry, March. Event, April.

264

Gasparilla Sidewalk Art Festival
Leslie Osterweil, Board President
P. O. Box 10591
Tampa, Florida 33679 U.S.A.
Tel: (813) 253-3292

Entry November

International; entry open to all; annual in March; established 1971. Named after Jose Gaspar, legendary pirate. Purpose: to bring quality craftswork to Tampa; provide funds for artists to continue work. Sponsored by Gasparilla Sidewalk Art Festival Board. Supported by art patrons, local businesses. Maximum 300 participants. Held by river in Tampa for 2 days.

CRAFTS FAIR: Ceramics, General Crafts. Completed in previous 3 years. Entrants provide and attend sales displays. Submit 3 35mm slides for entry review (winners of previous 3 years automatically accepted). No commercial molds. Competition includes visual art, photography, other crafts.

AWARDS: (Includes all sections): $3000 Best of Show Award. $2000 Gasparilla Award. 3 $1000 Merit Awards. 10 $400 Honorable Mentions. 10 $300 Juror Awards.

JUDGING: Entry review by selection committee. Awards judging by internationally known artist. Not responsible for loss or damage.

SALES TERMS: Sales compulsory.

ENTRY FEE: $10 jury fee. $25 (refundable) for 8x10-foot exhibit space. Entrant pays return postage.

DEADLINES: Entry, November. Acceptance, January. Event, March.

265

Halifax Art Festival
Museum of Arts and Sciences Guild
Art Festival Chair
P. O. Box 504
Ormand Beach, Florida 32074
U.S.A. Tel: (904) 255-0285

Entry August

International; entry open to all; annual in November; established 1972. Formerly called HALIFAX SIDE-

WALK ART SHOW to 1972. Sponsored and supported by Museum of Arts and Sciences, business leaders. Average statistics (all sections): 175 participants (maximum), 60,000 attendance. Held at Old Ormand Hotel (founded 1888) in Ormand Beach for 2 days. Have concessions, entertainment. Second contact: 1040 Museum Blvd., Daytona Beach, Florida 32074.

CRAFTS FAIR: Ceramics, Sculpture; 4 entries minimum. Completed in previous 2 years. Entrants provide and attend sales displays. Submit 3 slides of work in each category for entry review. No caricatures, jewelry, kits, copies; partners, group entrants, commercial reproductions. Competition includes visual arts, photography, other crafts.

AWARDS: (Includes all sections): $500 Judges' Choice Award. 8 $300 Distinction Awards. 30 $100 Merit Awards. $800 Museum Purchase Awards. Museum Aquisition Award. ($6700 total prize money).

JUDGING: By 2 art professionals. Not responsible for loss or damage.

ENTRY FEE: $35 for 10x10-foot covered, or 12x12-foot uncovered space.

DEADLINES: Entry, August. Acceptance, February. Event, November.

| 266 |

Mainsail Arts Festival
City of St. Petersburg
Phil Whitehouse, Coordinator
P. O. Box 2842
St. Petersburg, Florida 33731 U.S.A.
Tel: (813) 893-7732

Entry February

International; entry open to all; annual in March; established 1976. Formerly called MAINSAIL SIDEWALK ARTS FESTIVAL. Purpose: to present outstanding art to St. Petersburg area in informal atmosphere. Sponsored by City of St. Petersburg, St. Petersburg Art Commission, Junior League Art Center. Average statistics (all sections): 150 entrants, 30 awards, 20,000 attendance. Held in St. Petersburg for 2 days. Also sponsor Performing Arts Festival. Second contact: Glenn Anderson. St. Petersburg Arts Commission, 1450 16th Street North, St. Petersburg, Florida 33704.

CRAFTS FAIR: Ceramics, Sculpture, original; minimum 4 per entrant. Entrants provide and attend sales displays. Submit 3 35mm slides for entry review. No molds, kits, copies, commercially produced entries. Competition for some awards includes visual arts, photography, vanguard, other crafts.

AWARDS: $9000 in Cash Awards. $500 First, $250 Second Award to each category. *Includes all sections:* $1500 Best of Show Award. 15 $150 Merit Awards. Special Patron Award.

JUDGING: Entry review by community arts patrons. Awards judging by 2 judges. Based on quality of entire submission. Not responsible for loss or damage.

SALES TERMS: Sales optional. No commission charge.

ENTRY FEE:$7.50 plus $25 (refundable) for 12x12-foot exhibit space.

DEADLINES: Entry, February. Judging, event, March.

| 267 |

Space Coast Art Festival
Gloria Farinella, Registration Chair
P. O. Box 135
Cocoa Beach, Florida 32931 U.S.A.
Tel: (305) 783-4371

Entry August

International; entry open to all; annual in November; established 1964. Purpose: to promote furtherance of cultural development. Sponsored by Space Coast Festival, Cocoa Beach Women's Club, City of Cocoa Beach. Average statistics (all sections): 275 accepted entrants, 100,000 attendance. Held in Cocoa Beach (south of Kennedy Space Center) for 2 days.

CRAFTS FAIR: Ceramics, Sculpture, General Crafts, original. Produced in previous 2 years. Entrants provide and attend sales displays. Submit 35mm slides each section for entry review. No items produced from commercial molds, displays. Competition for some awards includes visual arts, photography, other crafts.

AWARDS: $500 each to best in ceramics, general crafts, sculpture. 2 $100 Merit Awards to ceramics, 2 to general crafts, 1 to sculpture. *Includes all sections:* $100 to best display. Purchase Awards. Honorable Mentions.

JUDGING: Entry review by jury. Awards judging by 2 art educators. Not responsible for loss or damage.

SALES TERMS: Sales optional. No commission charge.

ENTRY FEE: $35 per 12-foot exhibit space. Entrants pay return postage.

DEADLINES: Entry, August. Notification, September. Event, November.

| 268 |

Walt Disney World Festival of the Masters
Pat Phaneuf, Coordinator
P. O. Box 35
Lake Buena Vista, Florida 32830
U.S.A. Tel: (305) 824-5635

Entry July

International; **entry open to previous prizewinners;** annual in November; established 1975. Formerly called ART FESTIVAL IN THE VILLAGE to 1979. Purpose: to provide opportunity for public to purchase originals by award-winning artists; promote visual arts. Sponsored by Lake Buena Vista Communities Inc. Average statistics (all sections): 200 entrants, 27 states, 45 awards, 100,000 attendance. Held at Walt Disney World Village in Florida for 3 days.

CRAFTS FAIR: Ceramics, Sculpture, Mixed Media, original; limit 4 per entrant in each of 2 categories. Entrants provide and attend sales displays. Submit 3 35mm slides of work for entry review. No art supplies, picture frames, kits, molds. Competition includes visual arts, photography, other crafts.

ELIGIBILITY: Open to entrants having won best of show, first 3 places, merit, public, or exhibitors awards in a recognized art show, festival or fair in the previous 3 years.

AWARDS: (Includes all sections): $700 First, $350 Second, $175 Third Prize each to ceramics, sculpture, creative crafts, mixed media. 19 $100 Merit Awards. Judge's Selection Ribbons. Purchase Awards for Disney World Permanent Collection.

JUDGING: Entry review by selection committee. Awards judging by 3 experts. Sponsor may photograph entries for publicity. Not responsible for loss or damage.

ENTRY FEE: $100 (refundable) for 120-square-foot booth space. Entrant pays return postage. Sales optional.

DEADLINES: Entry, judging, July. Event, November.

269

Spring Fling
Wichita Falls Museum and Art Center
Guild
Two Eureka Circle
Wichita Falls, Texas 76308 U.S.A.
Tel: (817) 692-0923

Entry November

International; entry open to all; annual in April; established 1972. Purpose: to provide showcase for dedicated artists. Sponsored by Wichita Falls Museum and Art Center Guild. Average statistics (all sections): 80 entrants (maximum 90), 2 countries, 15 awards, 15,000 attendance, $1200 sales per entrant. Held in Wichita Falls for 2 days. Tickets: 50¢-$1.

CRAFTS FAIR: Ceramics, Sculpture, original; entry unlimited, maximum 2 sections. Pottery to be wheel-thrown or handbuilt. Entrants provide and attend sales displays. Submit 4 slides per category (1 slide of entrant and display), resume for entry review. No copies, molded ceramics, dough art. Competition includes photography, visual arts, other crafts.

AWARDS: 5 $100 Cash Awards and Gold Arch Medals. 10 $50 Cash Awards and Gallery of Honor Certificates to outstanding entries. Purchase Awards.

JUDGING: By professionals, academics, Based on quality, creativity. Not responsible for loss or damage.

SALES TERMS: Sales compulsory. No commission charge.

ENTRY FEE: $50 ($25 students) for 8x8-foot booth space or 12x12-foot table (1 booth space per entrant).

DEADLINES: Entry, November. Judging, event, April.

CRAFTS FAIRS, FESTIVALS (Clay, Glass)

Crafts Fairs, Festivals, Shows, sales accepting CLAY, GLASS, PLASTIC, PORCELAIN, RAKU, STONEWARE (listed alphabetically by state). Attendance usually required.

270

Citrus County Festival of the Arts
Citrus County Art League
Vivien Gross, President
1206 Paradise Avenue
Crystal River, Florida 32629 U.S.A.
Tel: (904) 795-2970

Entry November

International; entry open to all; annual in November; established 1971. Purpose: to improve community awareness of art; provide showcase for artists, performers. Sponsored and supported by Citrus County Art League, Citrus County Chamber of Commerce. Average 252 entrants (all sections). Held in Inverness, Florida for 1 day. Have entertainment, refreshments, participant demonstrations. Also sponsor monthly lectures, demonstrations, Fine Arts Auction Banquet. Second contact: Citrus County Chamber of Commerce, P. O. Box 416, Inverness, Florida 32650.

CRAFTS FAIR: Clay, Glass, original. Entrants provide and attend sales displays. Divisions: Adult, Junior (7th-12th grades). Competition for some awards includes other crafts. Also have visual arts, photography sections.

HANDIWORK FAIR: All Types (including mold-poured ceramics, greenware), original. Entrants provide and attend sales displays. Competition for some awards includes other crafts. Also have visual arts, photography sections.

AWARDS: (Includes all sections): $3000 in Best of Show, Excellence Awards. $3000 in Purchase Awards. Ribbons.

JUDGING: By 1 academic each division.

ENTRY FEE: $20 for 10x10-foot exhibit space. No sales commission charge.

DEADLINES: Entry, Judging, event, November.

271

Gainesville Spring Arts Festival
Lona Stein, Coordinator
Santa Fe Community College (SFCC)
P. O. Box 1530
Gainesville, Florida 32602 U.S.A.
Tel: (904) 377-5161, ext. 383;
372-1976

Entry January

International; entry open to all; annual in April; established 1970. Sponsored by SFCC, SFCC Endowment Corporation. Supported by NEA, Fine Arts Council of Florida. Recognized by Gainesville Area Chamber of Commerce. Average statistics (all sections): 225 exhibitors (maximum), 63,000 attendance. Held in Gainesville for 2 days. Have children's arts-crafts display, instruction areas; entertainment.

CRAFTS FAIR: 3-Dimensional Clay, Glass, original, handcrafted, appropriate for family viewing. Submit 3 35mm slides per category for entry review. No kits, molds, mass-produced work, imports. Competition includes other 3D crafts. Also have 2D section.

AWARDS: (Includes all sections): $500 Best of Show Award. 5 $200 Distinction Awards. 5 $100 Merit Awards. 5 $50 Honorable Mentions. $250 Excellence Awards each to clay, glass, other crafts.

JUDGING: By 2 nationally prominent judges. Not responsible for loss or damage.

ENTRY FEE: $5 per category. $35 for for 15x10-foot exhibit space.

DEADLINES: Entry, January. Notification, February. Event, April.

272

Saint Augustine Arts and Crafts Festival
Frederick White, Director
P. O. Box 547
St. Augustine, Florida 32084 U.S.A.
Tel: (904) 829-8175

Entry February

International; entry open to all; annual in April; established 1964. Purpose: to promote an understanding of arts and crafts; provide opportunity for artists to show and sell work. Sponsored by St. Augustine Arts and Crafts Council (nonprofit). Average statistics: 140 entrants (maximum), 21 awards. Held at Plaza de la Constitution in St. Augustine for 2 days. Also sponsor Fall Arts and Crafts Show.

CRAFTS FAIR: Clay, Blown Glass, Mixed Media. Entrants provide and attend sales displays. Submit 3 slides per medium and 1 of entire exhibit for entry review. No commercial kits, molds, patterns. Competition for some awards includes visual arts, photography, other crafts.

AWARDS: $650 Award of Distinction to best each section. 11 $250 Merit Awards (includes all sections).

JUDGING: By 2 jurors.

SALES TERMS: Sales compulsory.

ENTRY FEE: $5 jury fee plus $65 for booth space (one exhibitor per booth).

DEADLINES: Entry,   February, Event, March.

273

Baton Rouge Fall Crafts Festival

Arts and Humanities Council of
Greater Baton Rouge
Richard Sabino, Festival Director
427 Laurel Street
Baton Rouge, Louisiana 70801
U.S.A. Tel: (504) 344-8558

Entry August

International; entry open to all; annual in October-November; established 1975. Purpose: to provide market for top quality craftspersons; showcase local and national artisans' work. Sponsored by Arts and Humanities Council of Greater Baton Rouge. Average statistics (all sections): 4500 entries, 45 entrants (maximum), 25,-000 attendance, $1000 sales per entrant, $45,000 total sales. Held at Old State Capitol grounds in downtown Baton Rouge for 2 days. Have auction, entertainment, food and drink. Publish *Discover* magazine-newspaper.

CRAFTS FAIR: Clay, Glass, original; unlimited entry. Entrants provide and attend sales displays. Require artists to occupy at least 1 booth space. Submit 6 slides of work for entry review. Competition includes fiber, leather, metal, woodcrafts.

AWARDS: $2400 in Cash and Purchase Awards (includes all sections).

JUDGING: Entry review by 3 experts, based on quality and professionalism. Awards judging by 1 professional of national reputation, based on merit of entire presentation. Not responsible for loss or damage.

ENTRY FEE: $5 jury fee. $50 for

8x10-foot booth space, plus 1 art work for auction, or $70 only. No sales commission charge.

DEADLINES: Entry, August. Event, October-November.

274

Greater Columbus Arts Festival Street Fair

Greater Columbus Arts Council
Street Fair Committee
33 North Third Street
Columbus, Ohio 43215 U.S.A.
Tel: (614) 224-2606

Entry February

Regional; **entry open to Central Ohio;** annual in June; established 1957. Purpose: to showcase the arts. Sponsored by Greater Columbus Arts Council. Recognized by City of Columbus, Columbus Area Chamber of Commerce. Average statistics (all sections): 285 entries, 120 entrants, 100,-000 attendance, $1000 sales per entrant. Held in downtown Columbus Ohio State House grounds for 3 days. Have concerts, special performances, children's activities, art exhibitions, crafts demonstrations, free entrant parking, security. Also sponsor in-school artist residency program, seminars.

CRAFTS FAIR: Clay, Glass, original; limit 1 per entrant (for competition). Entrants provide and attend sales displays. Submit 3 slides, brief resume for entry review. No commercial molds, reproductions, kits, manufactured works. Competition includes photography, visual arts, other crafts.

AWARDS: (Includes all sections): $200 Best of Show Award. 6 $100 Juror's Choice Award. Best of Display Award.

JUDGING: By 5 art experts. Sponsor may photograph entries for publicity. Not responsible for loss or damage.

ENTRY FEE: $5 jury fee plus $80 for 10x10-foot booth space.

DEADLINES: Entry, February. Registration, April. Event, June.

275

Handmade: Old and New Ways Crafts Fair

Appalachian Center for Crafts
Faye Watts-Maxwell
Route 3
Smithville, Tennessee 37166 U.S.A.
Tel: (615) 597-6801

Entry July

International; entry open to all; annual in September-October; established 1981. Purpose: to present a meeting place for regional crafts tradition and contemporary practices. Sponsored by Division of Tennessee Arts Commission, Tennessee Technological University. Supported by Tourist Association of Upper Cumberlands, State of Tennessee, Junior Women's League, community groups. Average statistics: 100 entrants, 32 awards, 20,000 attendance. Held in Smithville for 2 days. Tickets: $2. Also sponsor workshops, summer and educational programs, apprenticeships, internships, auction.

CRAFTS FAIR: Clay, Glass (contemporary, traditional), handcrafted. Entrants provide and attend sales displays. Submit 5 slides representative of work for entry review. Also have visual arts, photography, other crafts.

AWARDS: $250 Best of Show Award (includes all sections). $100 First, $75 Second, $50 Third Place Award to each media. $25 Merit Awards. Purchase Awards.

JUDGING: By nationally renown juror. Not responsible for loss or damage.

SALES TERMS: Sales optional. 10% commission charge.

ENTRY FEE: $5 jury fee plus $75 booth fee (professional), $50 (amateur).

DEADLINES: Entry, July. Notification, September. Event, September-October.

276

Stratton Arts Festival

Tricia N. Hayes, Development Director
Base Lodge
Stratton Mountain, Vermont 05155 U.S.A. Tel: (802) 297-2200

Entry August

State; **entry open to Vermont professionals;** annual in September-October; established 1964. Purpose: to create cultural atmosphere, display and present new ideas and art forms. Supported by Agency of Development and Community Affairs, Vermont Council on the Arts Agency, NEA. Average statistics (all sections): 1500 entries, 300 entrants, 3 scholarships, 15,000 attendance, $120,000 sales. Held at Base Lodge in Stratton Mountain for 1 month. Having lodging, restaurants, lectures, demonstrations, performing arts programs, exhibits, Featured Artist Series. Tickets: $1-$2. Second contact: P. O. Box 251, Manchester Center, Vermont 05255.

CRAFTS FAIR: Clay (including porcelain, raku, stoneware). Submit slides for entry review. Competition includes visual arts, music, other crafts.

AWARDS: (Includes all sections): 3 $1000 Elinor Janeway Cash Awards.

Best of Show Award. Media Recognition Awards.

JUDGING: Entry review and awards judging by 1 judge. Based on technical excellence, creative use of medium. Sponsor insures against loss or damage.

SALES TERMS: 30% commission charge.

ENTRY FEE: None.

DEADLINES: Entry, August. Judging, September. Event, September-October.

277
Neptune Festival Art Show
Virginia Beach Arts Center
Entries Chair
1711 Arctic Avenue
Virginia Beach, Virginia 23451
U.S.A. Tel: (804) 428-9294
Entry August

Regional; **entry open to U.S. East Coast;** annual in September; established 1975. Sponsored by Virginia Beach Arts Center. Average statistics (all sections): 200 entrants, 15 awards, $100,000 in total sales, 30,000 attendance. Held on ocean boardwalk in Virginia Beach for 3 days. Also sponsor Virginia Beach Boardwalk Art Show.

CRAFTS FAIR: Clay, Glass, original. Entrants provide and attend sales displays. No commercial reproductions, objects made from kits. Competition includes arts, photography, other crafts.

AWARDS: $750 First, $500 Second, $250 Third Prizes. Honorable Mention Ribbons.

JUDGING: By 1 judge. Not responsible for loss or damage.

ENTRY FEE: $25 for 4x7-foot rail space; $30 for 4x7-foot lawn space. No sales commission charge.

DEADLINES: Entry, August. Event, September.

278
Wisconsin Designer Craftsmen Morning Glory Fair
Barbara Pelowski, President
2742 North 95th Street
Milwaukee, Wisconsin 53222 U.S.A.
Tel: (414) 774-6861, 425-2465
Entry May

State; **entry open to Wisconsin;** annual in August; established 1972. Purpose: to emphasize excellence in craftsmanship. Sponsored and supported by Wisconsin Designer Craftsmen, Charles Allis Art Museum. Held at 1630 East Royail Place in Milwaukee for 2 days. Have silent auction. Also sponsor annual exhibit, workshops, lectures, demonstrations. Second contact: 3927 North Maryland Avenue, Shorewood, Wisconsin 53211.

CRAFTS FAIR: Clay, Glass, Plastic, original. Entrants provide and attend sales displays. Submit 4 slides for entry review. Competition includes photography, other crafts.

AWARDS: Cash and Purchase Prizes.

JUDGING: Entry review by jury. Awards judging by 1 juror. Based on excellence in craftsmanship.

ENTRY FEE: $5 plus $30 for 8x10-foot exhibit space (includes membership).

DEADLINES: Entry, May. Acceptance, June. Event, August.

CRAFTS FAIRS, FESTIVALS (Clay, Glass, Pottery, Sculpture, Mixed Media)

Crafts Fairs, Festivals, Shows, Sales accepting CLAY, GLASS, POTTERY, SCULPTURE, MIXED MEDIA (listed alphabetically by state). Attendance usually required.

279

Leesburg Fun and Art Festival
Leesburg Chamber of Commerce
Bertha R. Walters, Chair
P. O. Box 1258
Leesburg, Florida 32748 U.S.A.
Tel: (904) 787-2131

Entry December

International; **entry open to age 14 and over;** annual in March; established 1978. Sponsored by Leesburg Chamber of Commerce, Leesburg Art Association. Average statistics (all sections): 230 entrant (250 maximum), 25,000 attendance. Held at Venetian Gardens in Leesburg for 2 days. Have entertainment, parking, security.

CRAFTS FAIR: Clay, Glass, Sculpture, original, handmade, ready for display. Entrants provide and attend sales displays. Submit photos or slides of work for entry review. No copies, kits, precast pottery from commercial molds, multiple units. Competition includes fiber, wood, metal; for some awards includes visual art, photography, other crafts.

AWARDS: $300 First Place Blue Ribbon, $100 Second Place Red Ribbon, $75 Third Place Yellow Ribbon, $50 Fourth Place White Ribbon to each section. *Includes all sections:* $1000 Best of Show Award. 4 $100 Green Ribbon Judges Awards. $1300 in Purchase Prizes.

JUDGING: Not specified.

ENTRY FEE: $25 for 8x10- or 10x12-foot booth space. No sales commission charge.

DEADLINES: Entry, December. Judging, event, March.

280

Plaza Arts Fair
Country Club Plaza Association
Catherine Rickbone, Public Relations Director
4625 Wornall Road
Kansas City, Missouri 64112 U.S.A.
Tel: (816) 753-0100

Entry July

International; entry open to all; annual in September; established 1932. Purpose: to provide opportunity for artists to exhibit, sell and demonstrate their work. Sponsored and supported by Country Club Plaza Merchants Association. Average statistics (all sections): 600 entrants, 140 finalists, 90,-000 attendance. Held at Country Club Plaza in Kansas City for 3 days. Have music, demonstrations, educational materials.

CRAFTS FAIR: Clay, Glass, Sculpture, original. Entrants provide and attend sales displays. Submit 6 35mm slides (including 1 of display) for entry review. No copies, mechanically produced reproductions, commercial molds, kits. Competition includes visual arts, other crafts.

AWARDS: $5000 in Cash Awards (includes all sections).

JUDGING: By panel of 4-5 national and local judges and 1 fair participant.

Based on excellence of entire presentation.

ENTRY FEE: $10 jury fee. $75 for 4x8-foot exhibit area. $10 for 6x8-foot screen or 3x8-foot table. No sales commission charge.

DEADLINES: Entry, July. Judging, event, September.

281

Independence Arts Council Art in the Park
Fran Allerheiligen, Secretary
P. O. Box 198
Independence, Kansas 67301 U.S.A.
Tel: (316) 331-4390

Entry May

National; **entry open to U.S.;** annual in July; established 1974. Purpose: to display and demonstrate artistic talent. Sponsored by Independence Arts Council, Kansas Arts Commission. Held in Riverside Park in Independence for 2 days. Have participant demonstrations, display facilities, security, hostesses, entertainment, sporting activities. Second contact: Independence Chamber of Commerce, 108 West Myrtle, Independence, Kansas 67301.

CRAFTS FAIR: Clay, Glass, Sculpture, original, handmade. Entrants provide and attend sales displays. Submit 3 35mm color slides, resume for entry review; monochrome photographs for publicity. No manufactured items, kits, machine reproductions, commercial casts. Competition for some awards includes visual arts, other crafts.

AWARDS: $50 First, $25 Second, $15 Third Place Awards. *Including all sections:* $100 Best of Show Award. $40 to most attractive exhibit. $20 Gift Certificate to best demonstration crafts (including sculpture).

JUDGING: By 1 experienced juror. Based on creativity and originality. Not responsible for loss or damage.

SALES TERMS: Sales optional. No commission charge.

ENTRY FEE: $20 for 7x9-foot exhibit space (including table or pegboard).

DEADLINES: Entry, May. Event, July.

282

Creative Artistic Marketing (CAM) Outdoor Arts and Crafts Festival
CAM Art Center
A. DiMartino, Director
Box 263-M
Bay Shore, New York 11706 U.S.A.
Tel: (516) 666-0025, 665-9047

Entry May

National; **entry open to U.S. professional artists;** annual in June; established 1978. Sponsored and supported by CAM, Greater Bay Shore Chamber of Commerce. Average 100,-000 attendance (all sections). Held on Main Street in Bay Shore for 2 days. Have participant demonstrations. Also sponsor CAM Juried Exhibits, Visual and Performing Arts Workshops, Holiday Gift Giving Miniature Works Sale. Second contact: Bay Shore Chamber of Commerce, 21-4th Avenue, Bay Shore, New York 11706.

CRAFTS FAIR: Clay, Pottery, Sculpture, Stain Lucite Etching, original. Entrants provide and attend sales displays. No imports, dealers. Competition includes visual arts, photography, other crafts.

AWARDS: $1000 in Cash Awards. Ribbons.

JUDGING: By 3 art critics. Not responsible for loss or damage.

ENTRY FEE: $25 for 25-foot exhibition space. $5 journal advertising. No sales commission charge.

DEADLINES: Entry, May. Event, June.

283

Fine Arts Association Outdoor Arts Festival
38660 Mentor Avenue
Willoughby, Ohio 44094 U.S.A.

Entry April

International; entry open to all; annual in July. Purpose: to develop interest in and understanding of arts in Northwestern Ohio. Sponsored by Fine Arts Association. Recognized by Ohio Arts Council. Average 100 entrants (all sections). Held in School of Fine Arts grounds in Willoughby for 3 days. Have theater performances, concerts, entertainment, exhibitions, security. Also sponsor fine arts, music and performing arts programs, exhibitions, classes for all ages.

CRAFTS FAIR: Clay, Pottery, Mixed Media (utilitarian items should have aesthetic quality), original; unlimited entry. Entrants provide and attend sales displays. Submit slides of each category for entry review. No kits, moldware, commercial patterns, manufactured pieces. Competition includes visual arts, photography, other crafts.

AWARDS: (Includes all sections): $150 Cash Award each to 2D and 3D work. $100 Cash Award to most attractively designed booth space.

JUDGING: Entry review by Board of Trustees Visual Arts Committee and Exhibits Director. Not responsible for loss or damage.

ENTRY FEE: $5 jury fee plus $25 for 12x15-foot booth space (additional $15 for electricity). No sales commission charge.

DEADLINES: Entry, April. Notification, May. Event, July.

284

Oklahoma City Festival of the Arts
Arts Council of Oklahoma City
Liz Eickman, Festival Coordinator
3014 Paseo
Oklahoma City, Oklahoma 73103
U.S.A. Tel: (405) 521-1426

Entry January

National; **entry open to U.S.;** annual in April; established 1967. Purpose: to celebrate arts, educate community in art, provide opportunity for art sales. Sponsored by Arts Council of Oklahoma City. Recognized by American Council on the Arts. Average statistics (all sections): 200 entrants, 400,000 attendance, $800,000 in total sales. Held at Civic Center Park in downtown Oklahoma City for 6 days. Have performing arts, children's activities, Youth Emporium, international foods. Also sponsor concurrent Print Tent, 3D Street Market ($150 for 10x10-foot exhibit space).

CRAFTS FAIR: Clay, Glass, Sculpture, original, handcrafted. Entrants provide and attend sales displays. Submit 5 35mm slides per medium for entry review. No commercial molds, kits. Competition includes visual arts, photography, other crafts.

AWARDS: Purchase Prizes.

JUDGING: Entry review by jury. Not responsible for loss or damage.

SALES TERMS: Sales compulsory. 20% commission charge.

ENTRY FEE: $50 for 6x8-foot vertical pegboard panel; fee refunded after $500 in sales.

DEADLINES: Entry, January. Event, April.

285

Williamsburg Sidewalk Art Jubilee
Williamsburg Shopping Center Merchants Association
Sandra Meadows, Promotions Director
6 Conway Road
Newport News, Virginia 23606
U.S.A. Tel: (804) 874-0067

Entry May

International; entry open to all; annual in June; established 1977. Sponsored by Williamsburg Shopping Center Merchants Association. Average statistics (all sections): 1000 entrants, 14 awards, 20,000 attendance. Held at shopping center in Newport News for 3 days.

CRAFTS FAIR: Clay, Glass, **Sculpture,** original. Entrants provide and attend sales displays. Submit photograph or slide for entry review. No work from professional plans or kits, premanufactured components, imported items, unfinished work, work in poor taste. Competition includes other crafts. Also have visual arts, photography sections.

AWARDS: $300 Best of Show Awards. $150 Awards of Distinction. 5 $50 Merit Awards. Honorable Mention Ribbons.

JUDGING: By 1 judge. Not responsible for loss or damage.

SALES TERMS: Sales optional. No commission charge.

ENTRY FEE: $20 (refundable) for each 12x5-foot (lxw) covered space (limit 2 per entrant).

DEADLINES: Entry, May. Judging, event, June.

286

Lakefront Festival of Arts
Milwaukee Art Museum at the War Memorial
750 North Lincoln Memorial Drive
Milwaukee, Wisconsin 53202 U.S.A.
Tel: (414) 271-9508, ext. 255

Entry January

National; entry open to U.S.; annual in June; established 1963. Sponsored by Friends of Art of the Milwaukee Art Museum, First Wisconsin Banks. Held on Milwaukee Art Museum lakefront for 3 days. Maximum 180 entrants. Have demonstrations, educational exhibits, silent auction, performances. Also sponsor design competition. Second contact: Sarah Wright Kinball, Barkin, Herman, Solochek & Paulsen, Inc., 777 East Wisconsin Avenue, Milwaukee, Wisconsin 53202.

CRAFTS FAIR: Clay, Glass, **Sculpture,** original. Produced in previous 2 years. Entrants provide and attend sales displays. Submit 6 slides of each entry, brief resume for entry review. Competition includes photography, visual arts, other crafts.

AWARDS: 10 $750 Cash Awards and Works of Art (includes all sections).

JUDGING: Entry review and awards judging by 3 art museum curators. Based on excellence of presentation. Not responsible for loss or damage.

ENTRY FEE: $12 per category. $75 for 5x12-foot outdoor, $100 for 5x14-foot indoor exhibit space.

DEADLINES: Entry, January. Acceptance, February. Event, June.

CRAFTS FAIRS, FESTIVALS (Glass, Pottery, Sculpture, Enamel, General Crafts)

Crafts Fairs, Festivals, Shows, Sales accepting GLASS, POTTERY, SCULPTURE, CLAY, ENAMEL, PLASTIC, PORCELAIN, RAKU, STONEWARE, GENERAL CRAFTS (listed alphabetically by state). Attendance usually required.

287

Honeysuckle Art Festival
Selma Art Guild
Beverly Letterman, Chair
4238 Dalley Drive
Selma, Alabama 36701 U.S.A.
Tel: (205) 875-7340, 874-6617

Entry April

International; entry open to all; annual in April; established 1972. Sponsored by Dallas County Chamber of Commerce, Selma-Dallas County Council on the Arts. Average 113 entrants (all sections). Held at George C. Wallace Community College in Selma for 1 day. Have participant demonstrations. Second contact: Rhea Smith, Registration Chair, 1109 Eighth Avenue, Selma, Alabama 36701; tel: (205) 872-3861.

CRAFTS FAIR: **Stained Glass, Pottery, Sculpture,** original; handmade, hand-tooled, handcrafted, or manmade by machine; limit 2 per entrant per category. Entrants provide and attend sales displays. Require hand-delivery. Submit 3 photographs, short biography for entry review plus monochrome glossy portrait for publicity. No kits, ceramics. Divisions:

Professional (including teachers), Amateurs. Also have visual arts, mixed media, other crafts sections.

AWARDS: Over $16,000 in Prizes. Historic Selma & Dallas County Art Award to Dallas County residents only.

JUDGING: By 2 jurors. Sponsor may withhold awards. Not responsible for loss or damage.

SALES TERMS: Sales preferred. No commission charge.

ENTRY FEE: $20 for 8x12-foot covered space; $15 for 12x12-foot uncovered space (1 entrant per booth).

DEADLINES: Entry, judging, event, April.

288

Castro Street Fair Art in the Park
Frank Pietronigro, Producer
140 Haight Street, #10
San Francisco, California 94102
U.S.A. Tel: (415) 552-5191

Entry June

Regional; **entry open to San Francisco Bay Area;** annual in October; established 1979. Purpose: to provide public education in art, exhibition and performance space for Bay Area artists. Sponsored and supported by Castro Street Fair. Average statistics (all sections): 2500 entries, 250 entrants, 3 awards, 30,000 attendance. Held in Golden Gate Park in San Francisco for 2 days. Have medical, childcare, security facilities; stage, display panels. Second contact: Linda Lorraine, Coordinator, 610 Cole Street #203, San Francisco, California 94117; tel: (415) 431-4872.

CRAFTS FAIR: **Glass, Sculpture.** Entrants provide and attend sales displays. Submit slides for entry review. Sculpture categories: Ceramics, Stone,

Mixed Media. Competition includes visual arts, photography, other crafts.

AWARDS: (Includes all sections): Best of Show Award. Second, Third Prizes.

JUDGING: By 3 judges. Based on originality. Not responsible for loss or damage.

SALES TERMS: Sales optional. No commission charge.

ENTRY FEE: $10.

DEADLINES: Entry, June. Notification, September. Judging, event, October.

289

Grand Junction Art Festival
Michael Shannon, Chair
P. O. Box 1774
Grand Junction, Colorado 81501
U.S.A. Tel: (303) 243-2411

Entry August

International; **entry open to professionals;** annual in September; established 1976. Purpose: to display and market professional art work. Sponsored by Grand Junction Art Festival Ltd. Supported by local business. Average statistics (all sections): 100 entrants, 25 awards, 10,000 attendance, $8500 sales. Held in Grand Junction for 2 days. Have entertainment.

CRAFTS FAIR: Glass, Pottery, Sculpture, original, handcrafted. Entrants provide and attend sales displays. Submit 5 slides per category for entry review. No works assembled from manufactured parts. Competition includes metalwork, textiles, visual arts, photography.

AWARDS: $1050 in Cash, Merit, and Purchase Awards (includes all sections).

JUDGING: By 2 judges.

SALES TERMS: Sales compulsory. No commission charge.

ENTRY FEE: $35 for unlimited space (on first-come basis).

DEADLINES: Entry, August. Event, September.

290

Great Gulfcoast Arts Festival
Pensacola Arts Council
Art Show Chair
P. O. Box 731
Pensacola, Florida 32594 U.S.A.

Entry July

National; **entry open to U.S.;** annual in November; established 1973. Formerly called FESTIVAL FEVER DAYS to 1975. Purpose: to bring quality visual and performing arts to Pensacola. Sponsored by Pensacola Arts Council, *Pensacola News-Journal.* Average statistics (all sections): 300 entrants, 200 maximum participants, 40 awards, 60,000 attendance, $100,-000 in total sales, $500 sales per entrant. Held in Pensacola for 2 days. Have food, entertainment, children's arts-theater, workshops, museum exhibits.

CRAFTS FAIR: Glass, Pottery, Sculpture, Mixed Media (including stained glass, porcelain, raku, stoneware, clay, plastic), original; minimum 4 works on display. Entrants provide and attend sales displays. Submit 3 35mm slides for entry review. No kits, proxy exhibitors, commercial entries. Competition for some awards includes visual art, photography, other crafts.

AWARDS: $500 Best of Show Award (all sections). $200 First, $100 Second, $75 Third Place, $25 Merit Awards to each section. Over $2000 in Purchase Prizes (all sections).

JUDGING: Entry review by jury. Awards judging by 3 out-of-town professionals. Sponsor may withhold awards. Not responsible for loss or damage.

ENTRY FEE: $5 jury fee plus $40 per 100-square-foot exhibit space.

DEADLINES: Entry, July. Notification, September. Event, November.

291

Chiaha Harvest Fair
Chiaha Guild of Arts and Crafts (CGAC)
Nancy L. Smith, Publicity Director
P. O. Box 1282
Rome, Georgia 30161 U.S.A.
Tel: (404) 295-4828
Entry October

National; **entry open to U.S.;** annual in October; established 1965. Purpose: to provide public with opportunity to buy quality artwork. Sponsored and supported by CGAC. Average statistics (all sections): 70 entrants, 12 awards, 10,000 attendance. Held during Heritage Holidays Festival at Heritage Park in Rome for 2 days. Have food booths, plants sales, children's activities, entertainment. Tickets: 50¢-$1. Second contact: Bambi Berry, Exhibits Chair, Rt. 10, Horseleg Creek Road, Rome, Georgia 30161.

CRAFTS FAIR: Glass, Pottery, Sculpture, original. Entrants provide and attend sales displays. Submit slides or photographs, description of each work for entry review. No slip molds, hobby kits. Competition includes visual arts, photography, other crafts.

AWARDS: (Includes all sections): $100 Best of Show Award. 10 $50 Merit Awards. $500 in Purchase Awards. CGAC Purchase Award.

JUDGING: By 1 professional. CGAC Purchase Award by Harvest Fair Committee. Not responsible for loss or damage.

ENTRY FEE: $30 for 8x15-foot exhibit booth (sharing permitted). No sales commission charge.

DEADLINES: Entry, event, October.

292

Harvest Heyday Arts and Crafts Show
Chattahoochee Valley Art Association (CVAA)
William B. Gay, Director
112 Hines Street
P. O. Box 921
LaGrange, Georgia 30241 U.S.A.
Tel: (404) 882-3267
Entry October

Regional; **entry open to Alabama, Florida, Georgia, Tennessee;** annual in October; established 1978. Sponsored and supported by CVAA. Held at West Georgia Commons Mall in LaGrange for 2 days. Maximum 50 entrants (all sections). Have participant demonstrations. Also sponsor LaGrange National Competition, Affair on the Square Sidewalk Art Show.

CRAFTS FAIR: Glass, Pottery, Sculpture, original. Entrants provide and attend sales displays. No imports, molds, kits, jewelry. Competition includes visual arts, photography, other crafts.

AWARDS: $500 in Purchase Prizes (includes all sections).

JUDGING: By 2 CVAA judges. Not responsible for loss or damage.

ENTRY FEE: $25 ($35 group) for 7x10-foot exhibit space, $35 ($50 group) for 7x20-foot exhibit space. No sales commission charge.

DEADLINES: Entry, event, October.

293
Madison Chautauqua of the Arts
Dixie McDonough, Chair
Green Hills Pottery
119 West Main Street
Madison, Indiana 47250 U.S.A.
Tel: (812) 265-5080
Entry August

International; entry open to all; annual in September; established 1970. Purpose: to give craftspersons a place to sell creations, and public an opportunity to buy craftsworks. Sponsored by Madison Chautauqua of the Arts. Recognized by Indiana Festival Association, Madison Chamber of Commerce, Indiana Artists and Craftsmen. Average statistics (all sections): 108 entrants, 30,000 attendance. Held on Madison's Vine Street for 2 days. Have festival of food, entertainment.

CRAFTS FAIR: Glass, Pottery, Sculpture, original. Entrants provide and attend sales displays. Require entrants demonstrate crafts skills. Submit minimum 3 35mm slides per medium of work and 1 of display, biographical sketch for entry review. No greenware, plastercrafts, kits, molds. Competition includes other crafts. Also have art, photography sections.

AWARDS: Best of Show, First, Second, Third Place Ribbons. $250 Purchase Award. Green Hill Pottery Trophy to best craft display.

JUDGING: Entry review by committee. Awards judging by outstanding artist judge. Participant vote on Best of Show Ribbon. Based on originality of design and execution.

ENTRY FEE: $30 for 10x8-foot exhibit space.

DEADLINES: Entry, notification, August. Event, September.

294
River Bend Art Fair
Atchison Art Center
Marilyn Buehler
P. O. Box 308
Atchison, Kansas 66002 U.S.A.
Tel: (913) 367-7337
Entry May

International; entry open to all; annual in May; established 1964. Sponsored by Atchison Art Association. Average statistics (all sections): 130 entrants, 10 awards. Held at Atchison Mall for 2 days. Have featured artist, demonstrations, entertainment.

CRAFTS FAIR: Stained Glass, Pottery, Sculpture, original; limit 1 entry for competition, unlimited for display. No ceramics from commercial kits. Competition includes visual arts, photography, other crafts.

AWARDS: (Includes all sections): $150 First, $100 Second, $50 Third Place Awards. 3 $25 Judges' Awards. $25 Best Display Award. 6 Honorable Mentions.

JUDGING: By 2 jurors. Not responsible for loss or damage.

ENTRY FEE: $20 for exhibit space or table, $12 for 4x8-foot panel. No sales commission charge.

DEADLINES: Entry, event, May.

295
Algonac Invitational Art Fair
Algonac Sponsors of the Arts
(ASOTA)
Vonnie Breck, Artist Chair
Box 133
Algonac, Michigan 48001 U.S.A.
Tel: (313) 794-5294, 794-5296

Entry July

International; entry open to all; annual in September; established 1973. Purpose: to increase community awareness of artworks. Supported by ASOTA, Blue Water Tourist Association. Average statistics (all sections): 100 entrants, 11 awards, 10,000 attendance, $300 sales per entrant. Held in Algonac City Park for 2 days.

CRAFTS FAIR: Glass, Pottery. Entrants provide and attend sales displays. Submit minimum 3 slides for entry review; resume, personal photo for publicity. No copies, kits, machine-made items, commercial molds, greenware. Competition includes other crafts. Also have photography, visual arts sections.

AWARDS: (Includes all sections): Best of Show, Second Place, Third Place Ribbons and Cash Awards to best local artists.

JUDGING: By jury. Sponsor may photograph entries for publicity. Not responsible for loss or damage.

ENTRY FEE: $25 for 16x16-foot exhibition space.

DEADLINES: Entry, July. Judging, August. Event, September.

296

Danish Festival Arts and Crafts Fair
Shirley Fries, Managing Director
327 South Lafayette Street
Greenville, Michigan 48838 U.S.A.
Tel: (616) 754-6369

Entry June

International; entry open to all; annual in August; established 1968. Purpose: to celebrate Danish Heritage. Sponsored by Danish Festival Inc. and businesses. Recognized by National Association of Festivals. Average statistics (all sections): 130 entries, 50,000 attendance. Have booth sites, music, dancing, parade, Danish food. Held on Lafayette Street in Greenville for 2 days. Second contact: Carolyn Frye, Chair, 319 West Oak Street, Greenville, Michigan 48838; tel: (616) 754-8778.

CRAFTS FAIR: Blown Glass, Pottery (hand-thrown, slab pottery), original. Entrants provide and attend sales displays. Submit 4 slides or photographs for entry review. No entries from kits, molds, for sale commercially. Competition includes visual arts, photography, other crafts. Also have nonjuried senior citizens division.

AWARDS: (Includes all sections): Cash Prizes. Trophy. Honorable Mentions. Outstanding Awards.

JUDGING: By 3 judges. Sponsor retains 1 slide. Not responsible for loss or damage.

ENTRY FEE: $15 for 1 day, $25 for 2 days, for 10x12-foot exhibit space.

DEADLINES: Entry, June. Event, August.

297

Laurel Day in the Park
Laurel Arts League
Mrs. Harry H. Bush, Chair
3303 Franklin Avenue
Laurel, Mississippi 39440 U.S.A.
Tel: (601) 428-1267

Entry April

National; entry open to all; annual in May; established 1972. Purpose: to increase exposure, opportunity for artists. Sponsored and supported by Laurel Arts League, City of Laurel, Mississippi Arts Commission. Average statistics (all sections): 100 entries,

37 awards, 30,000 attendance. Held in Mason Park in Laurel for 1 day. Have music. Second contact: Shirley Bush, 720 Sixth Avenue, Laurel, Mississippi 39440.

CRAFTS FAIR: Stained Glass, Pottery, Sculpture (including plastic, porcelain, raku, stoneware), original, 2D ready for hanging if appropriate; limit 2 per entrant (all sections). Entrants provide and attend sales display. Require hand-delivery. No copies, commercially molded work. Divisions: Adult, Student (K-6,7-12). Competition for some awards includes visual arts, photography, mixed media, and other crafts.

AWARDS: *Adult:* $750 Best of Show Award (includes all sections). $200 First, $100 Second, $75 Third Prize to each category. *Student:* $15 First, $10 Second, $5 Third Prize each to elementary, junior high-high school.

JUDGING: By 1 art director. Not responsible for loss or damage.

ENTRY FEE: $25 for 6x10-foot display booth. Students, $3 jury fee only. Organizational groups, $50 for 3 booth.

DEADLINES: Entry, April. Judging, event, May.

| 298 |

Boston Mills Art Festival
Don Getz, Director
7100 Riverview Road
Box 173
Peninsula, Ohio 44264 U.S.A.
Tel: (216) 657-2807

Entry March

National; **entry open to U.S.;** annual in July. Purpose: to exhibit fine works for purchase. Sponsored by Akron Society of Artists, Cleveland Plain Dealer. Average statistics (all sections): 500 entrants, 200 exhibitors, 20,000 attendance, $35,000 sales. Held at Boston Mills Ski Resort in Ohio for 4 days. Have accommodations for exhibitors, pre-show publicity.

CRAFTS FAIR: Glass, Pottery, Sculpture, Enamel, hand-produced. Entrants provide and attend sales displays. Submit 5 35mm color slides (1 slide of display), personal resume for entry review; glossy monochrome photograph of entrant for publicity. Competition includes visual arts, photography, other crafts.

AWARDS: $500 Best of Show Award; Certificates and Banners (includes all sections). $150 First Prize each to sculpture, ceramics, glass, miscellaneous.

JUDGING: Entry review by 6 professional artists and 1 gallery owner. Awards judging by 3 professional artists. Not responsible for loss or damage.

ENTRY FEE: $9; $15 for both exhibits. No sales commission charge.

DEADLINES: Entry, March. Judging, event, July.

| 299 |

Crosby Gardens Festival of the Arts
Beverlee Anderson, Program Director
Festival Arts Committee
5403 Elmer Drive
Toledo, Ohio 43615 U.S.A. Tel: (419) 536-8365

Entry April

International; **entry open to U.S., Canada;** annual in June; established 1965. Formerly called ROSE GARDEN OF THE ARTS to 1970. Purpose: to provide artists opportunity to display, demonstrate, sell works, Sponsored by George P. Crosby Gardens, City of Toledo, Toledo Artists Club, Garden Club Forum, Arts Commission of Greater Toledo. Supported by Owens-Illinois, Inc. Recognized by Ohio Arts Council. Average statistics (all sections): 600 entrants, 350 exhibitors, 80,000 attendance. Held at Crosby Gardens for 2 days. Have booth, easel, table, setup spaces, festival stage events, demonstrations, Children's Emporium. Tickets: $1. Also sponsor seasonal events.

CRAFTS FAIR: Glass, Pottery, original, ready for display. Completed in previous 2 years. Entrants provide and attend sales displays. Submit 3 slides of work, 1 photograph or drawing of display for entry review. No manufactured or commercially produced work, molds. Also have visual arts, photography, other craft sections.

AWARDS: $100 First Place Ribbons. Second, Third Place Ribbons. Honorable Mentions. $2500 in Crosby Garden Purchase Awards (includes all sections).

JUDGING: Entry review by 6 professionals. Awards judging by 4 regional professionals. Based on originality, creativity, technique, appropriateness, craftsmanship. Not responsible for loss or damage.

ENTRY FEE: $5 jury fee plus return postage. $50 (refundable) for 8x10-foot booth (maximum 130 booths). $20 for 2-1/2x8-foot table. $20 for 4x6-foot easel space. $30-$50 for 6x8- to 8x10-foot special setups. No sales commission charge.

DEADLINES: Entry, April. Event, June.

| 300 |

Toledo Festival
Arts Commission of Greater Toledo
Elizabeth A. Emmert, Coordinator
415 North St. Clair Street
Toledo, Ohio 43604 U.S.A. Tel: (419) 247-6651

Entry July

International; entry open to all; annual in September; established 1980. Formerly called TOLEDOFEST: A CELEBRATION to 1981. Purpose: to provide visual and performing artists with audience for display and sale of work. Sponsored by Arts Commission of Greater Toledo. Average statistics (all sections): 125 entrants, 10 awards, 125,000 attendance. Held at Civic Center Mall in Toledo for 3 days. Have entertainment, children's activities, special events, dressing rooms, ethnic food booths. Publish *Accent Arts* (monthly newsletter). Also sponsor workshop, arts festival for handicapped.

CRAFTS FAIR: Glass, Pottery, Sculpture, Enamel. Entrants provide and attend sales displays. Submit 3 slides, brief resume for entry review. No handicrafts, kits, commercial molds, manufactured works. Competition includes visual arts, photography, other crafts.

AWARDS: 7 $100 Awards (includes all sections).

JUDGING: Entry review and awards judging by committee. Not responsible for loss or damage.

ENTRY FEE: $5 plus $100 for 8x10-foot booth space (maximum 2 artists per booth or setup space). $50 for 4x6-foot easel (1 artist per easel). No sales commission charge.

DEADLINES: Entry, July. Registration, August. Judging, event, September.

301

Seawall Art Show
City of Portsmouth Department of
Parks and Recreation
Deborah Avant, Cultural Planner
801 Crawford Parkway
Portsmouth, Virginia 23704 U.S.A.
Tel: (804) 393-8481

Entry April

International; entry open to all; annual May; established 1970. Purpose: to provide exposure and sales for artists, craftspersons. Sponsored by Portsmouth Community Arts Center, Chamber of Commerce, Downtown Merchants Association, Seawall Festival Committee. Average statistics (all sections): 800 entries, 200 entrants, 10 awards, 20,000 attendance. Held on Portsmouth Seawall Boardwalk for 3 days. Have participant demonstrations, entertainment, nonjuried craft section, nearby shop and parking area in event of rain. Also sponsor Portsmouth Photography Show and Contest, Citywide Student Art Show.

CRAFTS FAIR: **Stained Glass, Pottery, Enamel,** original, unrestricted dimensions. Entrants provide and attend sales displays. Submit 3 slides for entry review. Divisions: Adult, Student (all media). Competition includes visual arts, other crafts.

AWARDS: (Includes all sections): $3000 in Purchase Prizes. $750 Best of Show Award. 10 $150 Excellence Awards. $150 Merit Awards. $50 People's Choice Awards.

JUDGING: Entry review by 3 artists or art educators. Not responsible for loss or damage.

SALES TERMS: Sales compulsory. No commission charge.

ENTRY FEE: $25 for 6x7-foot exhibit space ($35 for 2 spaces).

DEADLINES: Entry, acceptance, event, April.

302

Mountain State Art and Craft Fair
Charles Ryan Associates
Debby Sonis, Account Executive
P. O. Box 2464
Charleston, West Virginia 25329
U.S.A. Tel: (304)342-0161

Entry July

State; **entry open to West Virginia residents age 18 and over;** annual in July; established 1963. Purpose: to promote, develop, perpetuate improvement in arts, crafts; acquaint public with cultural aspects of West Virginia. Sponsored by West Virginia University Extension Service; Bureau of Vocational, Technical and Adult Education; GOECD; WV Artists and Craftsmen Guild; WV Departments of Agriculture and Natural Resources. Average statistics (all sections): 100 entries, 50,000 attendance, $315,000 total sales. Held at Cedar Lakes Conference Center near Ripley in West Virginia for 5 days. Have educational exhibits, demonstrations, hands-on activities for children, apprentice program, entertainment, refreshments, parking, variety of booth spaces, pegboards and counters. Tickets: $3 adults, $1 children. Publish *Mountain Heritage.* Also sponsor $1000 maximum training Grant-in-Aid programs for professionals, $50 grants for apprentices. Second contact: Don Michael, Bureau of Vocational, Technical and Adult Education, State Capitol Complex, Charleston, West Virginia 25305; tel: (304) 348-2347.

CRAFTS FAIR: **Glass, Pottery** (including folk toys). Entrants provide and attend sales displays. Require sufficient inventory for duration of show. Submit 5 works and any display units for entry review. No commercial molds, patterns, kits, works using manufactured parts (bottles, Styrofoam shapes, plastic forms), mass-produced novelty or bazaar items. Competition includes visual arts, photography, other crafts.

CRAFTS CONTEST: 2-Dimensional (including relief sculpture), ready for hanging; limit 2 per entrant. Other requirements, restrictions same as for Crafts Fair.

AWARDS: *Fair (includes all sections):* Best of Show Purchase Award. 3 Cash Awards to best booth displays. 3 Honorable Mentions to booth displays. Excellence Awards. *Contest (includes all sections):* 1 $200, 2 $100, 4 $25 Cash Awards.

JUDGING: Entry review by Exhibits and Demonstrations Committee. Awards judging by 3 qualified judges. Based on quality of work, presentation to public, booth design. Sponsor may photograph entries for publicity. Not responsible for loss or damage.

SALES TERMS: 15% commission charge.

ENTRY FEE: $5 plus return postage.

DEADLINES: Entry, July. Entry review, November-January. Event, following July.

| 303 |

Eagle River Artarama
Donna Schwartz
2684 Pickerel Lake Road
Eagle River, Wisconsin 54521 U.S.A.
Tel: (712) 479-8947

Entry date not specified

International; entry open to all; annual in July; established 1972. Purpose: to sell and display artwork.

Sponsored and supported by Eagle River Chamber of Commerce. Average statistics: 150 entrants (maximum), 6 awards, 25,000 attendance, $30,000 total sales. Held at Riverview Park in Eagle River for 1 day.

CRAFTS FAIR: Glass, Pottery, Sculpture, original. Entrants provide and attend sales displays. No commercial molds, kits. Divisions: Adult, Junior. Competition includes visual arts, photography, other crafts.

AWARDS: *Adult:* 6 $100 Awards of Excellence. $2500 in Purchase Prizes. Honorable Mention Ribbons. *Junior:* 3 $10 Awards of Excellence. Honorable Mention Ribbons.

JUDGING: By 2 judges. Not responsible for loss or damage.

ENTRY FEE: $25 for 12x18-foot exhibit space (adult). $3 for 6-foot exhibit space (junior).

DEADLINES: Entry, not specified. Event, July.

CRAFTS FAIRS, FESTIVALS (Sculpture, General Crafts)

Crafts Fairs, Festivals, Shows, Sales accepting SCULPTURE, CERAMICS, POTTERY, BLOWN and STAINED GLASS, GENERAL CRAFTS (listed alphabetically by state). Attendance usually required.

| 304 |

Art in the Sun Festival
Greater Pompano Beach Chamber of Commerce

Susan Hatcher, Director of Special Projects
2200 East Atlantic Blvd.
Pompano Beach, Florida 33062
U.S.A. Tel: (305) 941-2940

Entry January

International; entry open to all; annual in March; established 1972. Purpose: to encourage acquaintance with arts through juried show. Sponsored by Greater Pompano Beach Chamber of Commerce. Supported by local business. Maximum 200 exhibitors. Held at Jay-Cee Park, Pompano Beach for 2 days. Have food, free parking, security.

CRAFTS FAIR: Sculpture, General Crafts, original; entry limit not specified. Entrants provide and attend sales displays. Submit 4 35mm slides (including 1 of display) for entry review. No kits. Competition includes other crafts.

AWARDS: $300 First, $200 Second, $100 Third, 3 Honorable Mention Awards to each category. *Includes all sections:* $600 Best of Show Award. Merit Ribbons, Artist Ribbons, Purchase Awards.

JUDGING: Entry review by selection committee. Awards judging by 1 judge.

ENTRY FEE: $50 for 15x15-foot booth space (maximum 200 booths). Sales optional.

DEADLINES: Entry, January. Event, March.

| 305 |

Images Festival of the Arts
Holly Bivins, Executive Director
P. O. Box 767
New Smyrna Beach, Florida 32069
U.S.A. Tel: (904) 427-6975

Entry October

International; entry open to all; annual in February; established 1976. Sponsored by Images Festival of the Arts. Average statistics (all sections): 2000 entries, 225 entrants, 3 countries, 39 winners, 50,000 attendance. Held at Riverside Park in New Smyrna Beach for 2 days. Have music, theater, dance performances.

CRAFTS FAIR: Sculpture, General Crafts. Completed in previous 2 years. Entrants provide and attend sales displays. Submit for entry review 3 35mm slides (no glass, metal mounts), publicity information, biographical sketch. No commercial entries. Competition includes visual arts, photography.

AWARDS: $1000 Purchase Prize. 5 $500 Distinction Awards, 8 $250 Commendation Awards, 25 $100 Merit Awards. Honorable Mention Ribbons.

JUDGING: Entry review by selection committee. Awards judging by 2 art professionals. Not responsible for loss or damage.

ENTRY FEE: $5 jury fee plus $35 (refundable) for 12x12-foot exhibit space. No sales commission charge.

DEADLINES: Entry, October. Notification, December. Event, February.

| 306 |

Mount Dora Art and Crafts Festival
Harlow C. Middleton
P. O. Box 916
Mount Dora, Florida 32757 U.S.A.
Tel: (904) 383-8105

Entry December

International; entry open to all; annual in February; established 1975. Known as NEW ENGLAND FESTIVAL OF THE SOUTH. Purpose: to promote participation, education in the arts. Sponsored and supported by private donations, registration fees. Average statistics (all sections): 240 entrants (maximum), 5 countries, 70 awards, 40,000 attendance. Held in downtown Mount Dora for 1 weekend.

CRAFTS FAIR: Sculpture, General Crafts, Mixed Media, original; minimum 4 per category. Entrants provide and attend sales displays. Submit 3 slides of work and 1 of display, resume for entry review. No manufactured items, commercial molds, precarved work. Competition for some awards includes visual arts, photography, other crafts. Also have youth-student section.

AWARDS: (Includes all sections): $1000 Best of Show. 25 $50 Merit Awards. $50 Alderman Award to most original craft. $300 First, $200 Second, $100 Third Place to each category.

JUDGING: By committee of teachers, artists. Sponsor may withhold awards. Not responsible for loss or damage.

ENTRY FEE: $5 handling charge plus $25 (refundable) per category for 8x14-foot exhibit space. No sales commission charge.

DEADLINES: Entry, December. Notification, January. Event, February.

307

On the Green Art Festival
Fort Pierce Art Club
Dillard Bucklen
6485 Badger Court
Fort Pierce, Florida 33450 U.S.A.
Tel: (305) 464-3875

Entry December

International; entry open to all; an-nual in January; established 1971. Purpose: to promote art appreciation in area. Sponsored by Fort Pierce Art Club. Maximum 200 entrants (all sections). Held in Fort Pierce for 2 days.

CRAFTS FAIR: Sculpture, General Crafts, original. Entrants provide and attend sales displays. Submit 3 photos of work for entry review. No kits, molds, commercial, manufactured items, dolls, toys. 5 craft categories. Competition for some awards includes visual arts, photography.

AWARDS: $300 Best of Show Award (includes all sections). $200 First, $75 Second, $50 Third Place Awards each to crafts (all media), sculpture (includes visual arts). Honorable Mention Ribbons.

JUDGING: By 3 judges. May withhold awards. Not responsible for loss or damage.

ENTRY FEE: $30 for 15-foot space (1 space per entrant). No sales commission charge.

DEADLINES: Entry, December. Event, January.

308

57th Street Art Fair
Sue Goldhammer, Committee Head
5555 South Everett Avenue
Chicago, Illinois 60637 U.S.A.
Tel: (312) 644-5800

Entry March

International; **entry open to age 18 and over;** annual in June; established 1948. Sponsored by 57th Street Art Fair Committee. Average statistics (all sections): 300 entrants, 10 awards, 20,-000 attendance. Held in Hyde Park in Chicago for 2 days. Second contact: Sheila King, Public Relations, 400 North Michigan Avenue, Suite 904, Chicago, Illinois 60611.

CRAFTS FAIR: Sculpture, General Crafts (including ceramics, hand-blown glass), original. Entrants provide and attend sales displays. Submit 1 work sample (Chicago-area residents), 2 35mm slides (others) for entry review. Competition includes visual arts, photography, other crafts.

AWARDS: (Includes all sections): $500 Best of Fair Award. $200, $75 Cash Awards each to newcomers in sculpture, crafts.

JUDGING: Entry review by independent panel of artists, critics. Awards judging by 5 professionals. Not responsible for loss or damage.

SALES TERMS: Sales compulsory. No commission charge.

ENTRY FEE: $2 plus $20 for maximum 12-foot booth space.

DEADLINES: Entry, March. Event, June.

309

Sault Summer Arts Festival
Sault Area Arts Council
Jean K. Jones, Chair
P. O. Box 857
Sault Ste. Marie, Michigan 49783
U.S.A. Tel: (906) 632-7927

Entry May

International; entry open to all; annual in August; established 1974. Purpose: to promote the arts in Sault Ste. Marie. Sponsored and supported by Sault Area Arts Council, Lake Superior State College, community schools, Sault Ste. Marie Chamber of Commerce. Average statistics (all sections): 58 entries, 38 entrants (100 maximum), 3 countries, 7 awards, 3000 attendance, $10,000 total sales. Held at Lake Superior State College in Sault Ste. Marie for 1 day. Have security, indoor spaces, food service, lodging, demonstrations. Second contact:

Frank Atkinson, Cisler Center, Lake Superior State College; tel: (906) 635-2542.

CRAFTS FAIR: Sculpture, General Crafts (including pottery, stained glass), original. Entrants provide and attend sales displays. Submit 3 color slides of work (low, medium, high priced items) for entry review. No kits, molds. Competition includes fine arts, photography, all other crafts.

AWARDS: $100 Best of Show Award. Other unspecified prizes.

JUDGING: Entry review by Council. Awards judging by 1 judge.

ENTRY FEE: $10 for 8x8-foot exhibit space (limit 2 per entrant). No sales commission charge.

DEADLINES: Entry, May. Acceptance, June. Event, August.

310

Hampton Medley of the Arts
Peninsula Council of the Arts
Coliseum Mall, Suite A-12
Hampton, Virginia 23666 U.S.A.
Tel: (804) 826-6066

Entry August

National; entry open to U.S.; annual in October; established 1973. Sponsored by Peninsula Council of the Arts. Average 100 entrants. Held in Hampton for 3 days.

CRAFTS FAIR: Sculpture, General Crafts, display 10x10x6-feet maximum (lxwxh). Entrants provide and attend sales displays. Submit 1 photograph or slide of display, 3 of current work for entry review. No commercially produced entries. Competition includes visual arts, photography, other crafts.

AWARDS: (Includes all sections): $750 Best of Show Award. $300 Excellence Award. $200 Distinction Award. 3 100 Merit Awards. $130 Cash Award. $75 Artist's Award.

JUDGING: By nationally recognized figure. Artist's Award by displaying artists. Not responsible for loss or damage.

SALES TERMS: Sales compulsory. No commission charge.

ENTRY FEE: $5 plus $30 (refundable) for 10x10-foot exhibit space (limit 2 per entrant).

DEADLINES: Entry, August. Acceptance, September. Event, October.

CRAFTS FAIRS, FESTIVALS (Specific Subject-Type)

Crafts Fairs, Festivals, Shows, Sales, and Auctions accepting specific subject or type of crafts, including ARTISTIC and FINE ARTS CRAFTS, CONTEMPORARY, TRADITIONAL, and WESTERN THEME SCULPTURE (listed alphabetically by state). Attendance usually required.

311

Town and Country Village Art Fiesta
Sacramento Suburban Kiwanis Club
R. Jan Pinney, Committee Chair
5777 Madison Avenue, Suite 370
Sacramento, California 95841 U.S.A.
Tel: (916) 332-7831

Entry May

International; entry open to all; annual in June; established 1958. Sponsored by Sacramento Suburban Kiwanis Club. Supported by Town and

Country Merchants Association. Average statistics (all sections): 1000 entries, 300 entrants (maximum), 3 countries, 13 awards, 20,000 attendance. Held at Town and Country Village in Sacramento for 2 days. Second contact: Mary Morse, 9060 Central Avenue, Orangevale, California 95662; tel: (916) 988-8656.

CRAFTS FAIR: Artistic All Media, original. Entrants provide and attend sales displays. Submit photo for entry review. No agents, dealers, copies, commercially manufactured objects, hobby crafts. Categories: Art in Action, Mixed Media. Competition for some awards includes visual arts, photography.

AWARDS: $200 Kiwanis Purchase Awards (includes all sections). $100 First, $50 Second, $25 Third Place Awards. Honorable Mentions to each category.

JUDGING: By 2 local media celebrity judges, 1 art critic. Not responsible for loss or damage.

ENTRY FEE: $30 for maximum 3 exhibit spaces ($10, students under 18). No sales commission charge.

DEADLINES: Entry, May. Judging, event, June.

312

Parsons Kansas Outdoor Arts and Crafts Fair
Art Fair Board
Anne Malone
P.O. Box 995
Parsons, Kansas 67357 U.S.A.
Tel: (316) 421-4294

Entry July

International; entry open to all; annual in July; established 1961. Purpose: to provide opportunity for public to see and buy arts and crafts.

Sponsored by Art Fair Board. Average statistics (all sections): 1000 entries, 120 entrants, 28 awards. Held at Parsons Plaza for 2 days. Have entertainment, tables and pegboards at $5 each, nonjuried student display area.

CRAFTS FAIR: Fine Arts Crafts (including ceramics), original. Entrants provide and attend sales displays. Submit description of work for entry review. No commercial, manufactured items. Division: Open Competition (Adult, Junior-Senior High), Private Display (Junior-Senior High, Over 60). Competition for some awards includes visual arts, photography, other crafts.

HOBBY CRAFTS FAIR: All Types. Divisions: Open Competition, Private Display (Junior-Senior High, Over 60). Other requirements, restrictions same as for Crafts.

AWARDS: $100 Best of Show Award: $2000 in Purchase Pledges (includes all sections). $60 First, $30 Second, $15 Third Prize to fine arts crafts open division. $20 First, $10 Second, $5 Third Prize each to fine arts crafts age 60 and over, junior-senior high. $30 First, $15 Second, $10 Third Prize to hobby crafts open division. $15 First, $10 Second, $5 Third Prize to hobby crafts age 60 and over.

JUDGING: By qualified judges each category. Not responsible for loss or damage.

ENTRY FEE: $20 each category ($5 for private display, free for grade school through senior high) for 8x30-foot exhibit space.

DEADLINES: Entry, event, July.

| 313 |

Minnesota Renaissance Festival
Craft Coordinator
Route 3, Box 117
Shakopee, Minnesota 55379 U.S.A.
Tel: (612) 445-7361

Entry February

International; entry open to all; annual in August-September; established 1971. Purpose: to recreate ambiance and atmosphere of 16th century European marketplace. Sponsored and supported by Mid-America Festival Corporation. Recognized by IFA, Minneapolis Aquatennial Association, Minneapolis Chamber of Commerce. Average statistics (all sections): 200 entrants, 15 winners. Held at Shakopee for 6 weekends. Also sponsor visual arts, photography, writing scholarships. Have incentive program to provide financial assistance for authentic costumes, displays, demonstrations, workshops, Renaissance School, gallery, food, games, entertainment, horses. Tickets: $6.95 (adults), $3 (children 5-12).

CRAFTS FAIR: Traditional, original, handcrafted. Entrants provide and attend sales displays. Submit 5-10 35mm slides for entry review.

AWARDS: $5000 in Purchase Awards. $3500 in Participation Awards to those with best festival spirit.

JUDGING: Entry review and awards judging by crafts experts. Based on quality of craftsmanship.

ENTRY FEE: Not specified.

DEADLINES: Entry, February. Event, August-September,

314

Roberson Center Holiday and Arts Festival
Roberson Center for the Arts and Sciences
Laura B. Martin, Assistant Director
30 Front Street
Binghamton, New York 13905 U.S.A.
Tel: (607) 772-0660

Entry July

International; **entry open to U.S., Canada;** annual in September; established 1955. Purpose: to showcase visual arts, crafts, and performing arts. Sponsored by the Roberson Center for the Arts and Sciences. Recognized by American Association of Museums, Alliance of New York State Arts Councils, Northeast Museums. Average statistics (all sections): 300 entrants, 40,000 attendance, $65,000 total sales. Held in Binghamton for 2 days. " Have Children at Holiday" event. Tickets: 50¢. Also sponsor performing arts events, planetarium shows.

CRAFTS FAIR: Contemporary, Traditional, original, 300 entrants maximum. Entrants provide and attend sales displays. No commercial molds, kits, patterns, stencils. Competition includes paintings, graphics, sculpture, photography.

AWARDS: $1000 in Purchase Prizes. Certificates of Merit.

JUDGING: By 3 judges. Not responsible for loss or damage.

SALES TERMS: 10% commission charge.

ENTRY FEE: $75 for 8x6-foot display area.

DEADLINES: Entry, July. Judging, event, September.

315

Western Art Association (WAA) Show and Auction
Jacqueline Leinbach, Coordinator
100 North Ruby Street
P. O. Box 893
Ellensburg, Washington 98926
U.S.A. Tel: (509) 962-2934

Entry March

International; **entry open to U.S., Canadian artists and dealers;** annual in May; established 1972. Proceeds go to Elmsview Center for handicapped adults. Purpose: to promote Western art and heritage. Sponsored and supported by WAA. Average statistics (all sections): 2000 entries, 100 entrants, 7 awards, $16,000 total sales. Held at Holiday Inn in Ellensburg for 3 days. Have banquet, security, accommodations. Tickets: $15 (auction). Also sponsor Art Show at Ellensburg Rodeo, scholarships. Second contact: Dr. Darwin J. Goodey, President, 509 North Willow, Ellensburg, Washington 98926; tel: (509) 925-4666.

CRAFT FAIR-AUCTION: Western Theme Clay Sculpture. *Fair:* original, mounted; limit 3 artists, dealers per room. Entrants provide and attend sales displays. Submit slides or photographs for entry review. *Auction:* original, mounted, may place reserve price on entries; limit 3 per entrant (1 eligible for purchase award). Submit authentication of contemporary, deceased artists' work. Competition includes bronze and wood sculpture, fine arts. Also have small auction (for items valued at $500 or less), silent auctions.

AWARDS: Best of Show Award to sculpture (includes all media). *Main Auction:* $1000 Purchase Award. ACC Powell Award. Judges' Award. $100 Kittitas County CowBelles and Cattlemen's Association Award, Plaque,

WAA Ribbon to best portraying beef industry.

JUDGING: Entry review by 7 qualified non-WAA persons; purchase award by WAA Board of Directors; other awards by participants, qualified individuals. Sponsor may withhold awards. Not responsible for loss or damage.

SALES TERMS: Sales compulsory. 20%-35% commission charge. $25 charge on works of deceased if not sold.

ENTRY FEE: $200-$300 for room, functions (refundable). Entrant pays return postage on entries not accepted for auction.

DEADLINES: Entry, March. Event, May.

CRAFTS FAIRS, FESTIVALS (Including Specific Type)

Crafts Fairs, Festivals, Shows, Sales accepting ALL CLAY AND GLASS CRAFTS MEDIA, including CERAMICS, CLAY, BLOWN and STAINED GLASS, POTTERY, ENAMEL, SCULPTURE (listed alphabetically by state). Attendance usually required.

316

Helen Keller Festival Art-Craft Show
Tennessee Valley Art Association
Ann McCutchen, Chair
511 North Water Street
P. O. Box 474
Tuscumbia, Alabama 35674 U.S.A.
Tel: (205) 383-0522

Entry June

International; entry open to all; annual in June; established 1964. Purpose: to commemorate Helen Keller's birthdate, birthplace. Sponsored and supported by Tennessee Valley Art Association. Average statistics (all sections): 135 entrants, 40,000 attendance. Held in Spring Park in Tuscumbia for 2 days. Have booth assistants, camping, security.

CRAFTS FAIR: All Media (including pottery), original. Entrants provide and attend sales displays. Submit 3 photographs or slides for entry review; include 8x10-inch glossies, other promotional material for publicity. No commercial kits. Divisions: Adult, Junior (grade 1-12). Competition includes other crafts. Also have visual arts section.

AWARDS: (Includes all crafts): $100 each to most innovative crafts, best display. $75 Second, $50 Third Prizes. 3 $25 Merit Awards.

JUDGING: By 3-member jury. Not responsible for loss or damage.

ENTRY FEE: $30 for 12x10-foot booth; juniors $5. No sales commission charge.

DEADLINES: Entry, event, June.

317

Mayfair By-the-Lake Craft Celebration
Polk Public Museum
800 East Palmetto
Lakeland, Florida 33801 U.S.A.
Tel: (813) 688-7743

Entry February

State;**entry open to Florida;** annual in May; established 1979. Purpose: to provide showcase for Florida's finest craftspersons. Sponsored by Polk

Public Museum, Florida Phosphate Council. Average statistics: 100 entrants, 34 awards, 50,000 attendance. Held on shores of Lake Morton in Lakeland for 2 days. Have security services. Second contact: Florida Phosphate Council, 4406 South Florida Avenue, Lakeland, Florida 33803.

CRAFTS FAIR: All Media Contemporary, Folk, Traditional, (including ceramics, glass, enameling, sculpture, mixed media), original, professional quality. Entrants provide and attend sales displays. Submit 3 35mm slides per media for entry review. No kits, molds. Competition includes other crafts.

AWARDS: $500 Best of Show Award. 6 $150 Merit Awards. 6 $100 Honorable Mentions. $125 Chairman's Award. $75 to best presentation. 19 $100 Purchase Awards.

JUDGING: Entry review by 3 professional craftspersons. Awards judging by 1 juror.

ENTRY FEE: $3 jury fee. $25 for 15x15-foot display space.

DEADLINES: Entry, February. Acceptance, April. Event, May.

318

Miami Beach Outdoor Festival of the Arts
Miami Beach Fine Arts Board
Pearl Kipnis, Chair
P. O. Bin "O"
Miami Beach, Florida 33119 U.S.A.
Tel: (305) 673-7733

Entry November

International; entry open to all; annual in February; established 1975. Purpose: to foster appreciation of an increase in creative and performing arts in Florida. Sponsored and sup-

ported by City of Miami Beach, Miami Beach Fine Arts Board. Average statistics: 250 exhibitors, 200,000 attendance. Held outside Miami Beach Convention Center for 2 days. Also sponsor performing arts, children's corner, international foods.

CRAFTS FAIR: All Media (including ceramics), original. Entrants provide and attend sales displays. Submit 3 slides for entry review. Competition includes visual arts, photography, other crafts.

AWARDS: (Includes all sections): $5300 in Cash Awards. $1000 in Purchase Awards. $20,000 Community Patron Purchase Awards. Ribbons of Merit.

ENTRY FEE: $100. No sales commission charge.

DEADLINES: Entry, November. Event, February.

319

Belleville Area Arts Council Arts and Crafts Festival
Joan Renner, Chair
Box 551
Belleville, Illinois 62220 U.S.A.
Tel: (618) 234-6086

Entry May

International; **entry open to U.S., Canada;** annual in August; established 1982. Purpose: to promote visual arts. Sponsored by Belleville Area Arts Council. Supported by businesses, individuals. Average statistics: 200 entrants, 50 semifinalists, 7 finalists, 10,000 attendance. Held at downtown Belleville Center for 2 days. Second contact: Belleville Area Arts Council, 121 East Washington, Belleville, Illinois 62220.

CRAFTS FAIR: All Media (including clay, glass), original; minimum 6 works per entrant. Entrants provide and attend sales displays. Submit 3 35mm slides per category for entry review. No kits, studio or co-op work. Competition includes all crafts. Also have art, photography sections.

AWARDS: $300 Best Craft Award. 50 $100 Awards of Merit; $3200 in Purchase Awards (includes all sections).

JUDGING: Entry review by 3-person committee. Awards judging by panel of 3 professionals.

ENTRY FEE: $5 jury fee. $60 for 7x10-foot exhibit space (refundable). No sales commission charge.

DEADLINES: Entry, May. Acceptance, June. Event, August.

320

Greenwich Village Art Fair
Rockford Art Association
Burpee Art Museum
737 North Main Street
Rockford, Illinois 61103 U.S.A.
Tel: (815) 965-3131

Entry May

National; **entry open to U.S. residents age 18 and over;** annual in September; established 1948. Purpose: to raise funds for Burpee Art Museum. Average statistics (all sections): 200 entrants (maximum), 25,000 attendance. Held in Burpee Art Museum in Rockford for 2 days. Tickets: 50¢-$2. Also sponsor national annual watercolor competition, art exhibitions, regional small sculpture competition.

CRAFTS FAIR: All Media (including glass, sculpture, enamels), original. Entrants provide and attend sales displays. Submit 5 35mm slides for entry review. No commercial kits, molds, patterns, stencils, prefabricated forms. Competition includes photography,

visual arts.

AWARDS: (Includes all sections): $500 Best of Show Award. $300 each to 2D and 3D work. $50 Merit Awards. Purchase Awards.

JUDGING: By 1 judge. Based on quality of work, suitability to overall show.

SALES TERMS: Sales compulsory. No commission charge.

ENTRY FEE: $5 plus return postage. $50 for 10x15-foot exhibit space.

DEADLINES: Entry, May. Acceptance, June. Awards, event, September.

321

Tawas Bay Waterfront Arts and Crafts Show
Tawas Bay Arts Council
Paula Peterson, Chair
1115 Bay Drive
Tawas City, Michigan 48763 U.S.A.
Tel: (517) 362-3198

Entry July

International; entry open to all; annual in August; established 1960. Sponsored by Tawas Bay Arts Council. 225 entrants maximum. Held at Tawas City Park and Court House for 2 days. Have demonstrations, refreshments, hostesses, Court House (opposite park) in case of rain. Also sponsor annual Hobby Antique Show and Sale. Second contact: Joan Blust, tel: (517) 362-3230.

CRAFTS FAIR: All Media (including ceramics, pottery), original; unlimited entry. Entrants provide and attend sales displays. Submit slides or photographs, detailed explanation of work for entry review. No group entries, molds, kits, leaded pottery for utilitarian purposes, dough art. Competition includes other crafts. Also have visual arts, sculpture, photography sections.

AWARDS: First, Second, Honorable Mention Awards.

JUDGING: Entry review by Art Show Committee. Awards judging by 1 artist-teacher. Not responsible for loss or damage.

ENTRY FEE: $20 Seniors, $5 Juniors (16 and under) for 10x10-foot outdoor exhibit space or 2 card tables indoor space. No sales commission charge.

DEADLINES: Entry, July. Judging, event, August.

322

Gallery North Outdoor Art Show
Marjorie Bishop, Sharon Cowles, Chairs
North Country Road
Setauket, Long Island, New York
11733 U.S.A. Tel: (516) 751-2676

Entry date not specified

International; **entry open to age 16 and over;** annual in July; established 1964. Purpose: to provide artists an opportunity to exhibit works. Sponsored by Gallery North. Average statistics (all sections): 1500 entries, 200 entrants (225 maximum), 15 awards. Held at Gallery North in Setauket for 2 days. Have demonstrations, entertainment, children's programs, food. Also sponsor educational programs in summer. Second contact: Box 1145, Setauket, New York 11733.

CRAFTS FAIR: **All Media** (including pottery), original. Entrants provide and attend sales displays. No commercially produced entries. Competition includes visual arts, photography, other crafts.

AWARDS: $100 Best of Show Award. 2 $100, 5 $50, 2 $25 Awards (all sections). Ribbons. Winners in-

vited to exhibit 1 work in gallery during August.

JUDGING: Entry review by committee. Awards judging by 1 crafts specialist. Not responsible for loss or damage.

ENTRY FEE: $25 for 4x12-foot booth space. No sales commission charge.

DEADLINES: Event, July.

323

Fredericksburg Art Festival
MEDIA
Connie Ihlenfeld, Treasurer
P. O. Box 1704
College Station
Fredericksburg, Virginia 22402
U.S.A. Tel: (703) 373-2805

Entry May

International; **entry open to U.S., Canada;** annual in June; established 1972. Purpose: to encourage development in art; increase public awareness of local, original art. Sponsored and supported by MEDIA, Park & Shop Merchants Association. Average statistics (all sections): 2500 entries, 88 entrants (maximum), 17 awards, 5000 attendance, $300 sales per entrant. Held in Park & Shop Shopping Center in Fredericksburg for 2 days. Also sponsor monthly media demonstrations, field trips, workshops. Second contact: Megan M. Scott, Chair, 316 Braehead Drive, Fredericksburg, Virginia 22401; tel: (703) 373-6363.

CRAFTS FAIR: **All Media** (including ceramics, stained and blown glass), original. Entrants or proxies provide and attend sales displays. Competition includes sculpture, visual arts.

AWARDS: (Includes all sections): $1000 Best in Show Ribbon. 6 $150 Excellence Award Ribbons. 10 $75

Merit Awards Ribbons. Honorable Mention Ribbons. Purchase prizes.

JUDGING: By 1 artist, teacher, or architect. Not responsible for loss or damage.

SALES TERMS: Sales compulsory. No commission charge.

ENTRY FEE: $30 per entrant for 12x5-foot covered outdoor exhibit space or indoor table space (spaces may be shared). $25 for uncovered spaces.

DEADLINES: Entry, May. Judging, event, June.

CRAFTS FAIRS, FESTIVALS (All Media)

Crafts Fairs, Festivals, Shows, Sales accepting ALL CRAFTS MEDIA (listed alphabetically by state). Attendance usually required.

324

Chalaka Arts and Crafts Festival
Sylacauga Parks and Recreation Department
Pat Holmes, Coordinator
P. O. Box 1245
Sylacauga, Alabama 35150 U.S.A.
Tel: (205) 249-8561

Entry May

International; entry open to all; annual in June; established 1968. Purpose: to provide showcase for artists and craftspersons. Sponsored by Sylacauga Parks and Recreation Department, B. B. Comer Memorial Library and Public Information Center, Sylacauga Art League. Average statis-

tics (all sections): 175 entries, 3000 attendance. Held at Noble Park in Sylacauga for 2 days. Have participant demonstrations. Second contact: 2 West 8th Street, Sylacauga, Alabama 35150.

CRAFTS FAIR: All Media, original. Entrants provide and attend sales displays. Submit 2 photos or slides of work for entry review. No kits. Divisions: Adult, Youth (age 18 and under). Competition includes visual arts, other crafts.

AWARDS: $2000 in Cash Awards and Purchase Prizes. Cash Prizes to Youths.

JUDGING: By 1 professional craftsperson and 1 artist. Not responsible for loss or damage.

ENTRY FEE: $15 for 12x12-foot exhibit space. No sales commission charge.

DEADLINES: Entry, May. Event, June.

325

Tucson Festival Arts and Crafts Fair
Tucson Festival Society
Jarvis Harriman, Executive Director
8 West Paseo Redondo
Tucson, Arizona 85705 U.S.A.
Tel: (602) 622-6911

Entry February

Regional; **entry open to Southwest U.S., Mexico professionals;** annual in April; established 1951. Purpose: to celebrate Tucson cultural heritage and contemporary activity. Sponsored by Tucson Festival Society. Recognized by International Festivals Association. Average statistics (all sections): 100 entrants, 50,000 attendance. Held in Reid Park in Tucson for 3 days. Have security, refreshments, entertainment, display booths.

CRAFTS FAIR: All Media. Entrants attend sales displays; may provide own sales displays. Submit 5 35mm slides, brief biography for entry review. No commercial reproductions. Competition includes visual arts, photography.

AWARDS: Cash Awards. Ribbons to best of show, most attractive booth.

JUDGING: Entry review by jury. Awards judging by regional juror. Based on competence, professional quality.

ENTRY FEE: $75 for 8x8-foot booth space (refundable).

DEADLINES: Entry, February. Judging, event, April.

326

Tucson Fourth Avenue Arts and Crafts Fair
Fourth Avenue Merchants Association
Loraine Glazer, Coordinator
426 East 7th Street
Tucson, Arizona 85705 U.S.A.
Tel: (602) 624-2441

Entry February, October

International; entry open to all; biannual in April, December; established 1970. Purpose: to promote renewal, renovation of downtown Tucson by retail merchants. Sponsored by Fourth Avenue Merchants Association. Average statistics (all sections): 250 entrants, 4 awards, 100,000 attendance. Held in Tucson for 3 days. Have food section.

CRAFTS FAIR: All Media, original, handcrafted. Entrants provide and attend sales displays. Submit 5 slides for entry review. No manufactured items, copies, imports, found items,

hobby crafts, manufacturers. Competition includes other crafts.

AWARDS: Purchase Awards.

JUDGING: By 5 Directors of the Board. Based on craftsmanship, originality of design. Not responsible for loss or damage.

ENTRY FEE: $150 ($100 for Arizona residents) for 8x10-foot exhibition space. No shared spaces unless working in the same medium. No sales commission charge.

DEADLINES: Entry, February, October. Event, April, December.

327

Ozark Native Arts and Crafts Fair
Ozark Native Craft Association
Mrs. Jean Chase, Chair
Route 1, Box 260
Winslow, Arkansas 72959 U.S.A.
Tel: (501) 837-2391

Entry June

International; entry open to all; biannual in June, September; established 1972. Sponsored by Ozark Nature Crafts Association. Average statistics: 70 entries, 90 entrants, 6 participating countries. Held at Ozark Nature Craft Fair 4 miles south of Winslow for 3 days.

CRAFTS FAIR: All Media, handcrafted. Entrants provide and attend sales displays. No lewd or obscene work.

AWARDS: Awards to most attractive display, most unique craft, best of show.

JUDGING: Not responsible for loss or damage.

SALES TERMS: Sales compulsory. No commission charge.

ENTRY FEE: $20 for 10x6-foot indoor space or camper; $15 for outdoor space.

DEADLINES: Entry, judging, event, June.

328

Celebration of the Arts
St. John's in the Valley United Methodist Church
Mary Lou Trangmoe, Chair
20600 Roscoe Blvd.
Canoga Park, California 91306
U.S.A. Tel: (213) 716-5878,
341-6434

Entry April

International; entry open to all; annual in April; established 1970. Sponsored by and held at St. John's in the Valley United Methodist Church in Canoga Park for 2 days. Have children's area, performing arts, entertainment, refreshments.

CRAFTS FAIR: All Media, original; limit 1 per entrant for competition. Entrants provide and attend sales displays. Also have fine and commercial arts, sculpture, photography sections.

AWARDS: $50 Best of Show Award. First, Second, Third Place Ribbons.

JUDGING: By professional panel. Not responsible for loss or damage.

SALES TERMS: 10% commission charge.

ENTRY FEE: $15 for 10x12x6-foot display area.

DEADLINES: Entry, event, April.

329

Sacramento Festival of the Arts Outdoor Arts Show
Sacramento Regional Arts Council
Ennan West, Coordinator
562-A Downtown Plaza Mall
Sacramento, California 95814 U.S.A.
Tel: (916) 441-1044, 446-2885

Entry September-October

International; entry open to individuals, galleries, organizations; annual in September-October; established 1962. Purpose: to provide opportunity for artists to display, sell work; showcase performing artists. Sponsored and supported by Sacramento Regional Arts Council, City of Sacramento, Downtown Association. Average statistics (all sections): 250 entrants, 15 awards, 15,000 attendance. Held at K Street Mall in Sacramento for 2 days. Have performing arts.

CRAFTS FAIR: All Media, original. Entrants provide and attend sales displays. No kits, hobby crafts and collections. Competition includes visual arts, photography.

AWARDS: $1200 in Cash Awards.

JUDGING: Entry review based on originality, professionalism. Awards judging by 3 judges; based on technique, originality, overall excellence. Not responsible for loss or damage.

ENTRY FEE: $20 for 5x15-foot exhibit space. No sales commission charge.

DEADLINES: Entry, event, September-October.

330

Ocean Beach Park Arts and Crafts Show
Eleanor Butler, Administration
Assistant
Ocean Beach Park
New London, Connecticut 06320
U.S.A. Tel: (203) 447-3031

Entry July

International; entry open to all; annual in August; established 1976. Purpose: to promote arts and crafts in area. Sponsored by Ocean Beach Park. Supported by Friends of Ocean Beach Park Arts and Crafts Show. Recognized by Connecticut Commission on the Arts. Average statistics (all sections): 200 entrants (maximum 700), 14 awards, 50,000 attendance. Held on Ocean Beach Park Boardwalk for 2 days.

CRAFTS FAIR: All Media, original. Entrants provide and attend sales displays. Competition includes visual art, other crafts.

AWARDS: Purchase and Cash Awards. Ribbons.

JUDGING: By 3 local artworld figures. Not responsible for loss or damage.

ENTRY FEE: $20. No sales commission charge.

DEADLINES: Entry, July. Event, August.

331

Artists Showcase
Diane Stahl, Assistant Director of
Development
Baptist Hospital of Miami Foundation,
Inc.
8900 North Kendall Drive
Miami, Florida 33176 U.S.A.

Entry August

International; entry open to all; annual in November; established 1980. Purpose: to provide opportunity for craftspersons to display and sell creative work; to show current trends in visual arts. Sponsored by and held at Baptist Hospital for 2 days. Average statistics: 175 entrants, 80 awards.

CRAFTS FAIR: All Media, original, handcrafted; limit 2 per entrant for hospital Purchase Prize (collaborators count as 1). Entrants provide and attend sales displays. Submit 4 35mm slides, including 1 of display. No commercial molds, kits, copies, machine or mass reproductions. Competition for some awards includes fine and commercial arts, photography, sculpture, other crafts.

AWARDS: $5300 in Patron Purchase Prizes. $500 Baptist Hospital Purchase Prize. $350 First, $175 Second Prizes to each category. 14 $75 Awards of Merit.

JUDGING: By 2-3 local jurors. Sponsor may withhold awards. Not responsible for loss or damage.

ENTRY FEE: $80 for 15x15x8-foot exhibition space.

DEADLINES: Entry, August. Event, November.

332

Dunedin Art Harvest Show & Sale
Dunedin Junior Service League
Laurie Love, Chair
P. O. Box 593
Dunedin, Florida 33528 U.S.A.
Tel: (813) 734-0124

Entry September

International; entry open to all; annual in November; established 1963. Purpose: to provide opportunity for public to view, purchase original art. Sponsored and supported by Dunedin

Service League, Dunedin Parks & Recreation Department. Average statistics (all sections): 180 entrants, 23 awards, 35,000 attendance. Have participant demonstrations.

CRAFTS FAIR: All Media, original, handcrafted; minimum 4 works per category. Entrants provide and attend sales displays. Submit 5 35mm slides of work (actual display) for entry review. No copies, commercial reproductions, products or displays, kits, tiles, beads, novelty shell crafts, knitting, crochet, candles, decoupage, plants. Competition includes visual arts.

AWARDS: 4 $600 Awards of Distinction. 4 $325 Merit Awards. 15 $1000 Honorable Mentions. $2500 in Purchase Awards.

JUDGING: By 3 professionals, academics. Not responsible for loss or damage.

ENTRY FEE: $3 jury fee plus $25 (refundable) for 12x12-foot exhibition space.

DEADLINES: Entry, September. Judging, event, November.

333
Key Biscayne Art Festival
Norman Roberts
Suite 2
50 West Mashta Drive
Key Biscayne, Florida 33149 U.S.A.
Tel: (305) 361-5170

Entry November

International; entry open to all; annual in February; established 1963. Sponsored and supported by Rotary Club of Key Biscayne, Inc., Key Biscayne Elementary School. Maximum 150 entrants (collaborators count as 1). Held in Key Biscayne for 3 days. Second contact: Paul Kopp, 550 Ocean Drive, Key Biscayne, Florida 33149.

CRAFTS FAIR: All Media, original. Entrants provide and attend sales displays. Submit 4 35mm slides of recent work (including 1 of setup), brief resume for entry review. No commercial molds, agents, pornography. Competition includes visual art, photography.

AWARDS: (Includes all sections): $5000 in Purchase Awards. $1000 in Cash Awards. Special Prizes to sculpture, crafts.

JUDGING: By 7 art experts. Not responsible for loss or damage.

SALES TERMS: Sales compulsory. No commission charge.

ENTRY FEE: $60 (refundable) for 10x16-foot exhibition space.

DEADLINES: Entry, November. Judging, event, February.

334
Washington's Birthday Arts and Crafts Festival
Eustis Chamber of Commerce
David A. Fennell, Executive Director
P. O. Box 1210
Eustis, Florida 32726 U.S.A.
Tel: (904) 357-3434

Entry January

National; **entry open to U.S.;** annual in February; established 1902. Formerly called WASHINGTON'S BIRTHDAY CELEBRATION to 1979. Sponsored by Eustis Chamber of Commerce. Supported by City of Eustis. Average statistics (all sections): 100 entrants, 50,000 attendance. Held at Ferran Park in Eustis for 1 day. Have races, regatta, Miss and Tiny Miss Pageants, concert, antique show, aircraft fly-in, fireworks. Publish *Dateline* (monthly).

CRAFTS FAIR: All Media; unlimited entry. Entrants provide and attend sales displays. No commercially produced works. Competition includes visual arts, photography.

AWARDS: (Includes all sections): $100 First, $60 Second, $40 Third, $25 Fourth, $15 "Farthest Away" Prizes.

JUDGING: By 5 judges. Not responsible for loss or damage.

ENTRY FEE: $15 for 6x12-foot exhibit space. No sales commission charge.

DEADLINES: Entry, notification, January. Event, February.

335

Columbus Artists Guild Fine Arts and Crafts Show
Elsa Matzinger
1010 Oakcrest Drive
Columbus, Georgia 31904 U.S.A.
Tel: (404) 327-8197

Entry March

Regional; entry open to Alabama, Georgia, Florida; annual in May; established 1966. Purpose: to improve artistic skills, build public appreciation of art, promote and sell arts and crafts to public. Sponsored by Cross County Merchant Association. Average 75 entrants (all sections). Held at Cross County Plaza in Columbus for 2 days. Have continuous entertainment, nonjuried section. Also sponsor exhibits, workshops, lectures, demonstrations. Second contact: Columbus Artists Guild, P. O. Box 5142, Columbus, Georgia 31906.

CRAFTS FAIR: All Media. Entrants provide and attend sales displays. Submit slides for entry review. Divisions: Adult, High School Students. Competition includes visual art, photography, other crafts.

AWARDS: $500 First, $350 Second, $250 Third Place Awards to adults. 8 $50 Merit Awards to adults. $40 First, $30 Second, $25 Third Place Awards to students. 2 Merit Gift Certificates to students.

JUDGING: By 1 distinguished judge.

ENTRY FEE: $30.

DEADLINES: Entry, March. Judging, event, May.

336

Antioch Arts, Crafts and Antiques Fair
Antioch Chamber of Commerce and Industry
Dixie M. Sparks, Executive Secretary
880 Main Street
Antioch, Illinois 60002 U.S.A.
Tel: (312) 395-2233

Entry June

International; entry open to all; annual in July; established 1972. Purpose: to afford craftspersons an opportunity to exhibit their work in a diverse group of people. Sponsored and supported by Antioch Chamber of Commerce and Industry. Average 180 entrants. Held in Williams Park in Antioch for 1 day. Also sponsor various other shows.

CRAFTS FAIR: All Media, original, handcrafted. Entrants provide and attend sales displays. No mechanically produced entries, antiques. Competition includes other crafts. Also have art section.

AWARDS: $250 to best of show (includes all sections). $75 First, $50 Second, $25 Third Place Awards. Minimum $1250 in Purchase Awards. Ribbons.

JUDGING: By 1 professional. Not responsible for loss or damage.

SALES TERMS: Sales compulsory. No commission charge.

ENTRY FEE: $20 for 12-foot exhibit space.

DEADLINES: Entry, June. Event, July.

337

Cedarhurst Craft Fair
Mitchell Museum
Pat Lipps, Chair
Box 923
Mt. Vernon, Illinois 62864 U.S.A.
Tel: (618) 242-1236

Entry May

International; entry open to all; annual in September; established 1977. Purpose: to increase appreciation of traditional arts and crafts; provide showcase for artists. Sponsored and supported by Mitchell Museum. Average statistics: 120 entrants (130 maximum), 8 awards, 25,000 attendance, $300,000 total sales. Held at Cedarhurst Estate in Mt. Vernon for 2 days. Have traditional crafts, entertainment, children's creative area, refreshments, security guards. Second contact: Pat Doscher, Publicity Chair, 10 Hawthorne Hills, Mt. Vernon, Illinois 62864.

CRAFTS FAIR: All Media, original; unlimited entry. Entrants provide and attend sales displays. Submit 3 3x5-inch color slides per medium for entry review. No copies, kits, molds, hand-decorated or manufactured items, commercially made products, fabricated forms or settings in lapidary work.

AWARDS: $300, $200 Museum Awards. $75 Counselor Award. Several $75 "Friends of the Museum" Merit Awards.

JUDGING: Entry review by 5-person committee. Awards judging by 1 qualified judge.

SALES TERMS: Sales compulsory. No commission charge.

ENTRY FEE: $3 jury fee. $100 for 15x10-foot outdoor space.

DEADLINES: Entry, May. Judging, event, September.

338

Lincoln Square Art Fair
Lincoln Square Chamber of Commerce
David Cheesman, Chair
P. O. Box 25132
Chicago, Illinois 60625 U.S.A.

Entry August

International; entry open to all; annual in August; established 1971. Purpose: to promote the arts. Sponsored by Lincoln Square Chamber of Commerce. Supported by Lincoln Square Kiwanis, Lions Club, Ravenswood Jaycees. Held at Lincoln Square Plaza in Chicago for 2 days.

CRAFTS FAIR: All Media, original. Entrants provide and attend sales displays. No manufactured items. Competition includes fine art.

AWARDS: Gold, Silver, Bronze Medals.

JUDGING: Not specified. Not responsible for loss or damage.

ENTRY FEE: $20 for 8-linear-foot exhibit space.

DEADLINES: Entry, event, August.

339

Orland Square Fine Art and Craft Fair
Art Plus Associates
Irene Spaetzel
18W118 73rd Place

Westmont, Illinois 60559 U.S.A.
Tel: (312) 964-9062

Entry November

International; entry open to all; annual in March; established 1976. Purpose: to provide outlet and promotional show for craftspersons. Sponsored by Orland Square Associates. Average statistics: 171 entries, 10 winners. 100,000 attendance. Held at Orland Square Shopping Center in Westmont for 4 days. Have display equipment, demonstration areas, Heritage Crafts section. Also sponsor various arts and crafts shows. Second contact: Susan A. Rockouski, 1614 Laurel Lane, Darien, Illinois 60559; tel: (312) 985-2552.

CRAFTS FAIR: All Media, original, handcrafted. Entrants attend sales displays. Submit 5 slides or photographs (including display set up) for entry review, personal monochrome photo for publicity purposes (optional). No imports, kits, resale, manufactured items. Competition includes visual arts.

AWARDS: 10 $100 Excellence Awards. 6 Honorable Mention Ribbons Awards.

JUDGING: Entry review based on originality, workmanship, total display. Awards judging by 2 professionals and academics. Based on individual work and total display. Not responsible for loss or damage.

SALES TERMS: Sales compulsory. No commission charge.

ENTRY FEE: $75 for 6x12- or 8x10-foot exhibit space, plus $25 deposit.

DEADLINES: Entry, November. Judging, event, March.

| 340 |

Yorktown Crafts Showcase -- Yorktown Fine Arts and Craft Showcase
Art Plus Associates
Irene Spaetzel
18W118 73rd Place
Westmont, Illinois 60559 U.S.A.
Tel: (312) 964-9062

Entry January, May

International; entry open to all; biannual in April (crafts), October (fine arts and crafts); established 1974. Purpose: to offer opportunity for craftspersons to sell work, entertain public. Sponsored by Yorktown Merchants' Association, Art Plus Associates. Average statistics: 100 entrants, 100,000 attendance. Held at Yorktown Center in Lombard, Illinois for 4 days. Second contact: Yorktown Merchants' Association, 203 Yorktown, Lombard, Illinois 60148; tel: (312) 629-6186. Also sponsor other art, craft shows.

CRAFTS FAIR: All Media, original. Entrants provide and attend sales display. Submit 5 slides or photos (including 1 of display) for entry review. No manufactured work, imports, kits, reproductions, or work for resale. Competition includes fine art (Fine Art and Craft Showcase only), other crafts.

AWARDS: (Includes all sections): $550 in Cash Awards. $250 in Purchase Awards.

JUDGING: By 2 crafts specialists. Based on workmanship, originality, total display.

ENTRY FEE: Crafts Showcase: $80 for 6x12- or 8x10-foot exhibit space ($30 refundable deposit). Fine Art and Crafts Showcase: $75 ($25 refundable deposit).

DEADLINES: Entry, January, May.

Acceptance, February, June. Events, April, October.

341

Fourth Street Festival of the Arts and Crafts

Ruth Conway, Linda Knudsen, Chairs
P. O. Box 1257
Bloomington, Indiana 47402 U.S.A.
Tel: (812) 824-4217

Entry June

International; entry open to all; annual in September; established 1977. Purpose: to provide quality art and crafts fair to south-central Indiana. Sponsored by Bloomington Committee for the Arts, Area Arts Council, Business Committee for the Arts. Average statistics (all sections): 180 entrants, 80 exhibitors, 10 awards, 30,-000 attendance. Held in Bloomington during Labor Day weekend. Have musicians, performances.

CRAFTS FAIR: All Media, original, handcrafted. Entrants provide and attend sales displays. Submit 4 photographs or 35mm slides for entry review. No guilds or cooperatives, kits, commercially made entries. Competition includes visual arts, photography.

AWARDS: 12 or more $100 Purchase Awards (includes all sections).

JUDGING: Entry review by 6 community artists. Purchase Prizes by local organizations. Based on excellence and design. Not responsible for loss or damage.

SALES TERMS: Sales compulsory. No commission charge.

ENTRY FEE: $35 for 10x10-foot exhibit space (1 space per entrant; partnership considered 1 entrant).

DEADLINES: Entry, notification, June. Event, September.

342

Ohio River Arts Festival Crafts Fair at the Courthouse

Evansville Arts and Education Council
Joyse Briding Kramer, Executive Director
16-1/2 Southeast Second Street
Evansville, Indiana 47708 U.S.A.
Tel: (812) 422-2111

Entry March

International; entry open to all; annual in May; established 1969. Purpose: to provide exhibition and sale of fine craft work. Sponsored by Evansville Arts and Education Council. Supported by Indiana Arts Commission. Average statistics (all sections): 40 entrants, 15,000 attendance. Held at Old Courthouse Center in Evansville for 2 days. Have participant demonstrations, food, entertainment. Publish *Artstalk* (quarterly). Also sponsor Ohio River Writers Conference, Children's Art Fair at the Zoo, Walkway Festival. Second contact: William Leth, ISUE, 8600 University Blvd., Evansville, Indiana 47712.

CRAFTS FAIR: All Media. Entrants provide and attend sales displays. Submit 5 slides or photographs for entry review. No kits, work done under supervision. Competition includes other crafts.

AWARDS: $400 Evansville Art Education Council Purchase Award to first place. 1 $200, 2 $100, 4 $50 Cash Prizes.

JUDGING: By 1 reputable craftsperson.

SALES TERMS: Sales compulsory. No commission charge.

ENTRY FEE: $50 for 150-square feet of display space.

DEADLINES: Entry, March. Acceptance, April. Event, May.

343

Talbot Street Art Fair
Indiana Artist-Craftsmen, Inc.
Joe G. Lehman
2823 West 52nd Street
Indianapolis, Indiana 46208 U.S.A.
Tel: (317) 297-1632

Entry February

International; entry open to all; annual in June; established 1955. Purpose: to maintain reputation as oldest, largest, most popular show in area. Sponsored and supported by Indiana Artist-Craftsmen. Average statistics (all sections): 270 entrants, 3 awards, 50,000 attendance. Held in Indianapolis for 2 days. Also sponsor workshops, seminars.

CRAFTS FAIR: All Media, original, handcrafted. Entrants provide and attend sales displays. Submit 2 slides of work, 1 of display for entry review. Competition includes visual art, other crafts.

AWARDS: $100 First, $75 Second, $50 Third Prize to best booths.

JUDGING: By jury. Based on display impact.

ENTRY FEE: $40 for 10x6-foot exhibit space. No sales commission charge.

DEADLINES: Entry, February. Acceptance, March. Event, June.

344

Washington Park Art Fair
Michigan City Art League
Toni Clem, Director
P. O. Box 923
Michigan City, Indiana 46360 U.S.A.
Tel: (219) 874-6047

Entry July

International; entry open to all; annual in August; established 1960. Formerly called MICHIGAN CITY ART FAIR to 1980. Purpose: to promote art, artists, art appreciation in area. Sponsored and supported by Michigan City Art League (nonprofit, founded 1932). Held in Washington Park on Lakefront in Michigan City for 2 days. Have boat show, demonstrations. Also sponsor workshops, other art fairs. Second contact: Henrietta Kominairec, First Bank, Fifth and Franklin, Michigan City, Indiana 46360.

CRAFTS FAIR: All Media, original. Entrants provide and attend sales displays. Submit 4 slides of work (per medium), 1 slide of display, resume, explanation of technique, for entry review. No copies, reproductions, commercial molds, kits, patterns, plans, stencils, prefabricated forms, hobby crafts, commercial jewelry settings. Competition includes photography, visual arts.

AWARDS: $500 in Cash Awards.

JUDGING: By 1 judge. Sponsor may photograph entries for publicity. Not responsible for loss or damage.

ENTRY FEE: $35 for 15x30-foot exhibit space; $25 for 15x20-foot space. No sales commission charge.

DEADLINES: Entry, July. Acceptance, event, August.

345

DubuqueFest Art Fair
Dubuque Fine Arts Society
Ruth Nash, Co-Chair
422 Loras Blvd.
Dubuque, Iowa 52001 U.S.A.
Tel: (319) 583-6201, 588-9751

Entry March

International; entry open to all; annual in May; established 1979. Purpose: to create new art audience, sell juried arts and crafts. Sponsored by DubuqueFest (nonprofit) under auspices of Dubuque Fine Arts Society; Dubuque Artists Guild. Supported by government, private grants. Average statistics (all sections): 250 entries, 100 finalists, 45,000 attendance. Held in Washington Park in Dubuque for 2 days. Have indoor location in event of rain, food, demonstrations, entertainment.

CRAFTS FAIR: All Media, original. Entrants provide and attend sales displays. Submit 3 slides or color prints for entry review. Competition includes visual arts.

AWARDS: $100 to best of show. Purchase Awards.

JUDGING: Entry review and awards judging by college art faculty. Based on aesthetic quality. Not responsible for loss or damage.

ENTRY FEE: $35 ($20 for 1 day) per 10x10-foot exhibit space. No sales commission charge.

DEADLINES: Entry, March. Event, May.

346

Kingman's Sidewalk Art Fair
Kingman Area Chamber of Commerce
Helena Arnold, Secretary
322 North Main
Kingman, Kansas 67068 U.S.A.
Tel: (316) 532-3694

Entry date not specified

International; entry open to all; annual in September; established 1967. Sponsored by Kingman Chamber of Commerce. Average 60 entrants.

CRAFTS FAIR: All Media, original. Entrants attend sales displays. Competition includes other crafts.

AWARDS: $2100 in Purchase Awards.

JUDGING: Not specified.

ENTRY FEE: $7.50 for 8x12-foot exhibit space. No sales commission charge.

DEADLINES: Event, September.

347

Baton Rouge FestForAll
Arts and Humanities Council of Greater Baton Rouge
Richard Sabino, Director
427 Laurel Street
Baton Rouge, Louisiana 70801
U.S.A. Tel: (504) 344-8558

Entry February

National; entry open to U.S.; annual in May; established 1974. Purpose: to showcase local talent. Sponsored by Arts and Humanities Council of Greater Baton Rouge. Average statistics: 50,000 entries, maximum 165 entrants (collaborators count as 1), 200,000 attendance, $150,000 total sales. Held in downtown Baton Rouge for 2 says. Have performing arts, refreshments, participant demonstrations, auction, nonjuried section. Publish *Discover* magazine-newspaper. Also sponsor FestForAll Short Story Contest, Juried Art Show; Goudchaux's Design Competition.

CRAFTS FAIR: All Media, handcrafted. Entrants provide and attend sales displays. Require top 50 entrants donate 1 work for auction. Submit 6 slides of current work for entry review. No commercially manufactures items, imports, kits. Competition includes visual arts, photography.

AWARDS: (Includes all sections):

$500, $300, $200, $100 Cash Awards. $1650 minimum in Purchase Awards. 5 $50 Honorable Mentions.

JUDGING: Entry review by 3 gallery and school directors; based on points system. Awards judging by 1 national judge; based on merit of entire presentation. Not responsible for loss or damage.

ENTRY FEE: $5 plus $65 for 8x10-foot booth space. No sales commission charge.

DEADLINES: Entry, February. Judging, event, May.

348

Red River Revel Arts and Crafts Festival
Barnett Lipman, Executive Director
520 Spring Street
Shreveport, Louisiana 71101 U.S.A.
Tel: (318) 424-4000

Entry May

International; entry open to all; annual in October; established 1976. Purpose: to celebrate fine arts and crafts. Sponsored by Junior League of Shreveport, Louisiana Bank & Trust Company, City of Shreveport. Supported by Aetna Life & Casualty Foundation, Louisiana State Arts Council, NEA. Average statistics (all sections): 100 entrants, 200,000 attendance, $150,000 total sales, $1500 sales per entrant. Held along Red River in downtown Shreveport for 1 week. Have international food, entertainment, demonstrations, nonjuried show for 1 day, 24-hour security. Also sponsor Red River Revel Run, Children's Art Education Program, workshops. Second contact: 800 Snow Street, Shreveport, Louisiana 71101.

CRAFTS FAIR: All Media, original. Entrants provide and attend sales displays. Submit 4 35mm slides for

entry review. Competition includes photography, visual arts, other crafts.

AWARDS: Over $2000 in Purchase Awards.

JUDGING: By 3 professional jurors. Not responsible for loss or damage.

SALES TERMS: 20% commission charge.

ENTRY FEE: $25 ($35 shared) 1/2 week, $50 ($70 shared) 1 week, for 2 8x4-foot panels in triangular tent (2D work), 8-foot table in 10x10-foot tent (3D work).

DEADLINES: Entry, May. Event, October.

349

Minnesota Crafts Festival
Molly Hibbard, Coordinator
328 Hennepin Avenue, #210
Minneapolis, Minnesota 55403
U.S.A. Tel: (612) 333-7789

Entry March

International; entry open to all; annual in June; established 1973. Formerly called SMITH PARK CRAFTS FESTIVAL, MINNESOTA CRAFTSPEOPLE'S FESTIVAL. Purpose: to promote appreciation and sales of quality crafts. Sponsored by Minnesota Crafts Council (nonprofit). Average statistics: 93 entrants, 5 awards, 12,000 attendance. Held at College of St. Catherine in St. Paul, Minnesota for 2 days. Publish *Craft Connection* (quarterly).

CRAFTS FAIR: All Media, original. Produced in previous 2 years. Entrants provide and attend sales display. Submit 4 35mm slides of work for entry review.

AWARDS: 5 Prizes.

JUDGING: Entry review by Jury.

Awards judging by festival participants.

ENTRY FEE: $25. $40 (refundable) for 12x12-foot exhibit space. No sales commission charge.

DEADLINES: Entry, March. Acceptance, April. Event, June.

350

Rose Fete
Minneapolis Institute of Art
Jacquelyn Warner
2400 Third Avenue South
Minneapolis, Minnesota 55404
U.S.A. Tel: (612) 870-3221

Entry April

International; entry open to all; annual in June; established 1960. Purpose: to promote public awareness and sales opportunities for participants. Theme changes annually. Sponsored by Minnesota Arts Forum. Supported by Minneapolis Institute of Arts. Average 40,000 attendance. Held at Minneapolis Institute of Arts for 1 day.

CRAFTS FAIR: All Media. Entrants provide and attend sales displays. Submit 3-5 slides or photos for entry review. Competition includes fine arts, other crafts.

AWARDS: 3 $500 Awards.

JUDGING: By committee of art professionals. Based on excellence. Sponsor may photograph, exhibit entries for publicity. Not responsible for loss or damage.

SALES TERMS: Sales compulsory. No commission charge.

ENTRY FEE: $5 plus $35 for 15x15-foot exhibit space.

DEADLINES: Entry, April. Acceptance, May. Event, June.

351

Meridian Art in the Park Arts and Crafts Festival
Greater Meridian Chamber of Commerce (GMCC)
W. J. Johnson, Jr., Executive Vice President
2000 Ninth Street
P. O. Box 790
Meridian, Mississippi 39301 U.S.A.
Tel: (601) 693-1306

Entry March

International; **entry open to artists age 18 and over;** annual in April; established 1977. Purpose: to bring community closer together; educate it in fine arts. Sponsored by GMCC, Mississippi Art Commission, private donations. Average statistics (all sections): 68 entrants, 30,000 attendance. Held in Highland Park for 1 day. Have food, entertainment, demonstrations, shows, recreation. Second contact: Randy Shoults, Meridian Junior College, 5500 Highway 19 North, Meridian, Mississippi 39301; tel: (601) 483-8241, ext. 147.

CRAFTS FAIR: All Media, original, handmade. Entrants provide and attend sales displays. No commercial molds, kits. Competition includes arts.

AWARDS: (Includes all sections): $500 Purchase Prize to best of show. $100 Juror Awards. 3 $50 Merit Awards. $750 in Purchase Prizes.

JUDGING: By 1 juror. Not responsible for loss or damage.

SALES TERMS: Sales compulsory. No commission charge.

ENTRY FEE: $25 for 10x10-foot exhibit space.

DEADLINES: Entry, March. Event, April.

352

Atlantic City National Indian Summer Art Show
Atlantic City Art Center
Florence Miller, Director
205 North Montpelier Avenue
Atlantic City, New Jersey 08401
U.S.A. Tel: (609) 345-5491

Entry August

National; **entry open to U.S.;** annual in September; established 1963. Purpose: to support Atlantic City Art Center. Sponsored by Atlantic City Art Center, City of Atlantic City. Average 100 entrants (all sections). Held on boardwalk in Atlantic City for 2 days. Also sponsor Atlantic City on the Boardwalk National Art Show.

CRAFTS FAIR: All Media, original design, handcrafted. Entrants provide and attend sales displays. No manufactured articles, commercial metal belt buckles, bought jewelry settings with polished stone inserts, loose beads, Indian Jewelry. Competition for some awards includes visual arts, photography.

AWARDS: $550 Grand Prize to best of show (includes visual art, photography). $150 First, $100 Second, $75 Third Prizes. $25 Honorable Mention.

JUDGING: Entry review and awards judging by 4 judges. Not responsible for loss or damage.

ENTRY FEE: $25 for each 15-foot of boardwalk rail length (limit 2 spaces per entrant).

DEADLINES: Entry, August. Event, September.

353

Craft America Craft Fair
Vernon Valley Recreation Association
P. O. Box 614
McAfee, New Jersey 07428 U.S.A.

Entry May

International; entry open to all; annual in September; established 1981. Sponsored by Vernon Valley Recreation Association. Held in Vernon Valley, New Jersey for 4 days.

CRAFTS FAIR: All Media, original. Submit 5 35mm slides and description of each for entry review. No commercially manufactured objects assembled from kits, embellished or decorated items. Competition includes other crafts.

AWARDS: $5000 in Cash Awards.

ENTRY FEE: $5 jury fee plus $85-$150 for 8x10-foot or 10x20-foot booth space.

DEADLINES: Entry, May. Acceptance, June. Event, September.

354

Somerset Art Association Outdoor Art Show
Sally Bush
Peapack Road and Prospect Street
Box 734
Far Hills, New Jersey 07931 U.S.A.
Tel: (201) 234-2345

Entry September

National; **entry open to U.S.;** annual in September; established 1970. Sponsored by Somerset Art Association. Average 150 entrants (all sections). Held at Far Hills Fairgrounds for 1 day. Have participant demonstrations.

CRAFTS FAIR: All Media, original. Entrants provide and attend sales displays. No kits, copies, agents, dealers. Competition includes visual arts, sculpture, photography, other crafts.

AWARDS: $50 First, $25 Second, $15 Third Place Prize to sculpture, other media (includes all sections except oils, watercolors). Honorable Mention Ribbons.

JUDGING: By 1 judge. Not responsible for loss or damage.

ENTRY FEE: $14 for 10-foot exhibit space, plus return postage. No sales commission charge.

DEADLINES: Entry, event, September.

355

Binghamton Summer Arts and Crafts Festival
Binghamton Business Association
Rosemarie A. Henkle, Coordinator
84 Court Street
P. O. Box 995
Binghamton, New Jersey 13902
U.S.A. Tel: (607) 772-8860

Entry July

International; entry open to all; annual in July; established 1962. Sponsored and supported by Binghamton Business Association. Average statistics (all sections): 200 entrants, 25,000 attendance, $140,000 total sales. Held at Binghamton courthouse grounds and surrounding area for 3 days. Have parade, flea market, book sale, auction, music-dance-theater performances, children's entertainment. Also sponsor Pops on the River Day, Farmer's Market, Octoberfest, Tournament of Bands.

CRAFTS FAIR: All Media, original, handcrafted. Entrants provide and attend sales displays. Submit entry description, resume. Categories: Pottery, Miscellaneous Crafts. Competi-

tion includes fine arts, sculpture, photography.

AWARDS: $25 Best of Show Award (includes all sections). $15 First, $10 Second, $5 Third Place Ribbons each to pottery, miscellaneous crafts.

JUDGING: By 2 professionals. Not responsible for loss or damage.

ENTRY FEE: $25 for 10x3-foot exhibit space, $1 each additional foot. No sales commission charge.

DEADLINES: Entry, event, July.

356

Downtown Syracuse Arts and Crafts Fair
Downtown Committee of Syracuse
Laurie Reed, Public Information
Department
1900 State Tower Building
Syracuse, New York 13202 U.S.A.
Tel: (315) 422-8284

Entry May

International; entry open to all; annual in July; established 1971. Sponsored by Downtown Committee of Syracuse. Supported by local businesses. Average statistics (all sections): 150 entrants, 2 countries, 40 awards, 25,000 attendance, $500 sales. Held at Columbus Circle in downtown Syracuse for 3 days. Have 8x2-foot tables, 8x4-foot panels for hire.

CRAFTS FAIR: All Media, original. Entrants provide and attend sales displays.Submit 5 35mm slides (includes 1 of display) per medium for entry review. No agents, kits, dealers, commercially produced belts, manufactured or kits jewelry, decoupage, imports, dried or plastic plants, commercial molds, cut bottles, embellished objects, greenware. Competition includes visual arts, photography, other crafts.

AWARDS: $2000 in Cash Awards and guaranteed Purchase Prizes.

JUDGING: Entry review by screening committee. Awards judging by 3 judges. Not responsible for loss or damage.

SALES TERMS: Sales compulsory. No commission charge.

ENTRY FEE: $5 plus $45 for 8x10-foot booth space (maximum 2 per entrant).

DEADLINES: Entry, May. Judging, event, July.

357

Kenan Craft Festival
Kenan Center
Joan T. Radecke, Program Director
433 Locust Street
P. O. Box N
Lockport, New York 14094 U.S.A.
Tel: (716) 433-2617

Entry January

International; entry open to all; annual in June; established 1970. Purpose: to educate public about crafts, give craftspersons place to display, sell work. Sponsored and supported by Kenan Center. Average statistics (all sections): 1200 entries, 240 entrants, 90 exhibitors, 3 awards, 10,000 attendance, $80,000 total sales, $1000 sales per entrant. Held at Kenan Center in Lockport for 3 days. Have demonstrations, workshops, seminars, art gallery, theater. Tickets: $2.50 (adult), $1 (child), $6 (family). Also sponsor Snofest.

CRAFTS FAIR: All Media, original, traditional crafts used in contemporary ways. Entrants provide and attend sales displays. Submit 5 representative slides for entry review. No commercial kits. Competition in-

---

cludes other crafts.

AWARDS: $125 Mastercraftspersons Award. $50 First, $25 Second Place Award. Best of Show Prizes.

JUDGING: By 4 crafts experts.

ENTRY FEE: $7 jury fee. $60 for 10x10-foot exhibit booth. No sales commission charge.

DEADLINES: Entry, January. Acceptance, March. Event, June.

358

Charlotte SpringFest
SpringFest Inc.
Koni Kushman, President
2100 Southern National Center
Charlotte, North Carolina 28202
U.S.A. Tel: (704) 372-3560

Entry February

International; entry open to all; annual in April; established 1982. Purpose: to provide regional showcase for craftspersons. Sponsored by Springfest, Inc. Supported by local corporations. Limited to 200 entrants. Held in Charlotte for 3 days. Have performing artists, security.

CRAFTS FAIR: All Media, original. Entrants provide and attend sales displays. Submit slides, resume for entry review. No commercially manufactured items, kits, molds, plastic flowers. Competition includes art, other crafts.

AWARDS: $5000 in Cash Awards. Ribbons.

JUDGING: Entry review by screening committee. Not responsible for loss or damage.

ENTRY FEE: $25 (refundable) for 10x10x15-foot exhibit space (wxlxh). $35 for 2 craftspersons, $45 for 3. No sales commission charge.

DEADLINES: Entry, February. Acceptance, March. Event, April.

359

City Stage Celebration

United Arts Council of Greensboro
Helen Snow, Executive Director
200 North Davie Street
Greensboro, North Carolina 27401
U.S.A. Tel: (919) 373-4510

Entry July

International; entry open to all; annual in October; established 1980. Purpose: to spotlight arts in the community. Sponsored by United Arts Council of Greensboro, Miller Brewing Company. Supported by Miller Brewing Company, private donations. Average 200,000 attendance (all sections). Held in downtown Greensboro for 2 days. Have special exhibits, demonstrations, displays, nonjuried crafts sale, visual and performing arts, entertainment, recreation, ethnic food, refreshments. Also sponsor City Stage Photography Competition.

CRAFTS FAIR: All Media, original; unlimited entry. Submit 3 slides or prints, resume for entry review (except invited artists, group exhibitors), publicity. No imports, kits, commercial molds. Competition includes visual arts.

AWARDS: Minimum $1000 in Purchase, Cash Awards.

JUDGING: Entry review by committee. Sponsor may photograph entries for publicity. Not responsible for loss or damage.

ENTRY FEE: $35 for 12-foot-square space ($45 for 2 exhibitors per space, $55 for 3). $100 for 12x30-foot space for group exhibitors. No sales commission charge.

DEADLINES: Entry, July. Event, October.

360

Marietta Indian Summer Festival

Arthur Howard Winer, Director
Marietta College
Marietta, Ohio 45750 U.S.A.
Tel: (614) 373-4643

Entry April

International; entry open to age 18 and over; annual in September; established 1959. Began as a sidewalk painting exhibit. Purpose: to provide artists with opportunity to exhibit and sell work; educate public about quality craftsmanship. Sponsored by Indian Summer Festival, Inc. Supported by Marietta Area Arts and Crafts League, Marietta Area Chamber of Commerce, Marietta College. Average statistics (all sections): 125 entrants, 6 awards, 10,000 attendance, $74,000 total sales, $600 sales per entrant. Held at Washington County Fairgrounds in Marietta for 3 days. Have workshops, security, food, music. Tickets: $1.-50-$2 (children under 12 free).

CRAFTS FAIR: All Media, original. Entrants provide and attend sales displays; demonstrate crafts. Submit slides (2D 1, 3D 4) of 5 items (maximum) plus 1 of booth display for entry review (set counts as 1). No commercial kits, moldware, bazaar items. Competition includes arts, all crafts.

AWARDS: 6 Master Artisan Awards.

JUDGING: Entry review, awards judging by professional judges. Based on overall quality of work, booth display. Not responsible for loss or damage.

ENTRY FEE: $55 for 10x10-foot space. No sales commission charge.

DEADLINES: Entry, April. Acceptance, May. Event, September.

361

Westerville Music and Arts Festival

Sharon Martin, Executive Secretary
5 West College Avenue
Westerville, Ohio 43081 U.S.A.
Tel: (614) 882-8917

Entry May

International; entry open to all; annual in July; established 1974. Sponsored by Westerville Chamber of Commerce. Average statistics (all sections): 150 entrants, 50,000 attendance, 19 awards. Held at Otterbein College in Westerville for 2 days. Have Heritage Crafts invitational section, crafts demonstrations, auction, entertainment, children's activities, refreshments, security.

CRAFTS FAIR: All Media, original, minimum 70% handcrafted. Entrants provide and attend sales displays. Submit 5 slides or photos for entry review. No kits, moldwork, boutique items. Also have visual arts, photography.

AWARDS: $200 Best of Show Award. 7 $100 Awards.

JUDGING: Based on quality, appearance, creativity. Sponsor may photograph entries for publicity. Not responsible for loss or damage.

ENTRY FEE: $50 for 12 linear feet of exhibit space. Sales preferred.

DEADLINES: Entry, May. Judging, event, July.

362

Mount Hope Outdoor Art Show

Mount Hope Estate and Winery
R. Keith McNally, Public Relations Director
P. O. Box 685
Cornwall, Pennsylvania 17016 U.S.A.
Tel: (717) 665-7021

Entry May, August

International; entry open to all; biannual in June, September; established 1980. Purpose: to allow mixture of arts to be presented in new surroundings. Sponsored and supported by, and held at Mount Hope Estate and Winery. Average statistics (all sections): 200 entrants, 6 awards, 5000 attendance. Have Victorian mansion, winery, music, refreshments. Tickets: $2. Also sponsor music, dance, multicultural events.

CRAFTS FAIR: All Media, original, 10x5 feet (lxw) maximum. Entrants provide and attend sales displays. Submit 2 slides or photos for entry review. No imports, plants, manufactured or kit jewelry, commercial molds, commercially produced work, decoupage. Competition includes visual arts.

AWARDS: (Includes all sections): $200 to best of show (to be reproduced on wine label). $200 Center of Lebanon Association Award. 5 judges' Merit Awards. Purchase Prizes.

JUDGING: By 3 judges. Not responsible for loss or damage.

SALES TERMS: Sales compulsory. No commission charge.

ENTRY FEE: $50 for 1 space, $85 for 2. For both Spring and Autumn shows: $75 for 1, $135 for 2 spaces. Spaces may be shared.

DEADLINES: Entry, May, August. Event, June, September.

363

Philadelphia Craft Show
Philadelphia Museum of Art
Women's Committee
Mary Lee Lowry, Show Coordinator
P. O. Box 7646
Philadelphia, Pennsylvania 19101
U.S.A. Tel: (215) PO3-8100, ext. 365

Entry April

National; **entry open to U.S.;** annual in November; established 1977. Purpose: to expose public, art world to finest craft work done in nation; advance craft artists. Sponsored by the Philadelphia Museum of Art Women's Committee. Average statistics: 1000 entries, maximum 100 exhibitors selected, $3000 in awards, 20,000 attendance, $300,000 total sales, $2000 sales per entrant. Held in Philadelphia for 4 days. Tickets: $4 general, $3 students, $2 senior citizens and children under 12.

CRAFTS FAIR: All Media, original, one-of-a-kind or limited edition, handmade or with use of appropriate tools. Entrants provide and attend sales displays. Submit 5 35mm color slides for entry review. No painting, photography, graphics, dried or pressed flowers, seeds, pods, cut bottles, embellished objects, handmade reproductions, items made from commercial kits or plans.

AWARDS: 1 $1000 First, 2 $500 Second, 3 $250 Third, 1 $250 Artists' Choice Prizes.

JUDGING: Entry review and awards judging by artists and art professionals. Based on conception, execution, technical perfection, imagination, individuality, uniqueness. Not responsible for loss or damage.

SALES TERMS: Work must be for sale. No commission charge.

ENTRY FEE: $10 plus $200 per 10x10-foot exhibit booth.

DEADLINES: Entry, April. Event, November.

364

Show of Hands Crafts Fair
Jewish Community Center of Rhode Island
Lola Schwartz, Assistant Executive Director
401 Elmgrove Avenue
Providence, Rhode Island 02906
U.S.A. Tel: (401) 861-8800

Entry August

Regional; **entry open to Eastern U.S.;** annual in November; established 1976. Purpose: to encourage, exhibit fine crafts. Sponsored by Friends of the Jewish Community of Rhode Island. Average 38 entrants. Held at Jewish Community Center in Providence for 2 days.

CRAFTS FAIR: All Media. Entrants provide and attend sales displays. Submit minimum 6 slides or photos of current works for entry review. Competition includes all crafts.

AWARDS: 3 $100 Cash Awards.

JUDGING: Entry review by Craft Fair Committee. Awards judging by local experts.

SALES TERMS: 25% commission charge on first $2000 sales.

ENTRY FEE: $25 deposit (to be credited against sales) for 8x8-foot exhibit booth.

DEADLINES: Entry, August. Judging, event, November.

365

Westerly Arts and Crafts Festival
Westerly-Pawcatuck Area Chamber
of Commerce
Diane B. Howard, Secretary
159 Main Street
Westerly, Rhode Island 02891 U.S.A.
Tel: (401) 596-7761

Entry June

International; entry open to all; annual in June; established 1967. Purpose: to promote the arts. Sponsored by Greater Westerly-Pawcatuck Area Chamber of Commerce. Average 200 entrants (all sections). Held in Wilcox Park in Westerly for 2 days.

CRAFTS FAIR: All Media, original; limit 50 per entrant. Entrants provide and attend sales displays. Submit photo, description of work for entry review. No commercially produced work, kits, imports, dealers. Competition includes visual arts, photography, other crafts.

AWARDS: Best of Show Award. Ribbons. Cash Prizes.

JUDGING: By 3 judges. Not responsible for loss or damage.

SALES TERMS: Sales optional. No commission charge.

ENTRY FEE: $20, $2 students (through high school). $5 late fee.

DEADLINES: Entry, event, June.

366

Kingsport Sidewalk Arts and Crafts Festival
Downtown Kingsport Association
Peggy Turner, Executive Director
404 Clay Street
Kingsport, Tennessee 37660 U.S.A.
Tel: (615) 246-6550

Entry August

National; **entry open to U.S.;** annual in September; established 1977. Purpose: to improve status of arts; provide exhibition and sale of art. Sponsored and supported by Downtown Kingsport Association. Recognized by Tennessee Arts Commission. Average statistics (all sections): 100 entrants, 30,000 attendance. Held in downtown Kingsport for 2 days. Have stage and entertainment program, children's activities.

CRAFTS FAIR: All Media, original. Entrants provide and attend sale displays. Submit slides, prints, or samples for entry review. No kits, agents. Competition includes photography, painting, graphics sections.

AWARDS: $3000 in Awards and Purchase Pledges.

JUDGING: Not specified.

SALES TERMS: Sales compulsory. No commission charge.

ENTRY FEE: $30.

DEADLINES: Entry, August. Event, September.

367

Atlantic Designer Crafts Exhibition
Karen Eide and James Chalkley, Promoters
P. O. Box 1000-60
Virginia Beach, Virginia 23451
U.S.A. Tel: (804) 422-3268

Entry August

National; **entry open to U.S.;** annual in November; established 1982. Purpose: to provide craftspersons with opportunity to show and sell work to public, wholesalers. Held in Virginia Beach Convention Center for 3 days. Tickets: $2. Have security.

CRAFTS FAIR: All Media, original, handcrafted; limit 2 booths per entrant. Entrants provide and attend sales displays. Submit 4 slides for entry review. No dough, etched lucite, commercial kits, molds.

AWARDS: (Includes all sections): $100 to best of show. 5 $300 Awards of Excellence.

JUDGING: Entry review by committee. Awards judging by 1 juror. Based on overall excellence, design, execution. Not responsible for loss or damage.

SALES TERMS: Sales compulsory. No commission charge.

ENTRY FEE: $5 application fee. $80 booth fee (refundable).

DEADLINES: Entry, August. Acceptance, September. Event, November.

368

Southern Shopping Center Sidewalk Craft Show

Sandra Meadows, Promotions Director
6 Conway Road
Newport News, Virginia 23606
U.S.A. Tel: (804) 874-0067

Entry June

International; **entry open to individuals, clubs;** annual in June; established 1980. Sponsored by Southern Shopping Mall Merchant's Association. Average statistics: 100 entrants, 5 awards, 20,000 attendance. Held at Southern Shopping Center in Norfolk, Virginia for 2 days.

CRAFTS FAIR: All Media, original. Entrants provide and attend sales displays. No kits, professional plans, pre-cut patterns.

AWARDS: $150 Best of Show

Award. 2 $75 Merit Awards. 2 $50 Honorable Mentions.

JUDGING: By 1 qualified judge. Not responsible for loss or damage.

ENTRY FEE: $10. No sales commission charge.

DEADLINES: Entry, event, June.

369

Mayfair Summer Art Fair

Mayfair Associates, Inc.
Cathy C. Brown
2500 North Mayfair Road
Milwaukee, Wisconsin 53226 U.S.A.
Tel: (414) 453-6026, 771-1300

Entry June

National; **entry open to U.S.;** annual in August; established 1960. Sponsored by Mayfair Associates, Inc. Purpose: to create traffic for the mall. Average statistics: 90 entrants, 10 awards, 80,000 attendance. Held in the Mayfair Mall in Milwaukee for 2 days. Have participant demonstrations.

CRAFTS FAIR: All Media, original. Entrants provide and attend sales displays. Submit 4 slides or pictures, resume for entry review. No agents, dealers, imports, manufactured or kit jewelry, bead jewelry, commercial molds or kits, crafts supplies, paper or plastic flowers.

AWARDS: 10 $50 Cash Awards. Ribbons.

JUDGING: By 1 local academic. Not responsible for loss or damage.

ENTRY FEE: $35. No sales commission charge.

DEADLINES: Entry, June. Event, August.

370

Monument Square Art Fair
Mrs. John R. Hackl,
Secretary-Treasurer
223 Sixth Street
Racine, Wisconsin 53403 U.S.A.
Tel: (414) 637-7706, 633-3215

Entry January

National; **entry open to U.S. artists age 18 and over;** annual in June; established 1963. Purpose: to seek out, encourage new talent through competition. Sponsored by American Association of University Women, Racine Branch; Downtown Association of Racine; Racine Art Association. Average statistics (all sections): 140 entrants (maximum), 9000 attendance, $71,000 total sales. Held at YMCA in Racine for 2 days. Have participant demonstrations, entertainment, music, bus tours, children's activities. Second contact: Mrs. Allen Onnink, President; tel: (414) 639-1945.

CRAFTS FAIR: All Media, original. Entrants provide and attend sales displays. Submit 3 actual works or 10 slides for entry review. Competition includes photography, visual arts.

AWARDS: $400 Best of Show Award. $300 Second, $200 Third Prizes. 8 $75 Excellence Awards. $14,000 in Purchase Prizes.

JUDGING: Entry review by Art Fair Board of Directors. Awards judging by 2 art professionals. Not responsible for loss or damage.

SALES TERMS: Sales compulsory. No commission charge.

ENTRY FEE: $5 jury fee plus $40 for 12x5-foot exhibit space.

DEADLINES: Entry, January. Event, June.

371

Salon des Metiers d'Art du Quebec Craft Fair
Jean-Guy Monette, General Director
1030 Cherrier Street, Suite 300
Montreal, Quebec H2L 1H9 CANADA
Tel: 1 (514) 527-7915

Entry April

Regional; **entry open to members in Quebec;** annual in December; established 1968. Formerly called ASSOCIATION PROFESSIONNELLE DES ARTISANS DU QUEBEC to 1977. Purpose: to promote crafts. Sponsored by Salon des Metiers d'Art du Quebec. Average statistics: 400 entrants, 350,000 attendance, C$5 million total sales. Held in Place Bonaventure in Montreal for 16 days. Also sponsor exchange program to corporations outside Quebec. Second contact: Felicia Cavalieri, Administration Council Secretary, 8462 St. Urbain Street, Montreal, Quebec H2P 2P1, Canada.

CRAFTS FAIR: All Media. Submit 8 items for entry review. Competition includes visual arts.

AWARDS: C$5000 Jean Marie Gauvreau Molson Award (includes all sections).

JUDGING: By 3 examiners in each category, plus 4 polyvalent jurors.

SALES TERMS: Sales compulsory. No commission charge.

ENTRY FEE: C$25 membership, C$10 annual subscription. C$756 for 8x10-foot exhibit space for 16 days.

DEADLINES: Entry, April. Acceptance, November. Event, December.

ALPHABETICAL
EVENT/SPONSOR/AWARD INDEX

Alphabetical index to each EVENT, SPONSOR, and AWARD (followed by identifying CODE NUMBER of the event).

A

A Gather of Glass Exhibition: 110
A Pottery Course in Kent: 222
A-B Jamboree Crafts Contest and Fair: 83
Acton-Boxborough Community Education Program: 83
Affair on the Square Sidewalk Art Show: 255
Affaire in the Gardens Fine Art and Crafts Fair: 242
Akron Beacon Journal Charity Fund: 227
Akron Society of Artists: 298
Albuquerque United Artists (AUA) Craftworks Competition: 84
Algonac Invitational Art Fair: 295
Algonac Sponsors of the Arts (ASOTA): 295
All Broward Exhibition: 85
All Oregon Art Exhibition: 118
Allentown Outdoor Art Festival: 257
Allentown Village Society: 257
Allied Arts of Seattle Visual Arts Committee: 40
American Art Exhibition: 17
American Association of University Women: 29
American Indian Arts Residence Scholarships: 165
American National Miniature Show: 146
American-Scandinavian

Foundation(ASF) Awards for Study in Scandinavia: 156
Amish Acres, Inc.: 47
Anacortes Arts and Crafts Festival Nonprofessional Competition: 197
Antioch Arts, Crafts and Antiques Fair: 336
Antioch Chamber of Commerce and Industry: 336
Appalachian Center for Crafts: 275
Area Artists Annual: 51
Arkansas Arts Center Prints, Drawings and Crafts Exhibition: 37
Arkansas Arts Center Toys Designed by Artists Exhibition: 105
Arkansas Industrial Arts Association Student Project Competition: 198
Armstrong Award: 204
Arrowmont School of Arts and Crafts Spring and Summer Assistantships: 8
Art and the Law Exhibition: 96
Art Center Association Juried Exhibition: 99
Art Fair Board: 312
Art Fair USA: 251
Art Festival in the Village: 268
Art Harvest Show and Sale.: 332
Art in All Media Exhibition: 49
Art in Arizona Show: 69
Art in State Architecture: 98
Art in the Park: 281
Art in the Park Arts and Crafts Festival: 351

G

N

T

SUBJECT/CATEGORY INDEX

Index to AREAS OF SPECIAL INTEREST (followed by identifying CODE NUMBER of each event).